Borderline Personality Disorder:

A THERAPIST'S GUIDE TO TAKING CONTROL

Borderline Personality Disorder:

A THERAPIST'S GUIDE TO TAKING CONTROL

Arthur Freeman
Gina M. Fusco

 W. W. Norton & Company • New York • London

W. W. Norton & Company has been independent since its founding in 1923, when William Warder Norton and Mary D. Herter Norton first published lectures delivered at the People's Institute, the adult education division of New York City's Cooper Union. The Nortons soon expanded their program beyond the Institute, publishing books by celebrated academics from America and abroad. By mid-century, the two major pillars of Norton's publishing program—trade books and college texts—were firmly established. In the 1950s, the Norton family transferred control of the company to its employees, and today—with a staff of four hundred and a comparable number of trade, college, and professional titles published each year—W. W. Norton & Company stands as the largest and oldest publishing house owned wholly by its employees.

Copyright © 2004, by Arthur Freeman and Gina M. Fusco
All rights reserved
Printed in the United States of America
First Edition

For information about permission to reproduce selections from this book, write to Permissions, W. W. Norton & Company, Inc., 500 Fifth Avenue, New York, NY 10110

The text of this book is composed in Palatino with the display set in Optima
Manufacturing by Victor Graphics, Inc.
Production manager: Benjamin Reynolds
Book design by Julia Druskin
Page makeup by Carole Desnoes

Library of Congress Cataloging-in-Publication Data

Freeman, Arthur, 1942
Borderline personality disorder : a therapist's guide to taking control / Arthur Freeman, Gina M. Fusco.
p. cm.
"A Norton professional book"
ISBN 0-393-70352-5
1. Borderline personality disorder—Treatment. 2. Psychiatry—Differential therapeutics.
I. Fusco, Gina M. II. Title.
RC569.5.B67F74 2003
616.85'852—dc21   2003041231

W. W. Norton & Company, Inc., 500 Fifth Avenue, New York, NY 10110
www.wwnorton.com

W. W. Norton & Company Ltd., Castle House, 75/76 Wells St., London W1T 3QT
1 2 3 4 5 6 7 8 9 0

Contents

Acknowledgments

A project of this magnitude has many roots. First and foremost are our teachers and mentors who have over the years helped us develop insight, skills, empathy, and understanding.

Second are our patients who have entrusted us with their wellbeing and have taught us much about the human condition. It is to them that we have dedicated our professional careers.

Third are our students who have asked the questions that have driven our need to develop programs and protocols for treating the broad range of emotional and behavioral disorders.

Fourth are our colleagues, especially at Philadelphia College of Osteopathic Medicine who have served as sounding boards for our ideas. The support staff, especially Susan Hartman, have typed, copied, collated, and organized the various iterations of these manuscripts. Additional thanks are also due to Alternative Behavioral Services, a comprehensive behavioral healthcare program for high-risk adolescents, that provided Gina M. Fusco with flexibility and support for this and other projects.

Fifth is the staff at W.W. Norton, especially Michael McGandy, Deborah Malmud, and Casey Ruble who have given us the chance to share our ideas with you the reader. They have also given shape and clarity to our presentation.

Finally, we want to thank our families. Arthur Freeman would like to thank his wife, partner, and colleague, Dr. Sharon Freeman for her continuing support, ideas, and love. He would also like to dedicate these volumes to their children: Andrew, Russell, April, Laura, Aaron, Heather, and Rebecca. Gina M. Fusco would like to thank her family, especially her mother Jeanette, and her sisters Cynthia, Elizabeth, and Holly. They have and continue to provide the inspiration and guidance needed to continue this work. Additionally, she would like to thank Stephanie Widder and Marni Nutkowitz who through their friendship, have provided much laughter, support, and encouragement.

Borderline Personality Disorder:

A THERAPIST'S GUIDE TO TAKING CONTROL

Introduction

The Taking Control program is designed to aid the experienced therapist in performing the focused, structured work necessary with patients diagnosed with borderline personality disorder (BPD). BPD is often mistakenly viewed as a generic diagnostic phenomena with little variation within the presentation of symptoms. Although many diagnosed with BPD and other cluster B personality disorders exhibit a similar constellation of symptoms, we generally view BPD patients as constituting a very broad group. The various criteria may manifest in a number of combinations, permutations, and degrees of severity. The goal is for patients, working collaboratively with a therapist, to identify, define, and target the parts and particular symptoms of the disorder that most affect their personal comfort, interpersonal relationships, and occupational functioning. This Therapist Manual and the companion Patient Manual cover each of the nine criteria for BPD listed in *DSM-IV-TR* (APA, 2000). (With the exception of the ninth criterion, which for the sake of clarity has been divided into two chapters, each criterion is addressed as a single chapter.) This program is geared toward patients whose disorder is rated as mild to moderate. Patients with severe manifestations, who have had multiple hospitalizations, and who are noncompliant with therapeutic or pharmacotherapeutic regimens are least likely to do well in this program. We have tried to focus on the large number of patients whose interpersonal styles bring them into conflict with their immediate environment. Our aim is to help these patients develop more effective coping strategies.

BPD is a disorder that frequently creates much turmoil and impairment in the life of an individual and for all the people around them (Beck, Freeman, & Associates, 1990). Psychotherapy based on any theoretical or conceptual model with the BPD population can be quite complex, difficult, and frustrating for both the therapist and the patient. It often results in a series of failed treatment strategies, coupled with unrealistic treatment expectations by the therapist, the patient, and the patient's significant others. Psychologists treating BPD patients frequently assimilate the projective identification of hopelessness. Difficulty in interpersonal relations—one of the primary diagnostic criteria for BPD—often becomes an obstacle in meeting treatment goals. By providing parallel patient and therapist manuals, we hope to achieve a true collaborative approach to treatment and thereby empower both the patient and the clinician. The Therapist Manual is designed to assist the clinician in taking control of the treatment by offering treatment suggestions that parallel what the patient is, ideally, doing in their workbook. In concert with the Patient Manual, this book offers a step-by-step guide to our treatment program.

WHAT IS BORDERLINE PERSONALITY DISORDER?

A personality disorder is defined as "an enduring pattern of inner experience and behavior that deviates . . . from the expectations of the individual's culture, is pervasive and inflexible, has an onset in adolescence or early adulthood, is stable over time, and leads to distress or impairment" (APA, 2000, p. 685). Specifically, BPD is a "pervasive pattern of instability of interpersonal relationships, self-image, and affects and marked impulsivity beginning by early adulthood and present in a variety of contexts" (APA, 2000, p. 710). BPD patients typically present with longstanding problems that have affected many areas of their lives. They may be referred by a family member or a concerned family physician in order to seek treatment for symptoms arising from a prevalent Axis I disorder such as a mood or anxiety disorder. The chief goal of effective treatment is to help patients learn how to evaluate themselves and their problems more objectively and to address their problems in a more hopeful, constructive manner (Layden, Newman, Freeman, & Morse, 1993). Thus we begin the Patient Manual by prompting the patient to identify his or her relevant traits or patterns of behavior.

Identifying a Patient With Borderline Personality Disorder

Patients with BPD typically seek treatment due to acute symptoms related to an Axis I disorder as described in the *DSM-IV-TR* (APA, 2000). These disorders include depression, anxiety, panic disorders, and eating disorders. Some patients present with high-risk symptomology such as suicidal ideation or homicidality (Layden et al., 1993). Impulsivity is one of the hallmark diagnostic indicators, and many borderline patients seek treatment due to a negative consequence of some impulsive act, such as reacting dramatically to significant others, fighting with bosses or supervisors, or attempting to manage the aftermath of a breakup of significant relationships. Sometimes a feedback loop occurs in which an Axis I disorder such as anxiety or depression becomes inflamed or exacerbated by the faulty coping style resulting from the Axis II personality. Many borderline patients do not recognize that many of their problems stem from longstanding personality patterns of thinking and reacting. They may adopt an "other-blaming" style and be convinced that they are the recipients of incredible bad luck or misfortune. Others may be aware that they have some longstanding problems in managing situations and relationships but are at a loss as to how to change or adapt.

It may be difficult to identify patients who have BPD. This is due to the comorbid presentation of the Axis I pathology, which can mask or cloud more longstanding problems. Thus, it is imperative that the evaluation process include a complete and thorough history-taking that covers relationship histories, coping styles, and prior treatments.

Diagnosing a Patient With Borderline Personality Disorder

The *DSM-IV-TR* (APA, 2000) provides clinicians with a comprehensive method of diagnosing BPD. Utilizing a categorical classification system, the *DSM-IV-TR* lists criteria required to meet the diagnosis of the disorder; patients must exhibit five of the nine criteria to be diagnosed with the disorder. However, many clinicians find the wording of the criteria ambiguous. Thus, a clear explanation and definition of the criteria are needed in order to help clinicians better understand the psychopathology related to the disorder.

Diagnosing a patient with BPD is commonly achieved by two different means. First, the patient's symptoms need to meet the threshold of required diagnostic criteria identified in the *DSM-IV-TR* (APA, 2000). The *DSM-IV-TR* states that in order for the criteria to be met, "a pervasive pattern of instability of interpersonal relationships, self-image, and affects and marked impulsivity beginning by early adulthood and present in a variety of contexts must be present in addition to at least five of the following" (APA, 2000, p. 710):

1. Frantic efforts to avoid real or imagined abandonment.

2. A pattern of unstable and intense interpersonal relationships characterized by alternating between extremes of idealization and devaluation.

3. Identity disturbance: markedly and persistently unstable self-image or sense of self.

4. Impulsivity in at least two areas that are potentially self-damaging (e.g., spending, sex, substance abuse, reckless driving, binge eating).

5. Recurrent suicidal behavior, gestures, or threats, or self-mutilating behavior.

6. Affective instability due to a marked reactivity of mood (e.g., intense episodic dysphoria, irritability, or anxiety usually lasting a few hours and only rarely more than a few days).

7. Chronic feelings of emptiness.

8. Inappropriate, intense anger or difficulty controlling anger (e.g., frequent displays of temper, constant, recurrent physical fights).

9. Transient, stress-related paranoid ideation or severe dissociative symptoms.

A second means of identifying a patient with BPD is to recognize the heuristic markers generally present for those with this disorder. Layden and colleagues identify the following heuristic signs:

1. The patient states, "I've always been this way. This is who I am."

2. The patient demonstrates ongoing noncompliance with the therapeutic regimen.

3. Therapeutic progress seems to come to a sudden halt.

4. The patient is unaware of the negative effects of his or her behaviors.

5. The patient's personality problems appear to be acceptable and natural, creating low motivation to change.

6. The therapist has very powerful, potentially antitherapeutic reactions to the patient that obstruct the patient's ability to trust the therapist.

7. The patient misses many sessions, arrives late, and sometimes leaves abruptly.

8. The patient exhibits an extreme all-or-nothing style of thinking.

9. The patient has difficulty moderating or modulating emotional reactions, especially anger.

10. The patient frequently does things that cause some sort of self-harm.

In the Patient Manual we have translated the relevant diagnostic criterion into a checklist of symptoms for the patient to consider. Each chapter provides a description of the criterion and how it may manifest.

Some patients view diagnostic labels as somewhat judgmental or pejorative. Therefore, we suggest that if you discuss the patient's actual personality disorder (if he or she meets the criteria), it is imperative that you reframe *disorder* by describing the personality problems as a "pattern" of how he or she copes and interact with his- or herself and the world. In other words, instead of defining a personality disorder as a set of chronic and disabling problems, think of it as constituting the patient's unique pattern of behaviors.

Typical BPD Traits

Patients with BPD often present with a cluster of traits that are particularly specific to the disorder, including a crisis-prone style, heightened sensitivity, catastrophic thinking, and dichotomous thinking.

Crisis-Prone Style

Patients with BPD typically have a crisis-prone style (Freeman & Fusco, 2000). High-arousal, crisis-prone patients have a premorbid history of emotional or behavioral dyscontrol; they approach their lives as a series of brushfires or crises, tackling the most recent "crisis du jour" only to move on to the next. Their baselines often remain at a state of being overwhelmed. Poor coping and problem-solving combined with a borderline personality style, affective state, and behaviors tend to enlarge simple stressors into more formidable crises. Clinicians gathering patient history should look for a patient's inability to manage or cope and/or a tendency to wrestle with crisis on a daily basis (Freeman & Fusco, 2000).

Heightened Sensitivity

Those diagnosed with BPD are usually exquisitely sensitive. They are more physiologically attuned to others, more sensitive to nonverbal cues, and often react to perceived changes in their environment based on to minor or misread cues. Several theorists have proposed that those with BPD are physiologically reactive to stimuli, which can create a cascade of negative events including distorted thinking

(Stone, 1993). Throughout this program we attempt to address this facet of BPD. We do this by encouraging patients to self-monitor and learn to predict when they may respond in a way they are attempting to change or alter. By assisting patients in reading their own signals, we can help them integrate the challenges and disputations provided by the treatment exercises. And by arming patients with coping methods, we ultimately provide the tools for a more healthy, and functional lifestyle.

DICHOTOMOUS THINKING: CATASTROPHIZING & JUMPING TO CONCLUSIONS

Patients diagnosed with BPD often have distorted thinking. This type of distorted thinking is a form of dichotomous, all-or-nothing thinking (Layden et al., 1993). Dichotomous thoughts entail an interpretation of stimuli as black or white. For example, a patient may view her husband as completely irresponsible when he is late instead of considering situational explanations such as the possibility that he is stuck in traffic. One form of dichotomous thinking is catastrophizing; interpreting relatively innocuous stimuli or events (either internal or external) as catastrophic. Layden and associates provided an example of catastrophic thinking in the form of a patient who becomes suicidal after getting a bad haircut. Another form of dichotomous thinking is jumping to conclusions rather than processing or examining a situation or event fully. (For example, a patient may interpret her boyfriend's quiet mood as a sign that he is unhappy in the relationship.) These various forms of dichotomous thinking are discussed throughout the Therapist's Manual, and we offer various interventions designed to target, decatastrophize, and encourage more rational and realistic processing of stimuli.

TAKING CONTROL OF BORDERLINE PERSONALITY DISORDER: THE COGNITIVE-BEHAVIORAL TREATMENT STRATEGY

The treatment program presented in this manual is based on cognitive-behavioral therapy (CBT), which in the past several years has become an increasingly effective intervention in the treatment of BPD (McGinn & Sanderson, 2001). Beck, Freeman, and Associates (1990) proposed a cognitive-behavioral treatment strategy aimed at decreasing dichotomous thinking, improving control over emotions and impulses, addressing assumptions, and strengthening the identity of the patient. Linehan (1987) proposed a more behavioral conceptualization of BPD and identified the basis of dysfunction as related to emotional dysregu-lation. Dialectical behavior therapy is geared toward building patients' emotion-regulation skills and helping them create a more positive atti-tude toward themselves (Linehan, 1987). If cognitive-behavioral psy-chotherapy is to be effective, an understanding of cognitive-behavioral theory and its relative components is necessary. Cognitive-behavioral theory and psychotherapy techniques have been described extensively elsewhere (Freeman, Pretzer, Fleming, & Simon, 1990).

The following sections identify and define the major components of cognitive-behavioral thought. The remainder of the Introduction closely follows the Introduction of the Patient Manual and serves to guide the clinician in didactically defining treatment to the patient, an exercise that ideally should occur within the first few sessions, and certainly no later than the fifth session.

The major thrust of cognitive-behavioral therapy is toward under-standing and identifying patients' behavioral patterns, as well as the precipitating and accompanying cognitive processes. Cognitions include current thoughts, self-statements, perceptions, appraisals, attributions, memories, goals, assumptions, standards, and beliefs. Simply put, cognitions influence behavior, emotions, and physiologi-cal states, without the linear connection that "thoughts equal feelings" (Freeman, 1992).

Cognitive-behavioral perspectives, techniques, and interventions are designed to examine the content of patients' thoughts that exacer-bate or aggravate situations. Cognitive-behavioral approaches exam-ine how stimulus is perceived, interpreted, categorized, and responded to. These responses tend to be patterned reactions to learned beliefs, assumptions, expectations, and held beliefs systems known as *schemas* (Beck & Emery, 1979).

Literature indicates that cognitive therapy is one of the most widely used treatment modalities among mental health practitioners today (Ritter, 1985). Mayne, Norcross, and Sayette (1994) reported that approximately 50% of faculty in accredited clinical psychology doctoral programs have a cognitive or cognitive-behavioral orienta-tion. Specifically, cognitive-behavioral therapy has been applied suc-cessfully to the treatment of personality disorders (Beck et al., 1990; Young, 1990). However, BPD can be one of the most complex person-ality disorders (Layden et al.) and therefore warrants individual attention. Specific cognitive approaches to the treatment of BPD include Linehan (1987), Pretzer (1990), Turner (1989), and Millon (1987). Little empirical research examining the effectiveness of cogni-tive therapies in the treatment of BPD exists (Trull, Stepp, & Durrett,

2003). Studies by Linehan, Armstrong, Allmon, Suarez, and Miller (1988) suggested that specific cognitive-behavioral treatment based on Linehan's dialectical behavioral model yielded a lower dropout rate and significantly less self-injurious behaviors than "usual" treatments. Recent studies have domonstrated that CBT in combination with formal problem-solving skills training (PSST) reduces self-injurious behaviors (Raj, Kumaraiah, & Bhide, 2001). However, Rush and Shaw (1983) suggested that cognitive therapy is not effective with this disorder due to its complex and "vexing" (Trull, Stepp, & Durrett, 2003) presentation and chronic nature. Additionally, poor results have been reported when cognitive-behavioral interventions were used without consideration of the dynamics of BPD (Mays, 1985; Rush & Shaw, 1983).

Schemas: A Basic Tenet of Cognitive-Behavioral Therapy

A fundamental tenet of cognitive-behavioral therapy is that one's basic assumptions play a central role in influencing perception and interpretation of events and in shaping both behavior and emotional responses (Beck et al., 1990). *Schemas*, the basic assumptions or rules that govern individual thought and behavior, are developed over many years. Schematic material guides every aspect of the individual's life, both consciously and unconsciously. It provides meaning and structure to a world that bombards our senses with information. Schemas may also be active or inactive. Active schemas govern day-to-day behavior—for example, how to dress or how to respond to a compliment or a criticism. Inactive schemas are dormant until they are stimulated into activity by some internal or external stress—for example, "eat anything to survive"; this would be triggered by the stressor of approaching starvation. However, considering this last example, if one is just hungry, he or she probably will maintain normal ideas about what foods are appropriate to eat; the belief that "I will eat anything to survive" returns to its dormant state when the stress of starvation is no longer there.

Understanding schemas is an integral part of practicing cognitive-behavioral theory and psychotherapy. It is extremely important to discuss the concept of schemas with patients and to help them identify the schemas that govern their behaviors, thoughts, and feelings. Additionally, a possible goal for your patient is to learn how to reduce stress and stressful situations so that his or her inactive schemas *stay* inactive. Patients with BPD tend to react to stressors (both minimal and extreme) in an exaggerated and dramatic way. These dramatic reactions are often a result of inactive emergency or crisis-mode schemas becoming activated. This easy activation of emergency-mode schemas thus creates an overall crisis-prone style (Freeman & Fusco, 2000).

WHERE DO SCHEMAS COME FROM?

Existing schemas are created through years of development. They provide the blueprint or template through which received information is processed and filtered. Our everyday perceptions, therefore, are products of a biased system of our own creation and maintenance. As incoming information and stimuli are sensed and perceived, their interpretation is subject to unique, idiosyncratic templates that categorize, sort, and organize information according to a preexisting system complete with rules and meanings. What occurs, then, is a system of interpreting the world through strongly held beliefs, patterns, and attitudes. Schemas can be cultural, familial, religious, or related to gender, age, or personality. Schemas are stored not only as cognitive material, but also as emotional, behavioral, and physiological "chips" of data within our systems. As the creation of schemas depends upon both intrapersonal and interpersonal developmental aspects, unhealthy or maladaptive patterns may be nurtured or continued as methods of survival in a hostile environment.

HOW DO SCHEMAS DEVELOP?

Piaget described the development of cognitive beliefs through the process of adaptation (Rosen, 1989). As individuals interact physiologically and behaviorally with their environments, ideas are either shaped and solidified through a process of assimilating data to preexisting ideas (less radical change) or changed to accommodate a more complete set of data. All aspects of development include this process of adapting to the environment and attempts to manage the disequilibrium that results when stimulus contradicts what is already known.

These early response patterns are created to manage incoming stimuli and to assist in the individual's functioning and survival. These same patterns may later in life cause difficulty in functioning. As these basic rules of life govern all aspects of behavior, treatment is predicated upon the recognition and definition of the schema related to the currently manifested problem.

SCHEMAS ENCOUNTERED FREQUENTLY IN THE BPD PATIENT

Many varying schemas can be found in patients with BPD. Layden and colleagues agreed with Young's (1990) description of characteristic maladaptive schemas for BPD patients and stated that schemas most frequently encountered with patients with BPD are dependence, lack of individuation, abandonment, mistrust, unlovability, defectiveness, and incompetence. These schemas are typically compelling and pervasive, and they may have caused significant disruption and dysfunction for patients. Generally, patients with BPD maintain numerous schemas that may be incongruent or in opposition; this adds to the inherent difficulty in treating this disorder. For example, the two opposing schema patterns of dependence and mistrust can cause patients to experience a no-win therapeutic situation: They are motivated to meet their needs for dependence but their belief that trusting others is dangerous prevents achieving a deep connection. This double-bind also may cause the individuals upon whom they are becoming dependent to withdraw or become antagonistic. Ultimately these opposing schematic patterns cause patients to feel "torn, unhappy, and unsettled" (Layden et al., p. 20).

LEVELS OF SCHEMA CHANGE

Can schemas really be altered? Schemas are difficult to alter for five reasons.

1. Some beliefs are highly emotionally charged and inextricably tied to past experience.
2. Beliefs held for very long periods of time are generally more a part of one's identity than newly created beliefs.
3. Beliefs may have been instilled or reinforced by credible, important individuals.
4. How the schema affects behavior is defined by one's thought processes and images.
5. Learned behaviors are a result of schematic activation and therefore produce years of positive and negative associations that may be considered intractable to change.

The more compelling or intrinsic the schema is to basic identity and survival for the patient, the more difficult it is to modify (Freeman & Dattilio, 2000).

Although some rules are not generally subject to simple change (e.g., traditional gender roles), most schematic material is accessible to reconstruction, modification, reinterpretation, or camouflage. By examining the level of change upon a continuum from reconstruction to camouflage, we can set realistic goals for ourselves as clinicians while remaining task-focused for patients.

Reconstruction of schemas is the most radical level of change. It involves the systematic dismantling of the material and a total reworking and rebuilding of ideas and attitudes. It is not generally seen as a realistic option for those with personality disorders, although if the schema is not compelling to the patient it may be possible. Modification of schematic material allows the foundation of the schema to remain but involves smaller changes. Reinterpretation involves patients' allowing and forming challenges to their schemas with the intention of creating a more healthy, functional relationship to themselves and the outside world. Some patients can only deal with a small amount of alteration to a schema. This involves patients' disguising or camouflaging their traits. For example, a patient who experiences rapid mood changes may learn to monitor him- or herself at social functions so as not to overreact to others' statements (Freeman, 1992).

VULNERABILITY FACTORS

Patients who experience life as a series of brushfires or a neverending cascade of crises are particularly vulnerable to stress and therefore stress-related schemas (Freeman & Fusco, 2000). This increases the likelihood that these patients will interpret incoming stimuli as threatening or dangerous to their existence and therefore may trigger or exacerbate intrapersonal crises. When experiencing stress, patients may not be able to see the forest for the trees or specifically define the instigating problem. Vulnerability factors such as acute health problems, chronic illness, chronic pain, deterioration of health, hunger, anger, fatigue, loneliness, any major life loss or change, poor-problem solving, weak impulse control, substance abuse, traumatic life events, or psychological vulnerability (existing depression) wear down patients' adaptive coping responses and ultimately can activate unhealthy schemas. (Typical unhealthy schemas include "I'm powerless in this situation" or "everything is hopeless.") These factors can occlude productive problem-solving and can prevent patients from feeling they at least were able to begin the race. Vulnerability factors imbue related schemas. These can be healthy schemas ("I've beaten this illness before") or unhealthy schemas ("I'm worthless without a job"). Helping patients understand and identify their vulnerability factors assists them in conceptualizing why they sometimes are unable to cope and other times are able to cope quite well. In addition, defining schemas related to vulnerability factors provides information that can be utilized for future treatment interventions.

When identifying potential areas of intervention, keep in mind patients' vulnerability factors: Have they experienced any of the previously mentioned stressors?; Are they healthy?; Do they have a chronic mental health or medical problem? Considering the varying levels of vulnerability factors your patient may have will help you have more realistic expectations of your patient, yourself, and the treatment.

THE STRUCTURE OF THERAPEUTIC SESSIONS

Beck and Weishaar stated that cognitive psychotherapy is "a collaborative process of empirical investigation, reality testing, and problem-solving between the therapist and patient" (1986, p. 43). Generally, patients who enter outpatient psychotherapy require 1½ to 6½ months of weekly outpatient sessions; in cases where a personality disorder has been diagnosed more sessions may be warranted (Beck, 1995).

The only initial goal of cognitive psychotherapy is to build rapport with patients. This develops and enables the collaborative working relationship to which cognitive-behavioral therapy subscribes. Collaboration is essential throughout the therapeutic process and, in essence, allows patients to identify which aspects of their personality patterns they wish to address, modify, or change. Providing a rational and effective structure both for the course of treatment and for each individual session is also a fundamental tenet of treatment. Once structure has been established, collaboration allows continued focus and direction in reaching established goals.

The basic structure of each session, following Beck's protocol (1995), is as follows:

1. Rapport building.
2. Brief mood check and review of the prior week's events.
3. Transition to current session.
4. Setting of agenda and discussion of issues within agenda.
   Review of the last week's assignments.
   Discussion of the current week's criteria (per chapter topic).
5. Application of relevant treatment strategies and interventions.
6. Setting of homework for the next session.
7. Feedback from patient.

Each session usually begins with a brief mood check to establish how patients are feeling. This should be a brief exchange that includes questions like "How was your week?" and may involve either a ranking of mood on a subjective scale (e.g., a 0 to 100 scale on which 0 equals being best ever felt and 100 equals being worst) or the completion of an objective measure such as the Beck Depression Inventory (Beck & Steer, 1987). The therapist then transitions to the current session and asks if any of the prior week's events or the mood state should be added to the current agenda (Beck, 1995).

For each session, an agenda must be set. Early in treatment the agenda is set by the therapist, and later it becomes more of the patient's responsibility (Beck, 1995). An agenda drives the session by providing the outline or set path for it. In this way patients' often vague, ambiguous discomforts can rapidly be transformed into workable, concrete problems that can be tackled by cognitive and behavioral interventions. Agenda-setting also involves reviewing the prior week's assignments and adding new items to the current session plan. Specific interventions and strategies are then created to target the distorted automatic thoughts, beliefs, and held schemas, including dichotomous thinking and irrational beliefs that have resulted in poor coping. Addressing schemas during this part of the session allows for the identification of how the patient interprets, categorizes, encodes, and responds to stimulus. Each session requires the therapist to encourage patients to self-monitor for physiological, emotional, cognitive, and behavioral warning signs that indicate activation of schemas. The agenda section of the session should include the introduction and explanation of the chapter topics. The remainder of the session is devoted to reviewing prior homework, assigning homework for the next session, and eliciting feedback from the patient to ensure that therapy is continuing in a collaborative mode. Although cognitive-behavioral therapy is a structured approached to psychotherapy, caveats to maintaining structure include patients' demonstrating intense hopelessness and/or suicidality or any other high-risk behaviors that require immediate and appropriate intervention.

SOME BASIC TOOLS AND PRINCIPLES OF COGNITIVE-BEHAVIORAL THERAPY

Through observation, Socratic questioning, and patients' self-monitoring, you can assist patients in identifying the automatic thoughts derived from the schemas. Four avenues or areas of response (physiological, emotional, cognitive, and behavioral) provide clues about the activation of a schematic pattern or reaction your patients may wish to target. Patients' self-observation and self-monitoring of automatic thoughts that occur in problem situations ultimately provide a roadmap and treatment plan that targets patterns to be altered. In this way, recurrent patterns can be tackled and coping strategies can be suggested and experimented with to prevent recurrence. Once automatic thoughts are identified, the relevant schema that underlies the automatic thoughts can be assessed and the level of change necessary can be determined. Let's look at the four basic tools and principles of a cognitive-behavioral therapy model.

Observation. Through observation of both verbal and nonverbal behaviors, you can detect your patient's areas of distress. This not only includes what patients actually say, but also how they express it. As your patients discuss relevant situations and begins to tackle their assignments, note if your patients express any extremes related to a given area. Nonverbally, perhaps your patients choose angular body postures, poor eye contact, or is extremely fidgety when discussing problematic areas. These areas warrant further investigation.

Self-monitoring. Self-monitoring enables patients to learn more about themselves and is an intrinsic aspect of cognitive-behavioral treatment and taking control. Ultimately self-monitoring yields important information that can be utilized in treatment. Self-monitoring can be described as patients' watching and viewing themselves to see how they respond, think, feel, and react physically to certain events or situations. The goal is to learn to predict situations in which they may become distressed and to know how they typically react. Knowing these two variables establishes inroads to treatment interventions and prevents maladaptive responses. The patient manual refers to what we call the body's *alarm system*. The alarm system is an analogy to understand the body's reaction to felt distress and discomfort or, in keeping with the analogy, an *intruder* (see the Overview for further description).

Socratic questioning. Given that patients with BPD are hypersensitive and also may manifest a suspicious or even a paranoid style, we do not recommend the use of interpretation as a treatment tool. It can come across as crossing boundaries, "mind-reading," intrusive, or, even worse, one degree off target. Even if they are 99% correct, interpretations that are slightly off target will be viewed as 100% wrong. Socratic dialogue is the ideal technique with patients with BPD. It involves using simple, focused, closed-ended questions to move the patient toward a desired goal (either insight into a behavior's antecedents or recognition of a particular behavior) (Freeman, 1992).

Socratic dialogue makes the session easier for patients but forces the therapist to frame questions carefully and strategically. For example, suppose a patient comes into the consulting room appearing angry and falls into the chair. She is shaking her head and clenching and unclenching her fists. The therapist responds, "You seem upset." This may be either ignored or responded to negatively if the patient is experiencing anger rather than upset. Conversely, if the patient were upset and the therapist perceived that she seemed angry, the patient might deny the entire statement simply because it didn't encapsulate exactly what she was experiencing.

The Socratic dialogue in this situation could be as follows:

Therapist: I can see that there is some strong reaction. What is going on?
Patient: What's going on?
Therapist: Are you reacting to something that just happened or is this from much earlier?

For greatest effectiveness, the questions should elicit an affirmative or positive response. If the therapist asks easy questions, patients' anxiety will decrease, they will be more likely to respond, and the internal pressure (and anger) about working for the therapist will decrease. The therapist will also be able to initiate a more positive mindset or perception of the therapeutic process even when the patient has a more negative mindset or perception of the therapeutic process.

Automatic thoughts. One method of identifying underlying schemas involves having patients identify their automatic thoughts or thoughts they experience when they are anticipating or reacting to an event (Beck, 1995). Automatic thoughts are how patients experience or process incoming stimuli through their own systems and generate a thought directly derived from their schema. For example, if a young child has been bitten by a large, white, furry animal that makes a barking sound, when he or she is approached by this type of creature the child will probably experience an automatic thought related to fear and pain. The child will therefore act on that behavior (e.g., run or scream). Automatic thoughts and their related behavioral clues often provide the foundation for therapeutic intervention. These automatic thoughts and learned responses to stimuli may have created a personality style associated with poor social, coping, or modulating skills. Therefore, schemas are neither good nor bad but rather are a way of interacting within both internal and external environments.

Overview of the Method: The Taking Control Program

Taking Control is an eleven-step cognitive-behavioral treatment program in which patients are first introduced to the program and then complete a series of steps based on the nine *DSM-IV-TR* (APA, 2000) criteria for BPD. Patients who meet some or all of the criteria for BPD (mild to moderate) will probably find the Taking Control program therapeutically beneficial. Generally, patients who can cognitively grasp cognitive-behavioral therapy and are willing to utilize it as a treatment method will be amenable to the Taking Control structure.

Each step of the program may last anywhere from a single session to several sessions, depending on the degree to which the patient identifies with the criterion. The primary clinician's clinical judgment should drive the pace of treatment. If patients initially request that the treatment focus on issues not covered in the Patient Manual, it is the clinician's responsibility to decide how to proceed and how to integrate aspects of the workbook. As noted earlier, if patients present with any high-risk symptoms or statements, the structure must be accommodated to ensure the safety of the patient and others. We suggest a general format for the first few sessions; however, it is the primary clinician's task to determine the length of treatment. The Patient Manual is an adjunctive support to clinicians and can be useful even if cognitive-behavioral therapy is not the primary treatment model. The Therapist Manual that you have in your hand will cite the relevant pagination in the Patient Manual when addressing specific worksheets and exercises.

Taking Control is based on the basic tenets and techniques of cognitive-behavioral therapy, but it adds a new dimension: It specifically asks patients how they wish to focus treatment, what areas they feel they need help in, and how they want to alter, modify, and change maladaptive behaviors that have resulted in discomfort or difficulty functioning. The structure of the program is designed to be flexible in order to meet patients' needs. The goal is for patients, working collaboratively with a therapist, to identify, define, and target the parts of the disorder that most affect their personal comfort, interpersonal relationships, and occupational functioning. Part of accomplishing this goal is teaching patients how to self-monitor. Self-monitoring is a key component to cognitive-behavioral treatment. The Taking Control program utilizes self-monitoring as a means to identify the aspects and behaviors patients wish to address. More importantly, self-monitoring provides a roadmap of the patients' futures regarding what stimuli triggers certain responses. This gives patients the opportunity to choose whether they want to take control and react in positive, healthy, and adaptive ways.

The Patient Manual describes self-monitoring as follows:

> Self-monitoring provides a valuable window to our behaviors and also gives us something tangible to work with in creating a program that will work for you. You can utilize information that you have obtained from self-monitoring as a means of predicting how you may react or respond to a given situation. Once you have understood what your patterns are, you can then monitor yourself to determine what is problematic for you. Then you can protect yourself, alter your behaviors, or even try something different from what you have used before as a means of coping with the situation. Self-monitoring means listening to your body's own internal *alarm system*, which, when activated, allows you to control the events that subsequently happen. (p. 10)

How does this process begin? We begin by sensing through our basic system of five senses. Our sensory system is designed to physically detect things in the world around us. We use our senses of sight, hearing, touch, taste, and smell to pick up signals from our environment. Each of the senses then sends messages to our brain, which perceives the information and gives it meaning. By perceiving, we actually understand or define what is happening around us. As children we learn to sense, perceive, and evaluate our environment. As we gather information about events through our eyes, ears, mouth, nose, and skin, it is filtered through our own special physiological system and interpreted and given meaning in our brain. We then make decisions based on learning, experience, and patterns of thought, or schemas, that have been developing since we were born (and maybe before) (Layden et al., 1993). Remember, however, that as information becomes available to us, it has gone through our own filter, a filter created by both early and ongoing experiences. From our perceptions, we act. We respond to how we perceive our environment. For example, your eyes may sense a large furry animal with jagged teeth running toward you. This image is sent to your brain, which perceives a dangerous animal that could cause harm. Your reaction to that perception is to run.

Generally, we take in the environment and create solutions that will meet our needs and ensure our safety. We also, ideally, tend to follow societal standards in behavior. As children, we create patterned ways of perceiving and therefore responding to certain situations. Over time, these patterns of sensing and perceiving influence how we react in certain situations. If a child has been hit by an adult several times, his or her perception of someone yelling may cause extreme fear and a desire to hide. As adults, we can't hide when someone is angry. So our learned pattern, although necessary to protect ourselves growing up, may actually no longer be useful or relevant.

We all self-monitor. We do so every day. As children we learn to monitor what we say to our teachers, parents, and friends. We watch ourselves. In this way, self-monitoring provides an inroad to understanding ourselves, both physically and mentally, and learning to predict how we may react or respond to any given situation.

The goal of self-monitoring, therefore, is to learn how we sense, perceive, and react to situations and experiences. Again, we're all different. Self-monitoring will assist you in predicting situations that may distress you and in knowing how you may react. The overall goal is to find those inroads to understanding yourself better and, with the information you have learned about yourself, to help define specific treatment interventions aimed at changing the reactions you are not happy with or that have given you some problems. Self-monitoring will help you to understand yourself both physically and mentally.

Many of the exercise and worksheets in the Patient Manual are designed to improve the patient's self-monitoring skills. Techniques and interventions, including the alteration of schema, are specifically tailored to the patient based on these self-monitoring worksheets.

Following are some ways of explaining self-monitoring to your patients:

- Think of yourself as having your own internal alarm system.
- Think of yourself as a scientist gathering data.
- Write down or record varying patterns that occur.

EARLY SESSIONS

Up to three sessions should be devoted to describing and educating the patient about the cognitive-behavioral treatment model, schemas, and the patient's potential diagnosis. The Introduction to the Therapist Manual can be utilized during this time and relevant readings within the Patient Manual assigned as homework.

Educating the Patient About the Cognitive-Behavioral Treatment Model

As cognitive-behavioral therapy is described, many examples can help exemplify the model as an *in vivo* method of educating the patient. For example, when asking patients if they have any type of reaction or mood change in response to discussing the use of cognitive-behavioral therapy, the therapist can utilize the reaction by asking patients to identify the accompanying thoughts that occurred ("I hate structure" or "I don't like to be told what to do"). In asking patients about their reactions and correcting any misinterpretations, an example of utilizing cognitive-behavioral therapy has occurred.

Explaining Schemas

We suggest explaining how schemas work by likening it to the child's game of Whisper-Down-the-Lane. The game begins with one person whispering something to the next person, who then tells the next person. By the time the tenth or so person hears the statement, it has been changed or distorted. This is how schemas work: The cognitive processes of sensation, perception, association of related material, and categorization of material (assimilation and accommodation) are the basis for our reactions, and we channel incoming information through our own biased filtering systems. Our reactions, therefore, derive from a system tainted with our own memories, feelings, and prior reactions. So, as each child hears the statement, the information is processed through his or her own biased filter system, and then the distorted version passed along to the next child.

As you explain schemas to your patients, make sure they understand the following:

- Schemas are basic ways of processing information, like a computer processing incoming data and spitting out results.
- Schemas are not good or bad; they simply are learned patterns.
- There are many types of schemas.
- Schemas are individualized.

After the cognitive-behavioral treatment model, schemas, and the diagnosis have been discussed, sessions 4 and 5 may be utilized to familiarize the patient with the treatment manual. Session 6 can begin addressing the first chapter topic and symptom/criteria.

SUBSEQUENT SESSIONS

The subsequent sessions are dedicated to the eleven-step treatment process. Each chapter constitutes a step and covers a *DSM-IV-TR* (APA, 2000) BPD criterion. Each chapter/step may not necessarily warrant a full session if it is not relevant to the patient; similarly, problematic symptoms may warrant more than one session. For example, if a patient experiences particular difficulty with abandonment, two or more sessions may be devoted to uncovering the schemas related to abandonment and practicing the related interventions.

All sessions follow the same basic outline and integrate Beck's (1995) protocol:

1. Rapport building.

2. Brief mood check and review of prior week's events.

3. Transition to current session.

4. Setting of agenda: review of the last week's assignments and discussion of what will be covered in the current session.

5. Discussion of the current week's criterion (per chapter topic).
   Review and definition of specific *DSM-IV-TR* criterion
   Reading of vignettes
   Discussion of vignettes
   Worksheet 1: The Assessment
   Worksheet 2: The Assignment
   Worksheet 3: The Incident Chart
   Worksheet 4: The Dysfunctional Thought Record (DTR)
   Worksheet 5: Schemas
   Worksheet 6: Treatment Goals
   Completion of The Diagnostic Profiling System (DPS) (see Worksheet 18)

6. Application of treatment strategies and interventions.
   Worksheets 7 & 8: Physical Triggers and Suggested Interventions
   Worksheets 9 & 10: Emotional Triggers and Suggested Interventions
   Worksheets 11 & 12: Cognitive/Automatic Thoughts and Suggested Interventions
   Worksheets 13 & 14: Behavioral Triggers and Suggested Interventions

Worksheet 15: The Expanded Incident Chart (in selected chapters)
Worksheets 16 & 17: Situational Triggers and Suggested Interventions
Worksheet 18: The Diagnostic Profiling System (DPS)

7. Setting homework for the next session.
8. Feedback from the patient.

Rapport Building

Collaboration with BPD patients is vital to ensure treatment progress and gains. Rapport building begins with the first contact, and continues throughout the entire therapeutic process. Active listening, empathy, good eye contact, and consistency are all integral to this process. Given the vacillating nature of patients with BPD, therapy can prove to be extremely challenging. Remaining consistent will help provide structure and predictability to the session.

Brief Mood Check & Review of Prior Week's Events

Each session usually begins with a brief mood check to establish how patients are feeling (Beck, 1995). This should be a brief exchange that includes questions like "How was your week?" and may involve either a ranking of mood on a subjective scale such as a 0 to 100 (0 being best ever felt and 100 being worst) or the completion of an objective measure such as the Beck Depression Inventory (Beck & Steer, 1987). Once patients have identified their mood, questions related to their current mood can be addressed. Usually, patients will have an understanding as to why their mood is either good or bad. This is where the transition to reviewing the prior week's events ties in nicely. For example, the therapist might say "You've said that your mood is bad today. You've given it a 30 out of 100. Has something happened during the week that you're reacting to, or do have some idea why you don't feel as good as you did last week?" Many patients want to give their therapist a play-by-play rundown of their week's events. This is not usually productive, as much superfluous detail can mask larger themes. It is vital that the therapist not get drawn into each and every interaction that the patient experienced during the week, but rather piece together patterns and themes. For example, if the patient describes several arguments during the week with their significant other which appears to have contributed to their current depressed mood, the therapist can make a suggestion to include the patient's interaction style, relationships, and means of resolving conflict to the agenda. A mood check is meant to be a brief part of the session.

Transition to Current Session

After patients have described the week's relevant events, the therapist can then transition to the current session (Beck, 1995). This can sometimes be difficult to do, particularly if patients become entangled or perseverative about something that happened during the week. Again, it is vital that the therapist ensure that if there is an aspect of the prior week's events that is relevant to the patient, this topic should be included within the agenda. The therapist can move things along with statements such as "You've listed your mood as about an 80 today, a pretty good day. Your meeting with your supervisor yesterday seems to have contributed to this mood. However, you were disappointed about how your mother reacted to your promotion. Is that something you want to discuss more in detail today?" By moving the patient from the week's events to the current session, setting the agenda can begin.

Setting of Agenda

An agenda must be set for each session. The agenda is set by the therapist, and later it becomes more of the patient's responsibility (Beck, 1995). An agenda drives the session by providing the outline or timeframe for each topic. The agenda includes setting time in the session to review the prior week's assignments and adding new items to the current session plan. As each patient may require a different number of sessions, setting the agenda for each session should reflect the on-going and overall treatment plan. For example, if the patient is authorized by their insurance company for only 10 sessions, it will be important to utilize the sessions in a very discriminate and productive manner. The agenda therefore allows for an outline of each session which clarifies concrete and non-ambiguous goals to help to maximize the time available. It is a collaborative process which during the earliest sessions is structured by the therapist, and later more driven by the patient.

In the first few sessions, socialization to the cognitive-behavioral model and discussion of the use of the Taking Control manuals should occur. After brief mood checks and transition to new topics occurs, the therapist sets the agenda topics. In these earliest sessions, agenda topics include introducing patients to the basics (see Introduction). At approximately session 4 and 5, agenda topics should include familiarizing patients with the treatment manuals. At approximately session 6, the therapist adds to the agenda the current criterion and an explanation of the chapter topics to be covered within the session. (Please refer to Beck, 1995 for basic structuring of a cognitive-behavioral session).

At all times, the therapist is conceptualizing how patients construe their life-situations, accessing automatic thoughts, beliefs, and schema (Beck, 1995). Throughout the entire process, the therapist is vigilant to elicit automatic thoughts, beliefs, and held schemas, including dichotomous thinking. In this way, specific interventions and strategies are created to target any distortions which may be causing dysfunction or distress. For example, if the therapist suggests as a topic discussing the patient's depressed mood, the therapist may note that the patient is not receptive to this topic. The patient may have schemas related to their mood (e.g., "If I'm depressed, I'm weak") which helps the therapist create a more comprehensive case conceptualization. Addressing schemas during the session allows for the identification of how the patient interprets, categorizes, encodes, and responds to stimulus. Each session requires the therapist to encourage patients to monitor for physiological, emotional, cognitive, and behavioral warning signs that indicate activation of schemas. Any automatic thoughts that are identified in the agenda-setting process add valuable information for later discussion. Once the agenda is set, the session proceeds by beginning with the first identified topic.

Discussion of the Current Week's Criterion

After the mood check, transition to current session, and agenda-setting has been completed, the therapist then addresses (at approximately session 6) the current BPD criterion to be discussed within the session. Each chapter represents an identified *DSM-IV-TR* (APA, 2000) BPD criterion, and provides a relevant example. The therapist discusses the criterion and it's definition with the patient. The examples are provided to give patients clarity as to how the actual criterion may manifest itself in everyday life. The therapist elicits automatic thoughts related to the specific material, gathering and compiling information which adds to the overall case conceptualization. If the area is considered potentially problematic for the patient, he or she is later prompted to complete a mini-assessment to determine whether the symptoms described in the criterion have caused any distress or dysfunction.

REVIEW & DEFINITION OF SPECIFIC *DSM-IV-TR* CRITERION

Next, the specific criterion for the step is defined and reviewed. Each chapter begins with a detailed definition of the *DSM-IV-TR* (APA, 2000) criterion specific to the chapter. The purpose for this is twofold. First, the more pragmatic, objective definitions will give clinicians a more comprehensive understanding of what can be a very amorphous subject. Second, the definitions will enable clinicians to create more idiosyncratic treatment plans for their patients. Not all patients exhibit all of the *DSM-IV-TR* criteria. By establishing a clear understanding of what the criteria mean, you can begin to create unique treatment plans that target specific areas of distress or dysfunction for your patient.

Each detailed definition includes definitions and synonyms for critical words—as defined in *Webster's Dictionary* (1993)—that are found in the *DSM-IV-TR*. We suggest that as you investigate whether a specific symptom constellation exists for your patient, you utilize some of the synonyms provided. This will enable both you and your patient to gain a greater understanding of what the *DSM-IV-TR* attempts to define and categorize.

READING OF THE VIGNETTES

Reading the vignettes in the manuals will assist you and your patients in conceptualizing how a specific symptom may manifest. The characters in the vignettes exhibit extreme symptomology, which should help you narrow down and focus on the specific criterion. As much overlap exists among the criteria, it is imperative that you decipher the differences between them. The vignettes are designed to offer an opportunity for a discussion about whether your patients experience similar symptomotology. We suggest using the vignettes as follows:

1. Read the vignette.
2. Discuss the vignette and what the characters may be experiencing.
3. Determine whether your patients have had similar experiences and if they can identify with the characters by asking the following questions:
   - Is this a pattern for you?
   - Is this pattern of long or short duration?
   - Do you experience this pattern across situations?
   - Does this type of pattern cause you distress? How?
   - How do you cope with this pattern?
4. Ask patients to identify their automatic thoughts in relation to the vignette.
5. Ask patients if they would like to further assess whether this is a problem area.

WORKSHEET 1: THE ASSESSMENT

If patients identify strongly with the characters in the vignette or believe the symptom is relevant in their life and would like to assess the problem further, ask them to complete WORKSHEET 1: THE ASSESSMENT. (Refer to specific chapters for the various versions of this worksheet.) This worksheet offers approximately ten questions for patients to answer (on a Likert-type scale from 0 to 4) about whether a specific scenario has caused distress or dysfunction in their lives within the past 6 months. WORKSHEET 1: THE ASSESSMENT is only meant to be used as a heuristic marker, not as an emprically-based instrument. If patients rate five or more questions at 2 (moderate severity) or above, or if patients report extreme distress in response to a question, you should consider focusing on that criterion. For those patients who acknowledge that in the past they may have engaged in some of the behaviors within the assessment, but do so no longer, it is the clinician's judgment as to whether include the chapter in the treatment planning. Whether to address the topic largely depends upon whether the patient continues to exhibit distress or dysfunction in response to their past behaviors, or if they are at risk to relapse into these behaviors again, are they able to self-monitor for these responses, and if necessary seek help.

WORKSHEET 2: THE ASSIGNMENT

If WORKSHEET 1 indicates that the patient is exhibiting symptomology for the criterion, WORKSHEET 2: THE ASSIGNMENT (p. 28) should be given. This worksheet clarifies why certain areas are problematic for your patients by helping them identify the related schema. It does this by prompting patients to remember situations in which they experienced the feelings, sensations, and distress exhibited in the vignettes or derived from WORKSHEET 1. This assignment is similar to what Freeman (1992) described as the Critical Incident Technique. You can help patients complete this worksheet by:

- Asking them to "think of the *big scene* or experience that occurred due to your thinking, feeling, or behaving _____ [*specific to relevant criterion*]."
- Encouraging them to examine the context of the situation.
- Encouraging them to imagine themselves "turning back a clock" and placing themselves within the situation.
- Reminding them that they are in the present and safe.
- Redirecting them to the present if they become overwhelmed or upset.

WORKSHEET 2
The Assignment

The following lines are provided for you to write down your assignment of identifying a time or situation in which you experienced a symptom or situation addressed in each chapter. Think of the last experience (when you were alone or with others) that relates to the specific symptom you have identified as problematic. Try to get into the moment and imagine yourself there. Use the lines below to detail your experience. Be as specific as you can. You will compile your reactions in WORKSHEET 3: THE INCIDENT CHART.

_____

_____

_____

_____

_____

_____

_____

_____

_____

_____

_____

_____

_____

_____.

WORKSHEET 3: THE INCIDENT CHART

This worksheet (p. 31) adapted from Beck (1995) and builds on WORKSHEET 2: THE ASSIGNMENT by prompting patients to recall all specific aspects of the situation, including the environment (i.e., external surroundings) and peer groups involved, their thoughts, their emotions, and their behavioral and physiological responses to the situation. This worksheet attempts to demarcate various reactions and symptoms related to responses. To complete this worksheet patients must learn to self-monitor and increase their capacity for self-observation. Ultimately the worksheet will yield information regarding the relative beliefs and underlying schema that perpetuate the patterned reactions and responses causing distress or dysfunction.

Following are a series of tips to help patients complete WORKSHEETS 2 and 3:

- Have patients describe the scene in as much detail as possible.
- Be sure patients are armed with a notepad to write down experiences or sensations outside of the office.
- Be sure there is enough time allotted within the session for a full description of these events.
- Be sure patients are not in a current situation that is activating compelling schema related to the assignment.
- Prompt patients to consider the physiological, emotional, cognitive, and behavioral indicators, reactions, or responses both prior to and during the experience.
- Specifically help patients identify their automatic thoughts in relation to the incident.
- Use the vignettes to help patients conceptualize how schema may be activated.
- If patients have difficulty recalling a situation, use WORKSHEET 1: THE ASSESSMENT to prompt them.

After WORKSHEETS 1, 2, and 3 have been completed, patients must decide whether they wants to take control of the maladaptive behaviors identified in the worksheets. As change is very much a goal of psychotherapy, it is vital that patients understand that they hold the key to effective coping. Taking control, or the decision to take control, is a conscious and active process that at times may be difficult but provides later rewards. Before patients even attempt a new or existing treatment strategy, they must make a commitment to identify the aspects of their personalities they wish to address in treatment. The following questions can assist you in determining whether your patient wants to take control of the identified cognitive-behavioral pattern:

- Now that you understand and can identify the sensations and responses that occur prior to experiencing _____ [*relevant to criteria*], is this something you would like to work on?
- Do you want to change or alter your beliefs in relation to this problematic area?
- What percentage of treatment would you like geared toward this problem?
- What do you think potential barriers or impediments to working on this problem would be?

WORKSHEET 3
The Incident Chart*

This worksheet will help you begin uncovering the schema related to this criterion. Think about the situation you described in WORKSHEET 2 and ask yourself the following:

- What was I physically experiencing before, during, and after the situation?
- What was I feeling?
- What thoughts were running through my mind before, during, and after the situation?
- How was I behaving? [*name some specific behaviors*]

Now fill out the worksheet in as much detail as possible.

Situation: _____.

Prior to Incident

Physiological sensations	Emotions	Cognitions/ thoughts	Behaviors
_____.	_____.	_____.	_____.
_____.	_____.	_____.	_____.

During Incident

Physiological sensations	Emotions	Cognitions/ thoughts	Behaviors
_____.	_____.	_____.	_____.
_____.	_____.	_____.	_____.

After Incident

Physiological sensations	Emotions	Cognitions/ thoughts	Behaviors
_____.	_____.	_____.	_____.
_____.	_____.	_____.	_____.

*(Adapted from J. S. Beck, *Cognitive Therapy: Basics and Beyond.* Guilford Press, 1995©.)

WORKSHEET 4: THE DYSFUNCTIONAL THOUGHT RECORD (DTR)

This worksheet (p. 34) is adopted from Beck (1995) and prompts patients to identify their reactions to problem situations. It does this by assisting patients in identifying the automatic and dysfunctional thoughts associated with their experience of the situation described in WORKSHEET 2 and other similar events. Automatic thoughts are how patients experience or process incoming stimuli through their own systems and generate a thought directly derived from their schema. The goal of the DTR is not only to encourage patients to begin to understand their patterns of automatic thinking, but also to help them respond more effectively to these thoughts. It also assists patients in further developing their ability and skill to self-monitor.

A good assignment is to have your patients identify topics from material collected in the DTR for the next week's agenda. For example, if during the week a patient experiences an argument with a significant other, his or her associated automatic thoughts may include themes of self-loathing. The patient may note that this thought is highly distressing and causes a great deal of negative emotions. The identified automatic thoughts related to self-loathing can then added as an agenda topic for further discussion during the session.

The DTR asks patients to rank the intensity of their emotional responses to their thoughts in the situation on a scale from 0 to 100 (100 being most intense). This allows patients to practice connecting their thoughts to their emotions. The final two columns of the DTR ask patients to identify a more adaptive response and the outcome of that response. The DTR can be completed in two stages: The first four columns can be filled out as the patient completes WORKSHEET 2; the final two columns can be filled out as the patient completes WORK-SHEET 3.

The following general guidelines include suggestions by Beck (1995):

- Be familiar with the DTR before presenting it to patients.
- Refer to the DTR during the actual intervention.
- Ensure that patients grasp the concept of cognitive-behavioral theory.
- Demonstrate the use of the DTR by prompting patients to write down their automatic thoughts as if they were in the moment of the experience or situation described in WORKSHEET 2.
- Use questions such as "What was going through your mind then?"; "What was your stream of thoughts?"; "What were you thinking?"

The DTR s can also be used to tailor techniques and interventions to the specific needs of the patient. The "Adaptive Response" column can be integrated as part of the treatment plan by noting which responses can be used to challenge distorted beliefs. It is often helpful, especially during the first few sessions, to ask your patients to note when they experience a negative mood change during the week and complete a DTR when the mood change occurs.

WORKSHEET 4
The Dysfunctional Thought Record (DTR)*

This worksheet is designed to assist you in identifying your automatic thoughts. Automatic thoughts can help you identify what underlying schemas or beliefs relate to particular events or situations. What are your automatic thoughts relating to_____?

Date/Time	Situation	Automatic thought	Emotion	Adaptive response	Outcome

*(Adapted from J. S. Beck, *Cognitive Therapy: Basics and Beyond.* Guilford Press, 1995©.)

WORKSHEET 5: SCHEMAS

By compiling the information from WORKSHEETS 1 TO 4 (particularly from the DTR), you will be able to begin identifying the activated, compelling schema related to the criterion. For example, patients who identify with Criterion 1, chronic feelings of real or imagined abandonment, may decide that the criterion is relevant to their life (WORKSHEET 1), provide an example of how it has affected their life (WORKSHEET 2), determine the associated responses (WORKSHEET 3), and finally identify the automatic, dysfunctional thoughts that accompany incidents similar to the situation (WORKSHEET 4). You are then able to complete WORKSHEET 5: SCHEMAS (p. 37), which asks patients to hypothesize and test how their core schemas are related to their feelings of being abandoned. By directly asking patients about the beliefs associated with their automatic thoughts, you will be able to generate a list of held schemas. This worksheet prompts patients to identify the beliefs they are aware of, from whom those beliefs come, what meaning the beliefs have, and how easy it will be to change those beliefs. This will provide the raw material needed to implement treatment interventions.

The following tips will help you assist patients in completing the schemas worksheet:

- Provide examples of held schema that are clearly understandable— e.g., beliefs regarding not eating foods such as worms. Then transition to the beliefs relating to the criterion.
- Explain that beliefs are either *intermediate* (composed of rules, attitudes, or assumptions) or *core* (composed of ideas that are absolutist, rigid, or global) (Beck, 1995).
- Ask patients what "rules" of life they follow specific to the criterion.
- Encourage patients to write down beliefs.

Challenging or altering an existing belief requires patients to "step out on a limb" as they try new behaviors and experience new modes of thought. These challenges upset homeostatic equilibrium and can create periods of intense anxiety. As patients practice new behaviors and thoughts, and receive positive feedback from these changes, their anxiety will diminish. You can describe this process of change to patients as the activation of their fight, flight, or freeze responses to anxiety. Psychoeducation about the behavioral, physiological, cognitive, and emotional components accompanying this set of fear responses is helpful in that it prophylactically prevents severe anxiety responses.

After patients have compiled their relevant schemas, and the origins and strength of each, they must determine how much alteration of the schema is possible. For example, if you collaboratively determine that a particular schema requires reconstruction, is it at a major level (total reworking) or a minor level (minimal adjustments to aspects of a particular schema)? Generally, long-held schema that originate from primary caregivers are more difficult to alter. For instance, if a patient has identified strongly with abandonment due the belief that loved ones typically leave, this may be a highly entrenched belief. Total reconstruction may not be possible.

WORKSHEET 5
Schemas

What are your rules or schemas related to being _____?
Take a moment to write them down.

_____

_____

_____

Choose any of these specific rules and fill in each of the columns. Indicate what the rule is, where (or whom) it comes from, what meaning it has for you, and how likely or easy it would be to change that rule. Once you have identified your particular schema, how strong it is, and whether or not it can be changed, you can begin to create treatment goals.

Schema	Where it comes from	Meaning to me	Easy to change?

WORKSHEET 6: TREATMENT GOALS

Treatment goals should be based on an in-depth conceptualization of patients' presenting symptoms, causes of distress, and schemas related to the creation and expression of automatic thoughts. In other words you can ask the patient: "How do you envision a positive and effective outcome?" Identifying treatment goals will help you formulate your treatment strategies. Established goals are paramount to any treatment strategy and should be obtainable and reasonable. Expecting a highly impulsive individual never again to experience an urge to do something is not realistic. However, expecting an individual to put the brakes on before acting *is* reasonable. Setting realistic goals solves two aspects of treatment:

1. Patients will experience relief at knowing they are reaching treatment goals.

2. An accumulation of treatment gains will help clinicians maintain focus on completing more complicated treatment goals and will bolster the much-needed energy to reach those goals.

Setting realistic treatment goals involves collaboration with your patient; the therapist should not be doing all of the work. While the therapist occasionally may exert more effort than the patient, particularly early in treatment, it generally should not be the norm.

WORKSHEET 6: TREATMENT GOALS (p. 41) should be completed for each criterion the patient identifies as relevant to his or her life. The worksheet will enable you to set goals and consider whether they are realistic or unrealistic. To complete this worksheet, adhere to the following steps:

Step 1

Determine if the chapter criterion is relevant to your patient.

- In relation to the specific criterion, what is the identified goal? What does your patient hope to achieve? For example, if the patient has difficulty with experiencing chronic feelings of real or imagined abandonment, is the patient's goal to not feel this way? To experience it as less painful? The purpose of the identified goal column is only to identify the goal.
- What is the priority of working on this goal? Is it high, moderate, or low? This in effect will help define the treatment interventions.
- Is your patient realistically identifying a goal?
- Are you realistically identifying a goal?

Step 2

What symptoms are preventing the goal from being achieved? How does the symptom specifically manifest itself in the patient's life (derived from WORKSHEET 2: THE ASSIGNMENT)? The specific manifestations of the symptom can be utilized as a means of identifying when the patient's alarm system is activated. They also offer an inroad to underlying schema (derived from WORKSHEET 3: THE INCIDENT CHART and WORKSHEETS 7–17).

- What is an example of the manifesting symptom?
- Is this a realistic problem? Is this a pattern?
- Which area causes the most dysfunction or discomfort?

Step 3

What is the related schema? How strongly is it held?

- What is the schema associated with the symptom (derived from WORKSHEET 5: SCHEMAS and WORKSHEET 4: THE DTR)? Specifically identify schema that are problematic.
- Has the patient realistically and completely described the schema?
- Do you believe this is a realistic schema?
- What level of schema change (reconstruction, modification, reinterpretation, camouflage) should be considered? Does the change require complete reworking of the belief or simply a minor adjustment?

Step 4

What is the hoped-for change? What does the patient wish would occur?

- How does the patient conceptualize the hoped-for change?
- Does the patient connect the hoped-for change with the held schema?
- Do you believe the hoped-for change is congruent and on target with the patient's conceptualization of the problem?

Step 5

Is the hoped-for change realistic or unrealistic? What are the patient's expectations of change?

- Is the patient conceptualizing their change as realistic and possible?
- Are you conceptualizing the change as realistic?
- If the patient's hoped-for change is unrealistic, assist him or her in establishing more realistic goals.

Step 6

What is the anticipated outcome?

- What outcome does your patient expect? How are you and the patient conceptualizing the result of schema change?
- Are your expectations realistic?

Step 7

Finally, what is the overall goal? The overall outcome of the treatment should integrate all of the other factors and take into account what is realistic for your patient.

- Does your patient agree with the overall outcome and strategy?
- Do you agree?
- Once you have identified the final goal, you can utilize that information in developing the specifics of your treatment plan.

WORKSHEET 6
Treatment Goals

This worksheet asks patients and you to identify your treatment goals, the symptoms that prevent them from obtaining their goals, the schema that is associated with those goals, and the changes that are hoped for. Are patients able to imagine themselves completing their goals? Complete this chart with the help of your therapist and prioritize the importance of each of these goals.

	Symptoms that prevent you from obtaining goal	Schema associated with goal	Hoped-for change	Realistic or unrealistic?	How outcome looks if goal is reached
Goal 1: Highest priority					
Goal 2: High priority					
Goal 3: Moderate priority					
Goal 4: Low priority					

41

AN EXAMPLE OF GOAL SETTING

The following section describes how Katie, a patient, and her therapist set goals specific to her identified difficulty with chronic feelings of abandonment.

Katie's therapist had identified early in treatment that Katie probably had BPD because she met many of the diagnostic criteria for the disorder. With the encouragement of her therapist, Katie agreed to try the Taking Control program.

Katie had many interpersonal problems. She had a very intense relationship with her boyfriend in which she vascillated between feeling strongly connected and feeling completely alone, isolated, and uncared for. After Katie was oriented to the cognitive-behavioral model of treatment, and specifically to the Taking Control program and manuals, she agreed to read the criterion-based chapter on abandonment.

After a brief mood check, the therapist began to set the agenda. Katie stated that she very much identified with the vignettes contained within the manual and agreed that the topics discussed within the abandonment chapter should be included as part of the agenda. She reported a long history of feeling frightened, anxious, and at times infuriated when she perceived that others in her life were leaving her or changing the "status quo" of the relationship.

With the help of her therapist, Katie completed WORKSHEET 1: THE ASSESSMENT. She positively endorsed several of the worksheet's items, indicating that this was an area to address. Katie indicated that she experienced great distress in reaction to feelings of abandonment.

Katie easily completed WORKSHEET 2: THE ASSIGNMENT, and identified a recent incident that demonstrated her fears of being left or deserted. She wrote about a situation in which she mistakenly interpreted her boyfriend's not calling her as a sign that he no longer wanted to be in the relationship. As she waited late into the evening for his call, she recalled becoming increasingly anxious, distressed, panicked, and tearful. In response to these feelings, she drove to his home sometime past midnight and knocked on his door. His parents answered the door and were quite annoyed with Katie. Her boyfriend had had every intention of calling her, but had fallen asleep on the couch after watching a movie. Katie was mortified.

Katie completed WORKSHEET 3: THE INCIDENT CHART, and documented the physiological, emotional, cognitive, and behavioral components of her dramatic reaction to the situation. She identified the physiological reactions of a racing heart, hyperarousal, and stomach distress. She identified feeling both sad and angry. Her dichotomous thinking included catastrophic conclusions that she would be alone again and that her relationship was over. Finally, in response to these reactions, her behaviors were very impulsive. WORKSHEET 3 allowed Katie to view the incident with her boyfriend in a holistic way, as it delineated how her specific reactions led her to behave in a way she later regretted. Katie then completed WORKSHEET 4: THE DTR, and further described her dichotomous and catastrophic thoughts in relation to the incident.

With the help of her therapist, Katie was able to begin to explore her beliefs and schema related to abandonment. She began to recognize that the schema related to being abandoned was very powerful for her, and she recalled a long history of being fearful of being alone. She easily remembered incidents from her teenage years when she became intensely anxious if her friends didn't call or if someone changed recreational plans. She seemed to always make a negative assumption from these situations, often incorrectly.

As she began to discuss this strongly held schema, she agreed with her therapist that addressing her abandonment belief would be an important treatment goal. For WORKSHEET 6: TREATMENT GOALS, she identified her first goal as to not experience such intense feelings of fear and anxiety when something happens in a relationship. Her therapist helped her understand that no relationship will ever feel totally safe, as relationships typically undergo periods of conflict or change. Katie decided to question her catastrophic thinking in response to the conflict or stress in the relationship rather than reacting in such a dramatic way. She filled out WORKSHEET 6 as follows:

WORKSHEET 6
Treatment Goals

	Symptoms that prevent you from obtaining goal	Schema associated with goal	Hoped-for change	Realistic or unrealistic?	How outcome looks if goal is reached
Goal 1: Highest priority *No abandonment feelings*	*Panic reactions, Catastrophic thinking*	*Those who love me will leave me*	*Not to feel abandoned when in relationship*	*Unrealistic—will sometimes feel conflict or stress in relationship*	
Goal 2: High priority *Managing anxiety*	*Panic reactions*	*I am unable to stop the panic*	*To manage panic attacks*	*Realistic*	
Goal 3: Moderate priority					
Goal 4: Low priority					

COMPLETION OF WORKSHEET 18: THE DIAGNOSTIC PROFILING
SYSTEM (DPS)

Freeman (1998) proposed the Diagnostic Profiling System (DPS) as a means of gauging and scaling the extent of distress and dysfunction caused by each symptom relevant to the *DSM-IV-TR* criteria. WORKSHEET 18: THE DPS (pp. 46–47) should be completed at least twice during each step: first, after WORKSHEET 6: TREATMENT GOALS has been completed (to establish a baseline), and second, after the interventions have been applied (to test whether they were successful). As patients practice new techniques during the week between sessions, the DPS can be reintroduced during the review of homework from the preceding week. In this way, the clinician can determine if patients utilized the interventions appropriately or whether the interventions require reworking or alteration. In addition, the DPS can be used as a check-in measure several weeks after interventions have been learned to determine whether they have "stuck" or if the chapter needs to be revisited, the goals altered, or the interventions retargeted. Toward the end of treatment, completing the DPS on all symptoms can assist in determining termination.

The DPS prompts the clinician and patient to rate the severity of each criterion on a Likert-type scale from 0 to 10, with 10 being the most severe. To complete the DPS, begin by listing the relevant symptoms at the bottom of the worksheet. The individual assessments can guide you in identifying how each criterion is exhibited. Next, rank the levels of intensity of each symptom on the vertical axis. We suggest that the DPS be used in conjunction with WORKSHEET 1: THE ASSESSMENT, which helps measure the severity of the symptom before intervention.

Application of Treatment Strategies & Interventions

The next step involves formulating and applying treatment strategies and interventions. (Note, however, that interventions can be applied at any time during the session if the situation warrants it.) Patients' abilities to self-monitor is key to determining how underlying schemas are being manifested. WORKSHEETS 7, 9, 11, 13, 15, and 16 help patients self-monitor by asking them to identify their physical, emotional, automatic thought, behavioral, and situational triggers. WORKSHEETS 8, 10, 12, 14, and 17 correspond with WORKSHEETS 7, 9, 11, 13, 15, and 16 by providing specific interventions targeting areas requiring alteration. The overall goals are for patients to learn to identify when their discomfort occurs, how it presents itself, and how to arm themselves with interventions to thwart such discomfort. Long-term goals are to alter the dysfunctional thoughts and underlying

The Diagnostic Profiling System (DPS)

FREEMAN DIAGNOSTIC PROFILING SYSTEM

(© FREEMAN, 2003) REVISED EDITION

Date of Assessment: _____

Patient#: _____   Session#: _____   Location: _____   Evaluator: _____

Patient Name: _____

Age: _____   Race: _____   Gender: _____   Birthorder: _____   Marital/Children: _____

Birthdate: _____

Employment: _____   Education: _____   Disability: _____   Medication: _____

Physician: _____   Referral Question: _____

Instructions: Record the diagnosis including the code number. Briefly identify the criteria for the selected diagnosis. Working with the patient either directly as as part of the data gathering of the clinical interview, SCALE the SEVERITY of EACH CRITERION for the patient at the PRESENT TIME. Indicate the level of severity on the grid.

DIAGNOSIS (DSM/ICD) with Code:

Axis I: _____

Axis II: _____

Axis III: _____

HIGH

10
9
8
7

SYMPTOMS

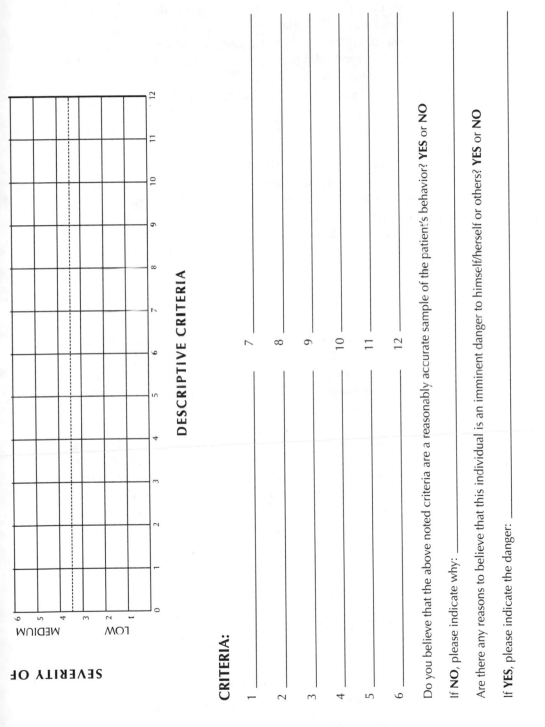

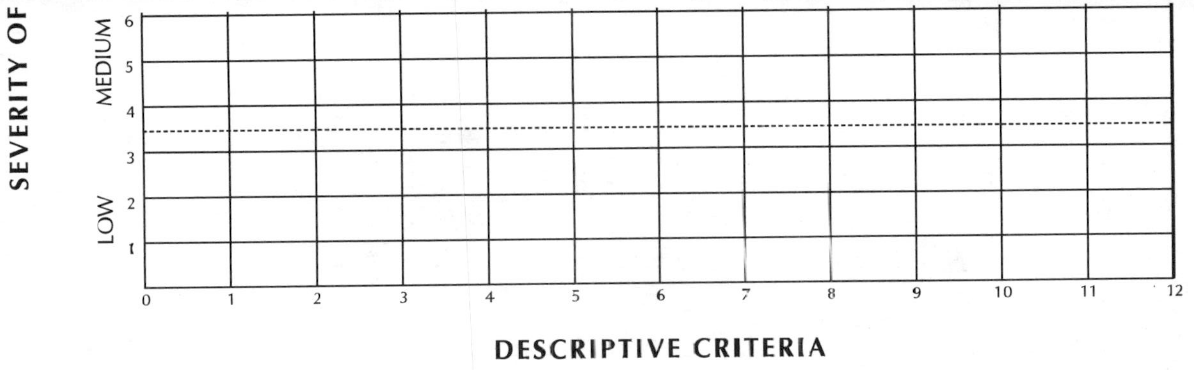
SEVERITY OF
MEDIUM
LOW
1 2 3 4 5 6
0 1 2 3 4 5 6 7 8 9 10 11 12
DESCRIPTIVE CRITERIA

CRITERIA:

1 ______________________ 7 ______________________

2 ______________________ 8 ______________________

3 ______________________ 9 ______________________

4 ______________________ 10 ______________________

5 ______________________ 11 ______________________

6 ______________________ 12 ______________________

Do you believe that the above noted criteria are a reasonably accurate sample of the patient's behavior? **YES** or **NO**

If **NO**, please indicate why: ______________________

Are there any reasons to believe that this individual is an imminent danger to himself/herself or others? **YES** or **NO**

If **YES**, please indicate the danger: ______________________

(From Freeman, 1998.)

schema related to the identified symptoms and triggers. This involves extensive use of cognitive interventions targeting the typical belief patterns and schema of BPD patients.

The Therapist and Patient Manuals suggest numerous cognitive-behavioral interventions relevant to the individual criteria and the responses that have become problematic for patients. These interventions were developed to combat or challenge cognitive distortions that lead to maladaptive behavioral responses. By challenging these distortions, subsequent change (assimilation and accommodation) within the schema occurs. Because each patient exhibits varying symptoms and therefore require different treatment methodologies, we encourage you to individualize the treatment plans. Although the interventions are presented here according to the various response categories (e.g., physical, emotional, cognitive, behavioral, and situational), they are flexible and can be used in combination or for any of the other targeted responses. In particular, the cognitive interventions can be utilized to address maladaptive beliefs and held schemas.

WORKSHEET 7: PHYSICAL TRIGGERS

This worksheet (p. 49) asks patients to consider the physical sensations they experience in relation to the particular criterion. Physical sensations are cues that can be used to identify when the patient's alarm system is being activated. They are often the earliest warning signs. For example, patients who have difficulty with abandonment issues may first become aware that something distressful is occurring when they begin to experience symptoms of anxiety, such as a pounding heart, sweaty palms, or gastrointestinal distress. Be sure your patient has been evaluated by a medical physician to ensure there are no underlying medical conditions presenting themselves as symptoms of anxiety. By self-monitoring for these earliest of warning signs, patients are taking initial steps to take control and thus can make informed choices about what their next move or reaction will be.

WORKSHEET 7
Physical Triggers

Physical sensations are clues to help you avoid future distressful situations. They may be very strong messages from your body, such as a pounding heart, stomach problems, or a general tenseness in your muscles. Think of the experience you described in WORKSHEET 2: THE ASSIGNMENT. What were you physically experiencing before, during, and after you perceived you _____?
You may have felt some of the following:

- queasy stomach.
- sweating/clammy skin.
- racing heart.
- tension.
- GI distress.

Use the lines provided below to describe your physical sensations.

_____

_____

_____

_____

_____

_____

_____

_____

_____

_____

_____

WORKSHEET 8: PHYSICAL TRIGGERS & SUGGESTED INTERVENTIONS
The primary interventions for physical triggers are:

- Thought-stopping.
- Relaxation.
- Relaxing imagery.

Thought-Stopping. Dysfunctional thoughts often have a snowball effect. They tend to accumulate and elicit a "second string" of dysfunctional thoughts that increase exponentially. If this process continues unimpeded, dysfunctional thoughts will run rampant, generating accompanying maladaptive responses. Some of these maladaptive responses can be in the form of a physiological reaction, such as those created by anxiety (e.g., shortness of breath, rapid heartbeat, sweatiness, and upset stomach).

Thought-stopping is based on a relatively simple premise. When patients experience distressful thoughts, they learn to stop and think something else. How is this done? Patients use the DTR to track particular thoughts that generate maladaptive responses. Patients' alarm systems have been activated as a result of the thought. They now can take note when the thought occurs and interrupt the flow of thoughts with a sudden stimulus (imagined or real), which prompts other thoughts. Patients can utilize a visual, auditory, or tactile stimulus, such as imagining a stop sign, hearing the word *stop*, or snapping a rubber band against the wrist when the thought occurs (Beck, 1995). You can demonstrate this during sessions by slapping your hand on the desk when patients have experienced a thought that causes uncomfortable physiological sensations. This hand-slapping technique effectively interrupts the physical sensations that arise from dysfunctional thoughts.

Relaxation. Relaxation and breathing exercises can bring considerable relief to anxious and/or tense individuals. Often the physical sensations accompanying anxiety can worsen the anxiety. Progressive muscle relaxation (PMR) techniques, first established by Jacobson (1962), have been proven to decrease anxiety consistently. PMR is easily taught in the clinician's office and patients can utilize the technique at home. Relaxation techniques can be taught with a variety of accessory methods including visual or auditory imagery combined with practiced breathing exercises to reinforce the belief that the patient can indeed control aspects of his or her body (Freeman, Pretzer, Fleming, & Simon, 1990). Bernstein and Borkovec (1976) provided a good primer for those unfamiliar with these widely used techniques.

Relaxing Imagery. In combination with the previous two techniques, employing relaxing imagery can decrease physiological arousal and subsequent anxiety. Encourage patients to identify a safe, relaxing image or scene, such as a beach or the woods, so that they can utilize that image when thought-stopping and relaxation techniques are being utilized. It is helpful to encourage your patients to imagine the situation in detail and to attempt to experience all of the sensations associated with the image. Audiotapes in combination with the relaxing image and PMR can be quite effective and can be self-administered outside the therapeutic setting (Freeman et al., 1990). Relaxing imagery is also described in the behavioral section. The following prompts can be used to assist patients in defining specific imagery:

I feel safe imagining _____.

I hear _____.

I feel _____.

I can see _____.

I can smell _____.

I can taste _____.

My safe person who can join me here is _____.

WORKSHEET 9: EMOTIONAL TRIGGERS

This worksheet (p. 52) asks patients to identify the emotions they experienced during the distressing situation. Emotions are very much a part of how we define ourselves and our personalities. Many make decisions based on their emotions without the added benefit of processing experiences with their mind. Merely recognizing and identifying what emotions they tend to experience will help patients understand and potentially change their reactions. By self-monitoring emotions, patients can determine which emotions have led to problematic thoughts or behaviors and make an informed choice about how they wish to react to them.

WORKSHEET 9
Emotional Triggers

How would you describe the emotions you felt during the distressful sit-uation? They may be very intense emotions such as sadness or anger. Use the emotions sections of WORKSHEETS 3 and 4 to identify some of the feelings you had when _____. They may include some of the following:

• fear.
• anger.
• sadness.
• disgust.

What were you feeling emotionally? Write down what those feelings were like.

_____

_____

_____

_____

_____

_____

_____

_____

_____

_____

_____

_____

_____.

WORKSHEET 10: EMOTIONAL TRIGGERS & SUGGESTED INTERVENTIONS
The primary interventions for emotional triggers are:

- Scaling Back.
- Improving Communication of Feelings.

Scaling Back. Often when patients feel very emotional about a situation or thought, they will react impulsively rather than thinking about how to respond. This technique is designed to assist patients in learning to "turn down" or lower the experience of a strongly felt emotion. By helping patients recognize the emotional response and its intensity *before* they react, they can learn to take a moment, scale the emotions back, and then choose how to react.

The Patient Manual describes this technique as follows:

> Because you are an exceptionally sensitive person, it would be unrealistic for you to try not to experience the emotions that accompany stress. You can, however, try to scale them back. Consider when you are experiencing a stressful situation turning those anxious feelings down a notch. Think of baking a soufflé. If the oven is too hot, the soufflé will overheat. If you yourself overheat, you may do or say something that you later regret. Before you react to the feelings you are experiencing, try to turn yourself down a few degrees—just like the oven. You can then learn to take control of what you consider to be damaging aspects of your relationships. Begin by rating the severity of emotion you are experiencing. Once you have tried to scale down your emotional response, take a moment to rate your emotion again and note the difference in the ratings. Scaling back takes practice. Do not be discouraged if you are unable to turn yourself down as quickly as you'd like to. (p. 12)

Clinicians can help patients with this exercise by:

- Encouraging them to wait a moment before they respond.
- Encouraging them to visualize "cooling off" or "turning down."
- Combining the exercise with relaxation techniques and/or relaxing imagery.

WORKSHEET 10 includes the following technique for assessing the emotions related to trigger experiences.
Consider the emotional response you wish to address. On a scale of 1 to 10 (1 being least intense and 10 being most intense), how would you rate the intense emotion you experienced before, during, or after

_____?

| 1 | 2 | 3 | 4 | 5 | 6 | 7 | 8 | 9 | 10 |

As you continue to have uncomfortable emotions related to _____, try to scale back or "turn the oven down." You may want to combine scaling back with some relaxation techniques described in the section on physical triggers. Once you have turned yourself down, rate your emotion again:

1   2   3   4   5   6   7   8   9   10

Ask patients if they feel different after scaling back, and to describe their feelings.

Improving Communication of Feelings. Assisting patients in communicating their feelings and emotions can help them improve their relationships. Furthermore, as patients learn to communicate with others, they also learn to communicate with themselves by rehearsing "self-talk". Self-talk is another form of self-monitoring. Meichenbaum (1977) encouraged the use of self-instruction, i.e., telling oneself what to do as a means of controlling impulsivity. Expressing oneself is not easy, and if patients have schema related to negative reactions when they express their feelings, they may have learned that saying or showing feelings is unsafe or threatening.

Building on the work of Satir (1967), communication involves three elements. It begins with the (1) "sender" of the message; the person trying to tell or show the other person something. Then there is the (2) message itself. The mission of the message is to reach the (3) receiver. To help your patients understand communication, remind them about their filter systems. The sender wants to say something to the receiver. However, the original message is subject to the sender's filter system. For instance, although the sender may be trying to say something kind to the receiver (a cheerful hello), his or her body language (poor eye contact) may communicate something else, like disinterest. This gives the message more than one possible meaning. Then, as the message is picked up by the receiver, it again is interpreted through a second filtering system. If the receiver misinterprets the message, his or her alarm system may become activated.

Misunderstandings can result from a simple exchange of words. Ask patients to listen to a conversation and note how often they hear expressions like the following: "Oh, I thought you meant"; "But you said"; "I don't remember it that way"; or "You mean what?" Prompting patients to examine how they send and interpret information with others can help them learn to examine their emotional expression. The following questions can help patients master effective communication:

• How do you send your messages? Watch how you communicate

nonverbally and verbally. Do you yell? Do you shake your fist? Does the pitch or loudness of your voice change?

- What kind of messages do you send? Do you make statements that are condescending or that put the other person down? Do they relate to the issue at hand? Do you make negative statements about yourself?
- How do you think the receiver is perceiving the messages? How do his or her responses contribute to your return messages?
- Do you ask if the other person understands your message? Do you prompt the other person to repeat what you just said in order to clarify?

The Communication Patterns Chart						
Sender of message	Receiver	Message	Verbal communication	Nonverbal communication	Type of communication (e.g., derogatory, self-deprecating)	Receiver's interpretation of message

Remember the typical distortions exhibited by borderline patients as you assist patients with these exercises, and keep in mind that they may provide additional information regarding underlying schema (see Introduction). For example, patients who demonstrate dichotomous thinking may need to be reminded to look for the "grays" in another individual's message before they react to it.

The following communication strategies are included in the patient manual and are integrated throughout the intervention worksheets:

Use "I" statements. Use "I" statements about how you are feeling in the moment. Let the other person know what kinds of feelings you are having. When you stay with "I" statements there really can't be any confusion about whom is feeling what!

I am feeling _____.

I am unsure if _____.

I _____.

Stay cool. In relationships, we tend to react with very strong emotions. Remember the scaling back exercise? Staying cool is reminding yourself that you need to turn yourself down before reacting to the other person. The other person will perceive not only what you are saying but also how you are saying it. For example, even though you may want to convince the other person that you aren't angry, yelling that you aren't angry sends a confusing and contradictory message.

No cursing allowed. Vulgar statements only add fuel to an already smoldering fire. Others usually remember cursing or crude things that are said to them even if it is in the "heat of the moment." By not cursing, you demonstrate that even though you may be hurt, afraid, or even angry, you respect others enough to not curse.

See what's coming. Do you and another person have a typical way of arguing or resolving conflict? Are you able to see what's coming? If you can, you will be able to prepare yourself and maybe even break the cycle by changing typical reactions.

I tend to resolve conflict by _____.

My arguments with others usually end with me

_____.

My arguments with others usually end with them

_____.

I would like to change the way I resolve conflict by

_____.

Bridge the gap. Is there room for compromise? Are you able to offer a compromise or help the other person come up with one? Have you both looked at ways to resolve the conflict?

I can compromise usually if _____.

Times I am unable to compromise include _____.

I would like to be able to compromise more about

_____.

See the grays in life. Is there something that you both may be missing? Is there something other than the two sides that you are both seeing or reacting to? What is the "gray" of the situation? This exercise is similar to the one that challenges black-and-white thinking in the cognitive section.

The black of the situation is _____.

The white of the situation is _____.

The grays of the situation are _____.

It doesn't have to end. Do you or the other person typically threaten to end or permanently change the relationship when you are emotionally charged up? When you are in the heat of the moment, you may feel so overwhelmed with emotions that you see no way out. By seeing the grays of situations and promising yourself and the other person that you won't threaten to end or permanently change the relationship, you build a path toward better communication of your feelings. This communication comes out of clear thinking and is not based solely on intense emotions.

Take turns. Are you letting the other person make his or her own "I" statements? Often miscommunication occurs because we don't hear each other or let the other person tell us how they are actually feeling. By allowing the other person to express him- or herself you are building a bridge to his or her perceptions and learning how your behaviors effect others.

I feel _____.

He or she responds _____.

I then say _____.

WORKSHEET 11: COGNITIVE/AUTOMATIC THOUGHTS TRIGGERS

This worksheet (p. 58) assists in patients identifying and utilizing the automatic thoughts that occur during situations that cause distress or difficulty. It largely serves to extend the DTR and provide additional writing space to detail the thoughts that occurred in response to the specific incident. Automatic thoughts provide an inroad to understanding underlying schema and therefore are a primary focus of cognitive-behavioral therapy interventions.

WORKSHEET 11
Cognitive/Automatic Thoughts

What thoughts were running through your mind before, during, and after you perceived _____? What primary thought seemed to make you increasingly distressed? Refer to WORKSHEET 4: THE DTR to identify the specific thoughts related to this topic.

WORKSHEET 12: COGNITIVE/AUTOMATIC THOUGHTS & SUGGESTED
INTERVENTIONS
The primary interventions for cognitive/automatic thoughts are:

• The Catastrophic Thinking Chart.
• Challenge Dichotomous Thinking.
• The Disputation Chart.
• The Negative and Positive Consequences Chart.
• The Impulsivity Chart.

Beck (1976) stated that errors in thinking, or "cognitive distortions," can wreak havoc and aggravate the establishment and maintenance of relationships for those with BPD. Individuals with BPD typically experience many types of cognitive distortions; the three most common distortions are: Catastropic thinking; dichotomous thinking; and jumping to conclusions.

Catastrophic Thinking. This form of thinking means assuming that the worst is going to happen. Individuals who engage in catastrophic thinking believe that when a situation arises, a catastrophy will probably occur. Challenging catastrophic outcomes is difficult, as we do not necessarily *know* the outcomes of situations. But you can help patients by asking: "Is it really likely that the dreaded event will happen?"; "Are you reacting to a catastrophy that has occurred only in your mind?"; "What is the evidence that it will happen?"; and, finally, "Worst case scenario: If it did actually happen, what would you do and how would you cope?" Using the DISPUTATION CHART (p. 61) and CATASTROPHIC THINKING CHART (below) will help generate alternative ideas related to the event.

The Catastrophic Thinking Chart

This chart helps patients challenge their assumptions that the worst is going to happen by asking them to imagine alternative outcomes to the situation.

Situation	Catastrophic Thought	Noncatastrophic Thought
_____ .	_____ .	_____ .
_____ .	_____ .	_____ .
_____ .	_____ .	_____ .

Dichotomous Thinking. This form of thinking means looking at things in an all-or-nothing way or in extremes. It is the tendency to "evaluate experiences in terms of mutually exclusive categories (e.g., good or bad, success or failure, trustworthy or deceitful) rather than seeing things on a continua" (Beck, Freeman, & Associates, 1990, p. 187). There is very little "gray" in this form of thinking, which sometimes blocks opportunities that may exist in the gray. Dichotomous thinking can also easily result in an abrupt shift to the opposite extreme, as there are no continua on which to base perceptions or interpretations of information. In order to help your patient conceptualize this, use the analogy of an artist's paint palette. Imagine that the palette has only has black and white paint. However, if the artist mixes black and white, he gets a broad array of different grays. The grays in life can be loosely translated as all the options or alternatives that one can consider. Ask your patient to try defining the grays in life. For example, if your patient views his or her partner or as either a terrible person or a perfect person, ask the patient to mix the black and white into a gray. Probably the person is both good and bad.

The Dichotomous Thinking Chart		
Black	**Gray(s)**	**White**
|--|--|		
He's terrible.	*He's not perfect but sometimes he's great.*	*He's perfect.*

Jumping to Conclusions. This form of thinking means that assumptions are made without looking at what the actual proof is. Often there is a rush to a conclusion without considering whether there is actual evidence to support it. As noted earlier, impulsivity is a typical symptom of BPD, and it can extend into thought processes as well. Interventions prompt patients to challenge themselves by producing evidence of what they fear is happening or could happen. Challenge patients to prove themselves wrong or to prove that the worst is unlikely to happen (see the DISPUTATION CHART). Encourage patients to think of themselves as scientists gathering data to support their conclusions.

The Disputation Chart

This chart prompts patients to write down what they are convinced has happened. Then they fill in the chart both with proof of their assumption and refuting statements contradicting the assumption. The purpose of the chart if for patients to weigh the evidence of their belief using objective information to challenge distorted subjective information. Once the DISPUTATION CHART is complete, you can suggest that patients carry the chart with them as a way to prevent their reactions to unsubstantiated negative thoughts.

Situation: _____ .

Belief: _____ .

Proof Supporting Belief   **Refuting Statement**

1. _____ .   _____ .

2. _____ .   _____ .

3. _____ .   _____ .

The Negative and Positive Consequences Chart

This chart challenges patients to examine their behaviors before they engage in them. Patients must have completed WORKSHEET 3: THE INCIDENT CHART and be able to read their physical and emotional warning signs. The NEGATIVE AND POSITIVE CONSEQUENCES CHART asks patients to list the positive and negative consequences of a particular behavior or response. For example, a patient may want to act impulsively by being sexually intimate with a stranger. Filling out the chart and discussing the weight and meaning of each behavior can help the patient assess the positive and negative consequences of that action. Next, challenge the patient to identify a specific behavior that he or she is considering changing. After the consequences have been carefully weighed, does the behavior seem worth doing?

Behavior	**Negative Consequences**	**Positive Consequences**
Going home with stranger.	*Dumped next day, sexually transmitted diseases, HIV, potential danger of rape, murder.*	*Sexual encounter, feeling close, not being alone, potential relationship.*
_____ .	_____ .	_____ .
_____ .	_____ .	_____ .
_____ .	_____ .	_____ .

After completing the chart, ask patients the following:
- Do the negative consequences outweigh the positive consequences?
- Is it worth it to decrease this behavior?
- Do you want to continue this behavior?

Impulsivity Chart*

Impulsivity is a key symptom of BPD. Impulsivity can wreak havoc for those who react and respond without careful consideration of the potential outcome or consequences. The IMPULSIVITY CHART helps determine the actual route of an impulsive act and offers several avenues to prevent it (Pretzer, 1990, p. 203).

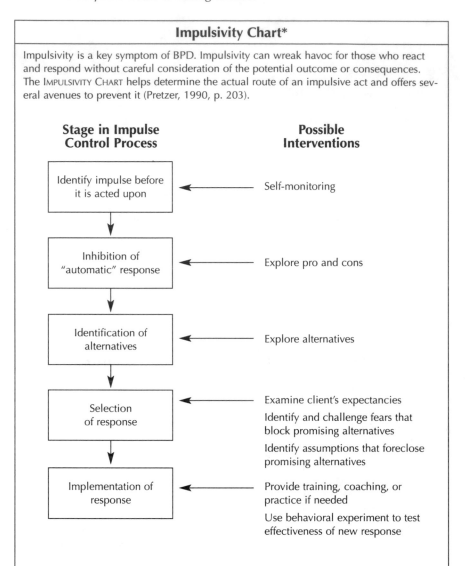

Stage in Impulse Control Process

Possible Interventions

Stage in Impulse Control Process	Possible Interventions
Identify impulse before it is acted upon	Self-monitoring
Inhibition of "automatic" response	Explore pro and cons
Identification of alternatives	Explore alternatives
Selection of response	Examine client's expectancies Identify and challenge fears that block promising alternatives Identify assumptions that foreclose promising alternatives
Implementation of response	Provide training, coaching, or practice if needed Use behavioral experiment to test effectiveness of new response

Following are steps needed to fill out the IMPULSIVITY CHART:

1. *Identify the impulse.* Encourage patients to identify impulses before acting on them by self-monitoring in all areas.
2. *Inhibit automatic responses.* What are the pros and cons of acting on a certain urge or impulse? How do they weigh out? Does a night of passion with a stranger outweigh the possibility of danger? When we enter situations, we usually have a preconception about how they will turn out. This is a result of our experiences growing up, living, and functioning in everyday society. For instance, we know that if we park in a

---

*(From J. Pretzer [1990]. Borderline personality disorder. In A. Beck, A. Freeman, & Associates [eds.], *Cognitive therapy of personality disorders* [pp. 176–207]. New York: Guilford Press. Reprinted by permission of the Guilford Press.)

no-parking zone, we may be able to get into the store more quickly (positive) but we are also likely to get a ticket (negative). Often we can predict an outcome just by examining the situation at hand in more detail and by taking the time to read and monitor ourselves better.

3. *Identify alternatives.* Now that the patient is aware that he or she can make an informed choice about urges, does that mean no more spontaneity? Of course not. It's all a matter of degree, or finding the middle ground. For example, what could the individual considering sexual intimacy with a stranger have done to avoid placing him- or herself in a dangerous situation while continuing to attempt to make a connection with the new person?

4. *Select a response.* Identify and challenge fears related to alternatives. How does the patient make the choice to act or not to act? What are the patient's expectations regarding the act? What are the hopes related to carrying out the impulse? What, if any, are the disadvantages to not acting on an urge? Does actually looking before you leap make you boring or not alive? These responses need to be challenged, as acting on certain urges may actually threaten the patient's safety.

5. *Implement a response.* This fifth and final step entails actually choosing a response. If your patient is learning to take control of his or her impulses, it will take practice, training, and learning to identify vulnerable times when the likelihood of acting on an impulse that may be regretted later is high.

Encourage patients to ask themselves common-sense questions such as "Is this really a wise choice?" or "Could I get myself into trouble with this?" Also ask patients to consider the current situation: Are there prior situations that are similar?; What were the decisions that were made in this similar situation?; What was the outcome of the decisions that were made?; Are there similarities to the current situation and the potential decisions that are going to be made?

WORKSHEET 13: BEHAVIORAL TRIGGERS

Behaviors; the actual ways in which we react, are often what we notice the most. Other than the physiological reactions patients may experience, behaviors are the easiest means of explaining what self-monitoring is and how it can be helpful. For example, an individual may not recognize that he or she is angry until he or she actually behaves angrily, e.g., hits something. By self-monitoring, patients can more easily identify subtler forms of behavior that occur prior to the explosiveness, such as pacing. Behaviors can also be the result of reacting to a physiological, emotional, or cognitive stimulus (for instance, yelling when having a particular thought). These actions may include yelling, hitting, throwing, or even fighting. They may also be behaviors such as withdrawing from others, drinking in excess, or spending money unwisely. WORKSHEET 13 asks patients to identify the specific behaviors they were engaging in prior to, during, and after the experience described in WORKSHEET 2: THE ASSIGNMENT. The following questions may help identify the behaviors the patient wishes to address:

- Did you regret anything you did?
- Were you embarrassed by anything you did?
- Did your behavior help or hinder your relationships with others?
- Did your behavior make you feel bad about yourself?
- Did your behavior cause any irreversible events?

WORKSHEET 13
Behavioral Triggers

What specific behaviors did you engage in prior to, during, and after you perceived you were _____? Were you yelling at your significant other? Holding on to him or her? Shaking your fist at him or her? Making repeated phone calls? Take a moment to jot down what you were doing during this very stressful time.

Before:

Behavior 1 _____.

Behavior 2 _____.

Behavior 3 _____.

During:

Behavior 1 _____.

Behavior 2 _____.

Behavior 3 _____.

After:

Behavior 1 _____.

Behavior 2 _____.

Behavior 3 _____.

Try to detail as much information regarding your behaviors as possible. Use the lines provided below.

_____

_____

_____

_____.

WORKSHEET 14: BEHAVIORAL TRIGGERS & SUGGESTED INTERVENTIONS
  The primary interventions for behavioral triggers are:

- Consider the consequence.
- Try something different.
- Remove yourself.
- Stop what you're doing.
- Relaxation.
- Relaxing imagery.
- Identify a friend (safe person).

Consider the Consequence. What is (or could be) the consequence of a behavior? Suggest that patients use means-end thinking. In other words, are patients' actions going to lead to the end they want? Ask your patients to consider the behavior by asking them: "Is it worth it?"; "Is it for the good of yourself and/or your relationship?" The NEGATIVE AND POSITIVE CONSEQUENCES CHART (p. 61) is helpful with this exercise.

Try Something Different. Encourage your patients to identify and try a different behavior. For example, a patient could, instead of yelling, try scaling back and lowering their voice to a normal speaking tone. Once they have listed alternative ways of acting in a situation, suggest that patients carry the list around with them as a reminder.

Remove Yourself. If patients can identify times when they are unable to control what they do or how they react, suggest that they don't give themselves the opportunity to lose control. They can try taking a walk, going into another room, or letting whomever may be exacerbating the problem know that a "time-out" needs to occur, as discussion is currently causing too much upset. In this way, patients avoid saying or doing something they may later regret.

Stop What You're Doing. Take a moment to stop. Often experiencing physiological sensations causes a reaction to something perceived (distorted or accurate). Once patients recognize the familiar "butterflies in the stomach," they should take a moment to just stop. By having a moment of not doing, analyzing, thinking, or reacting, one allows the body to regain its equilibrium and calm down. Take a seat, take a breath, and focus on nothing but taking control.

Relaxation. Behavioral relaxation techniques are identical to the physiological relaxation techniques described earlier. Feelings of anger, anxiousness, or upset respond well to relaxation techniques. Encourage patients to sit down in a comfortable chair after they have taken a moment to stop. Suggest that they relax all of their muscles, letting the chair hold their weight, and calmly breathe in, focusing deeply on the diaphragm filling up and exhaling air. They can do this three times. Encourage them to imagine beginning to relax and take control. The negative cycles of engaging in a behavior that they wish to change can be altered if patients relax and, once calm, consider their options and alternatives.

Relaxing Imagery. Help patients identify and imagine a comfortable place or a favorite place they love to visit. Some people like to imagine themselves on a beach or in a forest. Encourage them to imagine whatever scene makes them relax. Help flesh out the picture by asking them for example, to think of the smells, feel the breezes, and hear the sounds. Combine relaxing imagery with relaxation exercises.

Identify a Friend (Safe Person). If patients can identify times that are especially difficult, it is imperative that they identify someone that is close to them, supportive, and understands that they may be struggling. This person should be their "safe person"—someone they can turn to who generally does not cause more distress. Encourage your patient to carry the person's phone number and potentially have a set code word to signal when they "really need to talk."

WORKSHEET 15: THE EXPANDED INCIDENT CHART

This worksheet (pp. 68–69) is a means of advancing the patient's understanding of the relevant situation and its context. It expands upon WORKSHEET 3: THE INCIDENT CHART and includes recognizing the people that may be associated with the context of the incident. This chart is introduced in the Patient Manual only in the chapters relating to self-harm, learning to control anger, paranoid states, and dissociative experiences. Often the actions of others prompt potentially self-damaging, suicidal, or parasuicidal behaviors resulting from limited impulse control. The chart offers an additional "people" column to ensure that the patient fully contextualizes the situations that are known to be difficult. The ultimate goal is to change or avoid the responses that typically have accompanied specific people and specific situations.

WORKSHEET 15
The Expanded Incident Chart

As you complete this worksheet, ask yourself the following:

- What was I physically experiencing before, during, and after the situation?
- What was I feeling?
- What thoughts were running through my mind before, during, and after the situation?
- How was I behaving? [*name some specific behaviors*]
- Is there a specific person or group associated with this situation?

Situation: _____

Prior to Incident

People	Physiological sensations	Emotions	Cognitions-thoughts	Behaviors

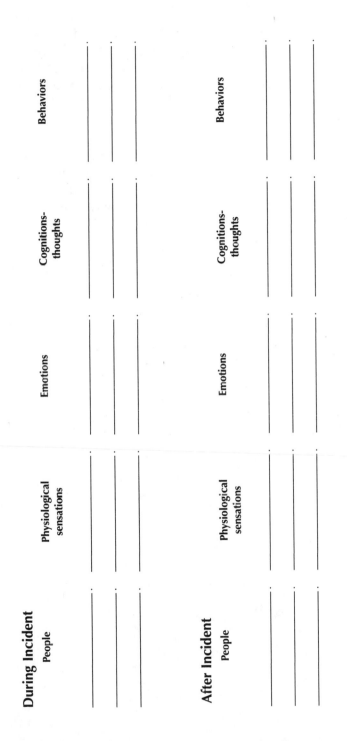

During Incident

People _____ Physiological sensations _____ Emotions _____ Cognitions-thoughts _____ Behaviors _____

After Incident

People _____ Physiological sensations _____ Emotions _____ Cognitions-thoughts _____ Behaviors _____

WORKSHEET 16: SITUATIONAL TRIGGERS

Certain events, people, and places can trigger patients' alarm systems. WORKSHEET 2: THE ASSIGNMENT prompts patients to recall or identify an incident that exemplifies symptoms of the criterion, and it is designed to help patients begin to understand the specific contexts in which they tend to experience difficulty. This worksheet builds on WORKSHEET 2 by delineating specific situations that have caused distress. By knowing what situations or contexts are problematic, patients can make decisions about how they want to handle the situation, which in some cases may mean removing themselves from the situation. WORKSHEET 1: THE ASSESSMENT can also be used to help patients identify the specific times, situations, events, and people that tend to cause distressing situations.

WORKSHEET 16
Situational Triggers

There may be times, individuals, events, and places that seem to cause a great deal of distress. Knowing which situations cause you difficulty can help you be prepared if a similar situation occurs, and you can be on extra alert for your alarms. You identified your four areas of warning signs in WORKSHEET 3: THE INCIDENT CHART. Now please list the situations in which you have experienced difficulty related to believing that

_____

_____.

Review WORKSHEET 1 if you need help identifying these situations.

1. _____

_____

_____.

2. _____

_____

_____.

3. _____

_____

_____.

4. _____

_____

_____.

WORKSHEET 17: SITUATIONAL TRIGGERS & SUGGESTED INTERVENTIONS

Through self-monitoring, patients may be able to identify which situations typically cause distress or exacerbate symptoms that may not occur at other times. Although not all situations are avoidable—for example, patients may have to go to the office even if it causes distress—they can avoid those that are and choose to change their reactions to those that are not. Following are brief descriptions of interventions that can be applied to any distressful situation:

• Remove yourself.
• Try something different.

Remove yourself. Removing yourself from a situation prevents you from losing control. Try taking a walk, going into another room, or taking a break from a conversation or situation.

When things get particularly difficult, I can _____ .

Try something different. Identify and list other behaviors that can help make you feel better. Carry a list of these "other things to do."

Instead of _____ [behavior],
I can try _____ [alternate behavior].

WORKSHEET 18: PATIENT PROGRESS & THE DIAGNOSTIC PROFILING SYSTEM

After patients have used the interventions described in prior sections, ask them to complete the DPS. The DPS can then provide an indication whether the interventions are actually working. If there is no decrease in distress compared to the prior related DPS in relation to the specific criterion, the therapist should revisit the specific interventions that patients are using, and determine whether new interventions should be applied or altered. The therapist should also review with patients how the interventions are being applied to ensure they are being used accurately. If there is an improvement, patients have concrete evidence (as shown on the DPS) that their efforts at reducing their distress is working.

The Diagnostic Profiling System (DPS)

FREEMAN DIAGNOSTIC PROFILING SYSTEM
(© FREEMAN, 2003) REVISED EDITION

Patient Name: _____ Patient#: _____ Location: _____

Date of Assessment: _____ Session#: _____ Evaluator: _____

Birthdate: _____ Age: _____ Race: _____ Gender: _____ Birthorder: _____ Marital/Children: _____

Employment: _____ Education: _____ Disability: _____ Medication: _____

Physician: _____ Referral Question: _____

Instructions: Record the diagnosis including the code number. Briefly identify the criteria for the selected diagnosis. Working with the patient either directly as as part of the data gathering of the clinical interview, SCALE the SEVERITY of EACH CRITERION for the patient at the PRESENT TIME. Indicate the level of severity on the grid.

DIAGNOSIS (DSM/ICD) with Code:

Axis I: _____

Axis II: _____

Axis III: _____

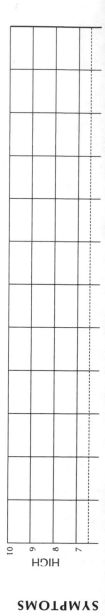

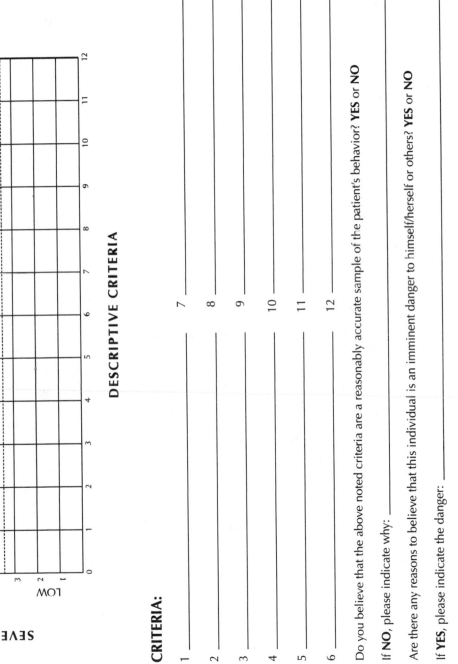

SEVERITY OF

DESCRIPTIVE CRITERIA

CRITERIA:

1 _____

2 _____

3 _____

4 _____

5 _____

6 _____

7 _____

8 _____

9 _____

10 _____

11 _____

12 _____

Do you believe that the above noted criteria are a reasonably accurate sample of the patient's behavior? **YES** or **NO**

If **NO**, please indicate why: _____

Are there any reasons to believe that this individual is an imminent danger to himself/herself or others? **YES** or **NO**

If **YES**, please indicate the danger: _____

(From Freeman, 1998.)

75

Setting Homework for the Next Session

Homework assignments are one of the most important features of cognitive-behavioral therapy. Homework should be designed to support the work that is completed within the session to outside of the session (Freeman, 1992). As patients learn new exercises and means of challenging dysfunctional behaviors, homework allows the opportunity for practice and use in everyday life. Initially, homework should be designed as a means of gathering additional information via self-monitoring. For example, within the earliest sessions, assigning a patient to utilize the DTR provides valuable information regarding distorted thoughts and related dysfunctional behaviors. As the sessions proceed and new interventions are learned, patients can practice these interventions when specific distressful situations occur. For example, if a patient has identified that arguments in a relationship causes much distress, he or she can practice relaxation techniques or use different communication strategies.

Setting a homework assignment is also an integral aspect of the collaborative process between the therapist and patient (Freeman, 1992). The therapist should ensure that the patient is in agreement and understand the reasoning behind the chosen homework. The assignments should be tailored to reflect the patient's skills (for instance, intellectual, cognitive, and processing ability). Overly ambitious assignments can result in failure, so the therapist should assess realistically the probability of the patient completing the assignment. This is a collaborative process, and requires the therapist to elicit any automatic thoughts related to the homework assignment which may prevent its completion (i.e., "I'll never be able to do this" or "It's too much"). Be sure to review the homework in the following session, and review the information obtained and whether the patient gained further insight into their particular patterns and behaviors. Additionally, if the patient was assigned to try a new strategy, did it work? What were the patient's thoughts in relation to the assignment?

Following are useful guidelines in setting homework assignments:

- Does homework reflect work completed in the session?
- Does the patient have the skill to complete the homework assignment?
- Does the patient understand the actual assignment and the reasoning behind it?
- What are the automatic thoughts related to the assignment?
- Is the assignment realistic or overly ambitious?

Feedback From the Patient

After homework is assigned for the following session, a brief summary of the session should occur, and feedback from patients regarding their experiences within the session. Feedback can help the clinician determine if treatment is proceeding collaboratively or according to the clinician's goals alone. Feedback is an integral aspect of the collaborative process. Without it, the clinician may proceed with his or her own agenda, and be uniformed as to the specific needs of the patients. When the clinician asks for feedback, it strengthens rapport, and allows patients to feel that their opinions matters and are important in the therapeutic process (Beck, 1995). It provides an opportunity for the therapist to gather additional information, clear up any misconceptions, and to ask if anything during the session was considered upsetting or disturbing.

Beck (1995) suggested that in addition to verbal feedback, patients can complete a written form, called the THERAPY REPORT. This report can be either read out loud or completed independently by patients:

1. What did you cover today that's important to you to remember?
2. How much did you feel you could trust your therapist today?
3. Was there anything that bothered you about therapy today? If so, what was it?
4. How much homework had you done for therapy today? How likely are you to do the new homework?
5. What do you want to make sure to cover at the next session? (Beck, 1995)

SUMMARY

The following chapters will guide you in deciphering which symptom(s) or criteria provide the most discomfort or difficulty for your patient. As noted earlier, the vignettes, assessment, and assignment will help you determine whether the criterion is a problem area. If it is, you can proceed to the four avenues of intervention (physiological, emotional, cognitive, and behavioral) and address the situations that appear to exacerbate problematic responses. Key information is provided to challenge, alter, and rework automatic thoughts and related schema. Understanding the driving force of schema will assist you in tackling and/or dismantling related distortions. Again, many symptoms exist on a continuum. Continued solicitation from the patient regarding which symptom(s) they are committed to challenging and changing is vital for the process to be effective. Secondary gain often plays a huge role in the maintenance of symptomotology. Asking questions such as "What do you want to accomplish by doing/thinking/feeling/reacting this way?" can help you and the patient explore the positive and negative consequences of maintaining a certain behavior.

CHAPTER 1	# Frantic Efforts to Avoid Real or Imagined Abandonment

This chapter addresses BPD Criterion 1: "frantic efforts to avoid real or imagined abandonment. Note: Do not include suicidal or self-mutilating behavior covered in criterion 5" (APA, 2000, p. 710). To some extent, most people fear being left alone and without interpersonal contact. However, for those with BPD, this criterion is almost considered a hallmark of the disorder. Patients describe desperate means to remain attached or connected to significant others, family members, friends, and even acquaintances.

These patients feel acute distress when they believe they may be deserted or abandoned. Their fears may drive them to intense levels of anxiety, only to be relieved by some sort of impulsive behavior. The impulsive behavior can manifest in many ways: for example, patients can appear desperate or clingy, or they may engage in self-mutilation. Patients may actually prompt the dreaded loss of a relationship by becoming overwhelmed by the fear of losing it.

Thoughts and perceptions related to abandonment are particularly difficult to challenge or dispute in treatment, often because the patients' fears stem from actual past abandonment. Additionally, cycles and patterns perpetuate themselves: Patients who suffered early losses or neglect tend to seek out individuals and situations that repeat those experiences. Differentiating distortions from real threats of abandonment often is a considerable challenge for both the clinician and the patient. It is even more challenging if the threat to the relationship is real.

Criterion 1
Frantic efforts to avoid real or imagined *abandonment*

Frantic
Definition: Marked by extreme excitement, confusion, agitation
Synonym: Frenetic, feverous, frenzied.
BPD: In addition to behaviors that are frenetic, intense, and powerful, emotions accompany the perception of real or imagined abandonment. These extreme emotions are often the harbinger of interpersonal difficulty and dysfunction.

Abandonment
Definition: The state of having been given up and left alone; the act of forsaking.
Synonym: Deserted, destitute.
BPD: Patients with BPD experience the feeling of abandonment as complete, total, and irreversible. Thus, the desperation associated with the feeling is related to the belief of the finality of the experience or the perception of the abandonment. Potential loss is not perceived as transient, but rather as irreversible, complete desertion.

VIGNETTES

The first vignette details Amy's desperate attempts to convince her boyfriend not to leave her for a weekend away with his friends. The vignette describes how her feelings turn into rage reactions, which ultimately force her boyfriend to distance himself—the exact opposite of what she is hoping for. The second vignette describes distorted thinking demonstrated by jumping to conclusions and catastrophic thoughts. In this vignette, Emily is convinced that because her boyfriend's call was unplanned, the news surely will be negative. This fear of the unknown is very difficult to deal with for someone with compelling schemes related to abandonment. This second vignette provides the opportunity for you and the patient to attempt to define what Emily's boyfriend might have intended to say instead of jumping to the catastrophic conclusion that he wants to end the relationship.

Both vignettes describe fears that a relationship with a significant other is threatened. After perceiving the innocuous data the characters concluded that a negative event was imminent. These conclusions led them to behave in manners that both would like to change but may feel powerless to do. Reactions such as rage and repeated calling result in distancing on the part of the significant other, thereby creating the conditions in which the patient's prophecy of abandonment will be fulfilled. It is important for your patient to understand that all levels of functioning are effected when schematic material is active.

Vignette 1: Amy

All Amy could think was, "I can't believe this is happening again!" Feeling upset and desperate, she sat by the phone and shakily dialed John's number. It was the third call that day. Her heart pounded in her chest. She was breathing so hard she wasn't sure she'd be able to talk, let alone make sense. He was going away without her on a two-day fishing trip with his friends. John finally answered the phone after four rings, but it seemed like an eternity.

"John, it's me. Honey, listen, I love you and I need you to cancel your trip. I absolutely have to see you this weekend."

John replied, "Amy, we've been through this again and again. I've been planning this trip for weeks. The arrangements have been made, I've paid for it, and the guys are counting on me; it's too late to back out now."

Suddenly her fear shifted to rage. "Goddammit John, we've been spending every weekend together for the past three months!" All she could see was red. She stopped planning what to say and the words just tumbled out. Demand followed insult. As her rage intensified, so did her use of profanity. John hung up after Amy threatened to end the relationship if he didn't stay with her that weekend. The last thing he said was that he welcomed the breakup.

"You bastard!" Amy said to the dead phone. Sobbing, she threw the phone across the room.

Vignette 2: Emily

The uneasiness Emily felt in her stomach was quickly changing to sensations of dread as she thought about what Mike wanted to say to her. His message on her answering machine said something about a change in their usual meeting time on Saturday night. She noticed her hands quivering as she poured a glass of water to relieve the dryness in her mouth. The lump in her throat made it hard to swallow. "What if he doesn't want to see me anymore? He's the only one who has ever really understood me. I'm not sure if I can go on without him!" she thought. Almost breathless, she repeatedly pushed her redial button every 30 seconds after her initial call to him and paged her therapist at least ten times.

Discussing the Vignettes & Prompting the Patient

In the first vignette, Amy exhibits intense fears of abandonment. She perceives John's trip as a complete and total desertion rather than a minor change or disruption in her routine; she sees an event signaling that the relationship is in serious jeopardy or about to end.

In the second vignette, Emily experiences a frenetic, frenzied response to what may be innocuous data. Her erroneous conclusion that Mike's message is a sign of potential abandonment leads her to behave in a frantic, desperate manner with repeated telephone calls, intense anxiety, and ruminations.

APPLYING TYPICAL BPD SCHEMAS & DISTORTIONS TO THE CRITERION

The relevant schemas in this case are related to abandonment and dependence. Frantic efforts to avoid real or imagined abandonment become greatly exacerbated by black-and-white thinking. Your patients may not identify with the word *abandonment*. Be sure to elicit if and when they too have experienced intense feelings related to being left or deserted. Inquire about the panic that may have occurred in response to that belief. A schema related to abandonment is easily activated, and dichotomous processing of information creates an immediate shift to the extreme polarity of complete abandonment. This intense feeling accompanying that belief drives patients to act so as to avoid or prevent the perceived abandonment.

As you discuss this criterion with your patients, be sure to elicit the automatic thoughts that accompany feelings of separation or detachment from others. Ask: "What was going through your mind?" These automatic thoughts will likely disclose the schema that defines the basic, intense fear of being deserted. Be sure to identify the behaviors that occur (e.g., frantic calling) when this schema is activated.

Clues to abandonment schemas usually become evident if patients identify feeling a pending loss *again*. This may relate to early losses of primary figures. By monitoring the feelings, thoughts, behaviors, and sensations that occur before and during the experience of fears of abandonment, patients can gain much insight into how they perceive their world and act upon the perceived information.

WORKSHEETS ONE & TWO: ASSESSMENT & ASSIGNMENT

As noted earlier, states of intense anxiety cause physical symptoms such as panic, GI distress, and sweating. WORKSHEET 1: THE ASSESSMENT (p. 84; and Patient Manual, p. 19) asks patients to consider a time when they, too, have felt that they may abandoned. We frame reactions to threats of abandonment as being acutely sensitive to changes in others' responses. Framing the patient's traits in a nonpejorative fashion allows the patient to feel less stigmatized.

WORKSHEET 1
The Assessment for Criterion 1

Rate the severity of the following problems as you think they may relate to you.

0 = none   1 = mild   2 = moderate   3 = severe   4 = extremely severe

1. There are times when I feel that I cannot tolerate being alone. ____

2. I often worry that the people close to me will leave me. ____

3. I find it distressing when others make changes in our plans. ____

4. I become obsessed with the threat that someone close to me may leave. ____

5. If other people reject me, I believe that I am bad, unlovable, or worthless. ____

6. I believe that if I'm not involved in a relationship, nothing matters. ____

7. I feel compelled to make repeated attempts to contact someone even when I've left messages. ____

8. I worry that I can't survive unless I have someone to depend on. ____

9. I continuously seek reassurance to allay my fears of rejection. ____

10. I force others to stay with me by acting out or saying things. ____

If the patient answers five or more prompts at level 2 or above, consider focusing on this criterion.

After patients complete WORKSHEET 1, then ask them to complete WORKSHEET 2: THE ASSIGNMENT. WORKSHEET 2 (Patient Manual, p. 20) prompts patients to identify an incident in which they believed abandonment was imminent. You can help your patients who have difficulty remembering such a time by framing the situation in terms of fears: "Do you ever remember a time when you were terrified of being left alone?" Using words related to *fear* will generally trigger some sort of memory of an incident related to this theme.

Help patients contextualize the experience by prompting them to consider when, where, with whom, and how this situation occurred. This will provide you with vital clues to underlying schemas related to abandonment. The goal of this exercise is to formulate a self-monitoring system in which patients identify the physiological, emotional, cognitive, and behavioral components related specifically to abandonment schemas. Patients' goals should be established around their reactions to distorted thoughts or the perceptions and/or beliefs that have lead to behaviors they later regret or that cause further dysfunction. Abandonment schemas can be activated by innocuous data. However, sometimes the patient is actually being abandoned. These are times when general coping skills are helpful; although some distortions may be present, the primary goal is to learn to manage and cope with the stressor.

SENSITIVITY & ABANDONMENT

Patients with BPD tend to be exquisitely sensitive. They are more physiologically attuned to others, more sensitive to nonverbal cues, and often react to perceived changes in their environment due to minor or misread cues. Individuals with BPD are particularly sensitive to any clues that may indicate a potential or real separation or loss. It is imperative that patients learn to utilize self-monitoring as a means of identifying when their abandonment schema is being activated. Once aware of its activation, they can then choose to take control and determine their responses.

WORKSHEETS THREE TO SIX, & EIGHTEEN: TREATMENT GOALS

A goal of treatment is considerable reality-testing aimed at resisting the impulse to dismiss the entire human race as neglectful and abandoning and remaining cautious enough to know when a situation may not be for the best. This approach allows patients to continually test their new ability to challenge and dispute distorted thinking. It is helpful for patients to be aware that the potential for upset exists in all relationships. How patients manage that upset is the key to maintaining and nurturing both their intrapersonal and interpersonal functioning.

After patients complete WORKSHEETS 1 and 2, assist the patient in filling out WORKSHEET 3: THE INCIDENT CHART (Patient Manual, p. 21). The four areas of self-monitoring (physiological, emotional, cognitive, and behavioral) offer avenues to treatment interventions and provide concrete examples of specific areas of change the patient can address. Assisting your patients in clearly describing how their systems react prior to what they perceive as abandonment provides the inroad to constructively managing fears rather than acting in ways that further complicate or deteriorate the situation. By clearly identifying warning signals, the patient can make a preemptive strike against acting on impulsive urges related to their fears.

Complete WORKSHEETS 4 and 5 (Patient Manual, pp. 22–23) to identify patients' automatic thoughts and schema. Then treatment goals can be identified. In order to assist and help organize this process, complete WORKSHEET 6: TREATMENT GOALS (Patient Manual, p. 24). Once treatment goals are set, complete WORKSHEET 18: THE DPS (Patient Manual, pp. 25–26) to determine a baseline level of distress or dysfunction for the particular criterion.

WORKSHEETS SEVEN TO SEVENTEEN: SUGGESTED INTERVENTIONS

Worksheets 7 & 8: Physical Triggers & Suggested Interventions

Some maladaptive responses can be in the form of physiological reactions such as those created by anxiety (e.g., shortness of breath, rapid heartbeat, sweatiness, and upset stomach). Again, these physiological signs and symptoms are often the first indicators that something is wrong. When patients first perceive that they may be left or deserted by someone, their thoughts tend to accumulate and cause extreme physiological distress that is very powerful and at times frightening. (This is particularly the case if the distress is accompanied by symptoms of anxiety.) Reducing physiological distress can combat the dysfunctional thoughts and/or distortions. Once they are able to identify and monitor particular physiological warning signs, patients then can choose their reactions and next step (Patient Manual, pp. 26–28).

THOUGHT-STOPPING

As noted earlier, thought-stopping is based on a relatively simple premise that when patients experience distressful thoughts related to being abandoned, they can take control and *stop* thinking those thoughts. Patients can use the DTR to identify which particular thoughts generate maladaptive responses in the guise of physiological distress. Then, when the thought occurs, they can simply interrupt the flow of thoughts with a sudden stimulus (imagined or real) and begin thinking different thoughts. Explain the thought-stopping technique to the patient.

RELAXATION

As reactions to the fear of being deserted usually lead to high levels of arousal, progressive muscle relaxation (PMR) techniques are particularly helpful. Encourage your patient to take a moment, stop, and practice deep breathing as explained. This exercise can be utilized if your patients are waiting to talk to someone or waiting for a phone call. As abandonment schemas are very compelling, having patients relax before considering how to react can help thwart behaviors that may have negative consequences. Relaxation techniques are also helpful for patients who have experienced real losses and are attempting to cope.

RELAXING IMAGERY

Encourage patients to use relaxing imagery as explained. It is not a good idea for patients to imagine the persons by whom they feel they are being deserted or abandoned; these images may create false expectations or hopes. Including those persons in their imagery also may cause additional anxiety and counteract their attempts to relax.

Worksheets 9 & 10: Emotional Triggers & Suggested Interventions

For patients who are both physiologically and psychologically sensitive, feelings can become intense and exaggerated. WORKSHEET 9 (Patient Manual, p. 29) prompts patients to describe the feelings they experience when they perceive they are about to be abandoned. These emotions may relate to an intense moment with a significant other due to a change in their perception of the person and the relationship. As abandonment schemas are very compelling and powerful, the emotions connected to them may surge forth in reaction to sometimes-distorted perceptions of change in a relationship. These specific emotional states, however, can provide clues about the schemas that abandonment issues ignite.

Scale Back

Using Worksheet 10 (Patient Manual, p. 30) ask patients to identify the intensity of the emotion they experienced when they perceived a potential change or loss in a relationship. Keep in mind that patients with BPD are sensitive and are likely to catastrophize their related emotional components when abandonment schemas are activated. Once you have encouraged patients to scale back, have them "take their temperature" on the Likert Scale again to note the differences and their ability to affect some change. Be sure to ask patients to consider their whole system, including their levels of physiological arousal. Would their response to the situation be different now that they have "turned themselves down"?

Worksheets 11 & 12: Cognitive/Automatic Thoughts & Suggested Interventions

Be sure that patients are able to describe the automatic thoughts related to abandonment. These can be derived from the DTR. Assist patients in identifying the extremes or their catastrophic conclusions and help them consider the middle ground. Finally, challenge patients to be "scientific" about weighing the evidence supporting their conclusions.

Challenge Catastrophic Thinking

Challenge the catastrophic thoughts related to the patients themselves, their significant others, and their relationships. Ask: "What is the true likelihood the event will happen?" For example, if patients experience someone changing plans at the last minute, do they have catastrophic thoughts such as "They don't want to be friends with me anymore?" Challenge patients with the thought "Perhaps they had difficulty making the time we set." Utilize The Catastrophic Thinking Chart (Patient Manual, p. 32).

Challenge Dichotomous Thinking

Help patients see the grays that exist when they are fearful of being abandoned (p. 89; Patient Manual, pp. 32–33). Keep in mind that thought processes tend to shift rapidly between extremes. For example, a patient may be thinking something like:

partner goes out → *means only that* → *patient is being abandoned*

Ask patients if this is necessarily true. What is the middle ground? Is it possible that the partner may be going out to do something that won't damage the relationship? Once patients have determined where the grays in the relationship may lie, ask them if they are experiencing any changes in how they are perceiving the relationship or events surrounding the stressor.

The Dichotomous Thinking Chart

Black	Gray(s)	White
He's leaving me.	He's late because he's stuck in traffic.	He's perfect.
_____ .	_____ .	_____ .
_____ .	_____ .	_____ .

WEIGH THE EVIDENCE

Help patients examine their thoughts and try to prove themselves wrong. Dysfunctional and self-defeating thoughts and beliefs flourish when negative presumptions are not subjected to analysis or testing. A negative bias allows contrary evidence to be overlooked. As patients with BPD tend to perceive stimulus in a dichotomous fashion, they may have already jumped to one extreme. Help patients not only weigh the evidence, but also draw conclusions from that evidence. All pertinent evidence must be reviewed. This requires diligence on the clinician's part, as patients may place a disproportionate emphasis on negative presumptions (Freeman, Pretzer, Fleming, & Simon, 1990). Following is an example of a DISPUTATION CHART (Patient Manual, p. 33) that challenges assumptions related to abandonment:

The Disputation Chart

Situation: *Boyfriend didn't call when he said he would.*

Belief: *Boyfriend wants to break up.*

Proof Supporting Belief	**Refuting Statement**
1. *Boyfriend didn't call.*	1. *One late phone call doesn't mean the end of the relationship.*
2. *Boyfriend forgot about me.*	2. *Boyfriend had busy day at work.*
3. _____ .	3. _____ .
4. _____ .	4. _____ .

Worksheets 13 & 14: Behavioral Triggers & Suggested Interventions

WORKSHEET 13 (Patient Manual, p. 34) prompts patients to describe how they reacted both before they assumed they were being abandoned and after. It is imperative that patients clearly identify which of these behaviors they wish to take control of, change, or eradicate. When helping patients review their patterns of behavior, encourage them to identify how they felt or thought about the behaviors they exhibited. Ask: "Did you regret anything they did?" "Did you feel embarrassed or were they told their significant other was particularly offended by anything specific?"

CONSIDER THE CONSEQUENCES

Using WORKSHEET 14 (Patient Manual, p. 35) challenge patients to imagine the consequences of their patterned behavior. Many patients experience difficulty because they do not foresee the consequences of their behaviors. Often patients with BPD have an externalized attribution style that affects their interpretation of events. In other words, they do not consider their own control over events but rather place the responsibility on outside or external sources. Problem-solving that utilizes thinking of consequences involves attending to and accurately assessing how behaviors and actions influence ourselves and others. In addition, means-end thinking can be useful for patients who have difficulty conceptualizing hypothetical constructs. In other words, ask your patient: "Is it worth it?" Utilize The NEGATIVE AND POSITIVE CONSEQUENCES Chart.

STOP

Ask patients to try to take a moment to stop. Often we experience physiological sensations in reaction to something we are perceiving. Once patients recognize that they are experiencing that familiar physical sensation, they can remember to take a moment to just stop.

RELAXATION

Anxiety is often associated with experiencing upset and distress. Symptoms of anxiety usually involve some sort of physical reaction. These could be stomach problems, a rapid heartbeat, or sweating. These types of feelings and bodily reactions respond well to relaxation techniques.

RELAXING IMAGERY

While they utilize relaxation techniques to relax their muscles, have patients imagine their safe place. Be sure to ask patients to describe their safe place in detail with the accompanying sounds, smells, and textures. They may also want to imagine a "safe person" such as a good friend or confidant whom they can imagine being there with them.

Worksheets 16 & 17: Situational Triggers & Suggested Interventions

WORKSHEET 16 (Patient Manual, p. 37) prompts patients to specifically identify those situations which have activated their belief that they were being abandoned. These situations can include interactions with not only significant others, but also family members and friends. Worksheet 17 (Patient Manual, p. 38) suggests that patients remove themselves from the situation, or, if the situation is unavoidable, that they try something different.

REMOVE YOURSELF

For those times that patients identify as very distressful, suggest that they don't give themselves the opportunity to lose control. In order to avoid making any type of "scene" where they may later regret, they can try taking a walk or going into another room. For instance, if your patient knows that when her partner is late in returning home she becomes overwhelmed with anxiety, be sure that she can go somewhere she considers herself to be supported.

TRY SOMETHING DIFFERENT

For those times that patients identify as highly stressful due to their belief of being abandoned, have them try a different type of reaction to the situation. For example, if your patient knows she feels especially anxious in between the times she sees her boyfriend, instead of calling him repeatedly for reassurance, ask your patient to do something constructive with her time. This could be a household project she's been wanting to complete or catching up with friends.

WORKSHEET EIGHTEEN: THE DPS

Complete WORKSHEET 18: THE DPS (Patient Manual, p. 39). Compare the results of the DPS after treatment goals were set. Is there a difference in the level of distress the patient is experiencing in response to the criterion? If not, reexamine the interventions chosen to target the symptoms, and collaboratively determine whether changes or alterations should be made.

CASE EXAMPLE

In the first vignette, excessive abandonment fears caused Amy to react in a negative, damaging manner. To help Amy control her outbursts, the therapist began by examining to what extent fears of abandonment were an issue in Amy's life. Amy was able to tell her therapist that she not only experienced these types of fears with her boyfriend, but also with her parents. By examining prior experiences in which she reacted to these uncomfortable feelings in a negative way, Amy was able to identify the compelling nature of the schema, which she then associated with her father. Throughout Amy's childhood, her father, an alcoholic, would often miss family events. Additionally, Amy's mother vacillated in her caretaking as she struggled to manage her own marriage and feelings of abandonment. Amy always felt as if the carpet was about to be pulled out from under her, which created a very compelling abandonment schema. By learning to monitor her physiological responses to the incredibly strong feelings associated with her fear of abandonment, Amy was able not only to challenge her catastrophic thinking but also to begin trusting herself to manage stressful times. Reviewing her DTR, she began to dispute and dismantle her belief that those who care about her will eventually leave her (she had several long-term friendships) as well as practice decatastrophizing. She applied stopping techniques as soon as her body registered anxious symptoms, relaxed, and viewed her situations rationally. Her initial DPS scores were well above the midpoint, but after consistent monitoring of her escalating catastrophic thinking, the score dropped to below the midpoint within three sessions.

CHAPTER 2

Unstable Relationships
Characterized by Idealization
& Devaluation

This chapter addresses BPD Criterion 2: "a pattern of unstable and intense interpersonal relationships characterized by alternating between extremes of idealization and devaluation" (APA, 2000, p. 710). Intrinsic to our being human is the capacity to relate or attempt to relate to others. However, for those with BPD, this very basic need for steady, consistent relationships is often not met. This is not for lack of effort or desire, but rather for lack of relationship-building and coping skills. This criterion encapsulates two very important aspects of BPD. First, it identifies a clear and traceable pattern of unstable relationships, many of which are highly emotionally charged and of short duration. This intensity often repels others, thus activating abandonment schemas. Second, the criterion identifies the cognitive-affective tendency to view significant others and relationships in all-or-nothing terms. This creates a dichotomous mode of approaching relationships. In other words, basic relationship schemas consist of a pattern of vacillation between perceiving significant others as idealized caregivers and cruelly punitive persons. These dramatic shifts are often a result of patients' perceptions that emotional and psychological needs were not met. These needs may include the rudimentary nurturance and care from significant others they crave. Once patients have perceived that their partner might not completely meet their needs, intense feelings of rejection and abandonment are triggered, resulting in behaviors that further complicate already-compromised situations.

Examining schemas related to how patients perceive, interpret, and respond in relationships is a vital and integral aspect of treatment. Most patients have had early caregivers who were usually able to meet most demands of their for nurturance. However, there is a catch: At

Criterion 2

A pattern of *unstable* and *intense* interpersonal relationships characterized by alternating between extremes of *idealization* and *devaluation*.

Unstable
Definition: Not physically or emotionally steady or firm.
Definition of *instability*: The quality or condition of being erratic and undependable.
Synonym: Capricious, changeable, insecure.
BPD: The definition of *instability* captures the capricious and changeable nature of how patients with BPD operate within a relationship. For individuals with BPD, the basic rules that guide most relationships are undependable and vague. Relationships themselves therefore become continually vulnerable to the erratic shifts associated with instability.

Intense
Definition: Extreme in degree, strength, or effect.
Definiton of *intensity*: Exceptionally great in concentration, power, or force.
Synonym: Fierce, vehement.
BPD: Within relationships, emotions and behaviors for patients with BPD are generally experienced in extremes. A concentrated or forceful emotional realm exists within relationships. This emotional intensity affects both interpersonal and intrapersonal reactions.

Idealization
Definition To envision things in a perfect but unrealistic form.
Synonym: Quixotic, romantic, unrealistic.
BPD: Patients with BPD often experience others in idealized or perfect form. Significant others are perceived through an idyllic lens despite evidence that may dispute this belief. This idealization is inherently detrimental to the relationship, as unrealistic expectations cannot be met.

Devaluation
Definition: To make less or become less in value.
Synonym: Depreciate.
BPD: The definition of *devalue* assumes that the object being devalued originally had a higher status. The key to understanding devaluation for borderline patients is to conceptualize it as a shifting process from an originally different or more idealized representation of the other to a lower or depreciated status. This shift usually creates much confusion for both patient's with BPD and the significant others. The devaluation can be precipitated by patients simply experiencing the mere humanness of the other or by the other's inability to meet the the emotional needs of BPD patients. Both the ideal and the negative are experienced as extremes.

times that caregiver invoked fear or threatened to abandon the relationship. Patients who have had experiences of this sort view relationships as either perfect and all-nurturing or as deeply flawed and invoking intense fear, anger, and turmoil. In the latter circumstance abandonment schemas are activated. During childhood this dichotomous thinking leads to the formation of powerful and often intractable schemas for understanding relationships. As maturation continues, patients continually seek out those who they believe can meet their needs, only to be completely devastated when their idealized caregiver is unable to meet their unrealistic demands. Often in the beginning of a relationship, those with BPD rapidly and intensely attach themselves to the caring and nurturing part of another individual. As most people are trying to put their best foot forward in the beginning of a relationship, the other person's caring or giving side is usually more evident. Borderline individuals react to this like to a starving child, ingesting as much as they can only to learn later that the apparent nurturance they have ingested may or may not be good for them. Those with BPD have difficulty moderating their attachment to others. "Two shall become one" is the modus for relationships and often the harbinger of the relationship's fatality. Acute sensitivity to shifts in the relationship or the significant other's feelings often instigates intrapersonal and interpersonal crises. If a significant other begins to want space, those with BPD may experience an acute feeling of rejection, which prompts them to devalue the partner. They also may retaliate impulsively. Retaliation can take the form of angry outbursts, ending the relationship, self-harm or mutilation, or even threats of suicide; all these acts are performed in an attempt to avert the abandonment of the relationship and to reactivate nurturance. This ongoing cycle of dramatic shifts creates intense, unstable relationships that cause much distress.

COMBINATION OF DEFINITIONS

Patients with BPD experience erratic, changeable, and forceful perceptions and emotions within interpersonal relationships in which partners are seen as idyllic caretakers but are quickly devalued when they fail to live up to unrealistic expectations. This shift is bidirectional, intense, and can occur rapidly.

VIGNETTES

The first vignette describes Sandi, who feels that Pete places his parents' needs before hers. Her initial idealized view of Pete quickly erodes; she now experiences intense rage with respect to Pete. She then storms out and threatens to end the relationship. The second vignette introduces Barbara, who is terrified of disappointing Tom, her spouse, and therefore neglects her own feelings out of fear that he will abandon her. However, much anger boils beneath the surface because she feels that her own needs are not being validated or met.

Vignette 1: Sandi

Sandi was devastated. How on earth did she misjudge someone so badly? She had thought about how wonderful Pete was—so sweet, genuine, and unselfish—all day long. She knew she had found the man with whom she would spend her life. Driving home almost euphoric, Sandi expected that he, too, would feel her excitement about their budding relationship. As she opened her door, Pete met her in the hallway, apologizing that he had forgotten to tell her that he had dinner plans with his parents that evening. That feeling Sandi knew so well started to take over again. He wanted to go to his mother's for dinner and he was rejecting her. He forgot about her. He was selfish, rejecting, and mean. How could he do this to her? She had had a wonderful evening planned. Now he had ruined it! Her thoughts began to spiral into a rage. He thought more of his parents than of her. As that thought came to her mind again and again, she picked up her coat, walked toward the door, said, "Go ahead to your parents, you mama's boy, but forget about coming home because I won't be here!," and stormed out.

Vignette 2: Barbara

Barbara was furious. Once again Tom had asked her to entertain his business partner and his wife. Tom had just casually sauntered over and said, "Darling, do you really mind having them for dinner?" Barbara couldn't say no, but she surely wanted to. She never could say no. Not to Tom, not to her boss, her friends, family, and especially her parents. She felt a tight feeling in her chest and had a hard time swallowing. The thought that kept spinning in her mind was that no one recognized, acknowledged, or loved her. She was just there to be used. If she didn't do what everyone wanted, she'd be alone with no one to love her, right? Barbara tried to swallow her fury, but she felt so utterly discarded and rejected that she stood in the kitchen weeping hysterically.

Discussing the Vignettes & Prompting the Patient

The key to discussion of both vignettes is the idea of compromise. Sandi and Barbara do not think in terms of the "gray area" of compromise. Both characters exhibit dichotomous thinking, which is demonstrated by their extreme shifts between idealization and devaluation of the significant other. Sandi and Barbara subsequently experience intense emotional responses including rage, sadness, and feelings of abandonment and rejection. These feelings cause behaviors that damage communication and, ultimately, the relationship.

APPLYING TYPICAL BPD SCHEMAS & DISTORTIONS TO THE CRITERION

If patients identify that relationships are problematic after they complete WORKSHEET 1: THE ASSESSMENT, they should begin to learn to self-monitor their perceptions of significant others, particularly during conflicts. Patients can discover clues to erratic, volatile relationship schemas by identifying typical BPD cognitive distortions such as dichotomous thinking, catastrophic thinking, and jumping to faulty conclusions. Schemas related to this criterion may include dependence, lack of individuation, and feelings of unlovability, mistrust, and abandonment. General themes are related to connectedness and may be complicated by the tendency to polarize. Help patients recall conflicts that arose largely due to dichotomous thinking. Include all-or-nothing structures in your questions: "Do you remember a time when you wanted to break off a relationship due to something that later seemed inconsequential?"; "Do you remember a time when you were totally convinced you had found the perfect person, only to be incredibly disappointed later?" Words related to idealization and devaluation often trigger memories of incidents related to this theme. Encourage patients to remember highly emotional scenes in which they felt unsupported or perceived that their needs were not being met.

WORKSHEETS ONE & TWO: ASSESSMENT & ASSIGNMENT

As noted, states of intense anxiety can cause physical symptoms of panic, GI distress, and sweating. WORKSHEET 1: THE ASSESSMENT (p. 98; Patient Manual, p. 44) asks patients to consider times when they, too, have experienced feelings of being unsupported, left out, or slighted. As relationships are a very important part of life, disappointments, tension, or turmoil within an important relationship can cause much distress and subsequent anxiety.

WORKSHEET 1
The Assessment for Criterion 2

Rate the severity of the following problems as you think they may relate to you.

0 = none   1= mild   2 = moderate   3 = severe   4 = extremely severe

1. Your relationships largely consist of major ups and downs. ____

2. You have found it difficult to remain in a romantic relationship for any length of time. ____

3. Your sets of friends tend to change more quickly than those of most people. ____

4. You frequently argue with your significant other. ____

5. You resolve conflicts with others by arguing, leaving, or crying. ____

6. You tend to believe your relationship is either wonderful or horrible. ____

7. You use derogatory or insulting words during arguments. ____

8. You feel completely out of control when you disagree with others. ____

9. You tend to have exceptionally high standards for your significant other. ____

10. You have become involved with someone extremely quickly, only to discover shortly thereafter that he or she wasn't right for you. ____

If the patient answers five or more prompts at level 2 or above, consider focusing on this criterion.

After patients complete WORKSHEET 1: THE ASSESSMENT, ask them to complete WORKSHEET 2: THE ASSIGNMENT (Patient Manual, p. 45) which prompts patients to identify an incident in which they experienced extreme distress related to a relationship.

SENSITIVITY & UNSTABLE RELATIONSHIPS

Because they are extremely sensitive, borderline patients often perceive minor changes in relationships to indicate pending disappointment, abandonment, or loss. Patients who detect a pending loss (either real or distorted), may dichotomize incoming information leading to polarized thinking and a devaluation of significant others. Thus relationships generally are intense, and views of partners typically shift between idealization and devaluation.

WORKSHEETS THREE TO SIX, & EIGHTEEN: TREATMENT GOALS

A goal of treatment is to assist patients in seeing that their significant others cannot always measure up to an unrealistic ideal. There are grays. Finding the grays requires patients to challenge their methods of interpreting incoming information by self-monitoring and discovering when their relationship schemas are activated. The potential for conflict exists in all relationships. However, self-monitoring and problem-solving skills aimed at improving communication can help patients avoid perceiving relationships as all-or-nothing ventures fraught with disappointment and upset.

After patients complete WORKSHEETS 1 and 2, assist them in filling out WORKSHEET 3: THE INCIDENT CHART (Patient Manual, p. 46). The four areas of self-monitoring (physiological, emotional, cognitive, and behavioral) offer avenues to treatment interventions and provide concrete examples of specific areas of change patients can address. By assisting patients in clearly describing how they react prior to what they perceive as a disappointment, rejection, or conflict within a relationship, you can help them constructively manage their fears rather than act in ways that further complicate or deteriorate the situation. By clearly identifying warning signals, patients can make a preemptive strike against acting on impulsive urges related to their fears.

Complete WORKSHEETS 4 and 5 (Patient Manual, pp. 47–48) to identify patients' automatic thoughts and schemas. Then treatment goals can be identified. In order to help organize this process, complete WORKSHEET 6: TREATMENT GOALS (Patient Manual, p. 49). Once treatment goals are set, complete WORKSHEET 18: THE DPS (Patient Manual,

p. 50) to determine a baseline level of distress or dysfunction for the particular criterion.

WORKSHEETS SEVEN TO SEVENTEEN: SUGGESTED INTERVENTIONS

Worksheets 7 & 8: Physical Triggers & Suggested Interventions

Once they are able to identify and monitor for particular physiological warnings signs (WORKSHEET 7; Patient Manual, p. 51), patients can choose their reactions and next steps (WORKSHEET 8; Patient Manual, pp. 52–53). In the context of relationships, a heightened physiological arousal, often felt throughout the body, can be prompted by feelings of fear, anger, and sadness.

THOUGHT-STOPPING

Once patients have identified the maladaptive thoughts that tend to occur within their relationships (e.g., a tendency to idealize or devalue their significant other), they can flag themselves when the thoughts occur and interrupt the flow of dysfunctional thoughts with a sudden stimulus (imagined or real). This allows them to begin considering a more realistic option (e.g., that no one is entirely good or entirely bad). Patients can also think of stopping as "putting on the breaks" prior to reacting to a thought and giving themselves the opportunity to consider the *whole* situation rather than the polarized parts.

RELAXATION

Relationships often trigger intense physiological and emotional states, and the physical sensations that accompany anxiety can compound or worsen the anxiety. Progressive muscle relaxation (PMR) techniques consistently have been proven to decrease anxiety. If difficulty in relationships has caused patients to experience secondary symptoms such as poor sleep, fatigue, restlessness, or a general increased anxiety state, PMR can help reduce anxiety and relax the body. Patients may also benefit from knowing that if they are in a more relaxed state, they will be better able to grasp and process confictual situations; thus, they may be able help the relationship by being more appropriate and less reactive.

RELAXING IMAGERY

As mentioned previously, it may be detrimental for patients to include significant others or those with whom they are having difficulty in their relaxing image. In addition to stirring anxiety and being countertherapeutic, the inclusion of significant others in their relaxation imagery encourages patients to rely on others to provide nurturance rather than helping them to help themselves.

Worksheets 9 & 10: Emotional Triggers & Suggested Interventions

WORKSHEET 9 (Patient Manual, p. 54) prompts patients to describe the specific feelings they experience when perceiving an extreme shift in how they view their partner or someone they are relating to. By considering whether they were, for example, fearful, angry, or sad, patients can learn to prepare themselves for future situations. Additionally, the specific emotional state provides clues about the schema ignited by relationship issues.

SCALE BACK

Have patients utilize WORKSHEET 10 (Patient Manual, pp. 55–58) to gauge their emotional state when distressed about relationships. Ask patients to rate the emotions they experienced when they felt as if their significant others (or other persons in a relationship) disappointed them, causing them to immediately change their perception of persons and relationships.

Keep in mind that patients with BPD are very sensitive and likely to catastrophize their related emotional components. These emotional components occur as a result of an activation of schemas containing vacillating and polarized views of others within relationships.

IMPROVING COMMUNICATION OF FEELINGS

Ask patients to consider how they express themselves. Often, when patients perceive that their egos or interpersonal relationships are threatened, their entrenched schemas begin playing a very active role. Perhaps as children your patients learned that when they did express how they really felt, they were met with anger, rejection, or even abuse. Encourage your patients to try communicating the fear or sadness beneath the outburst, the retort, or the threat.

Worksheets 11 & 12: Cognitive/Automatic Thoughts & Suggested Interventions

The Taking Control program attempts to challenge and dismantle distorted thinking as it relates to relationships. Ask patients to describe their automatic thoughts about themselves and those with whom they are involved (WORKSHEET 11; Patient Manual, p. 59). These can be derived from the DTR. Automatic thoughts related to relationships are typically intense, polarized, and catastrophy-oriented. Assist patients in identifying the extremes or the catastrophic conclusions they draw. Also assist them in considering the middle ground. Encourage patients to list as many alternative explanations as possible regarding why their partners may have behaved in a particular manner. Finally, challenge patients to be scientific and weigh the evidence supporting their conclusions.

CHALLENGE CATASTROPHIC THINKING

What aspects of their relationships are your patients catastrophizing? Using WORKSHEET 12 (Patient Manual, pp. 60–61) assist patients in assessing the probability of the catastrophic outcome, and challenge patients' catastrophic thoughts related to themselves, their significant others, and their relationships. For example, if an argument occurs, do patients have thoughts such as "If we fight then it's over?" Challenge this type of thought with a statement such as "All relationships have conflict at one time or another." Utilize The CATASTROPHIC THINKING CHART.

CHALLENGE DICHOTOMOUS THINKING

Help patients see the grays when they are viewing others and speculating about others motives. Use the DTR to identify maladaptive thoughts.

For example:

$$\begin{array}{ccccc} \textit{partner} & & \textit{means} & & \textit{partner} \\ \textit{disappoints} & \rightarrow & \textit{only that} & \rightarrow & \textit{is bad} \end{array}$$

Ask your patients "Is this necessarily true?"; "What is the middle ground?"; "Is it possible the partner may *not* want to damage the relationship?"; "What are the grays?" Use the painter's palette metaphor to help patients assess the black, white, and grays. For example:

The Dichotomous Thinking Chart		
Black	**Gray(s)**	**White**
|--|--|		
He's terrible.	He's not always bad.	He's perfect.
_____ .	_____ .	_____ .
_____ .	_____ .	_____ .

WEIGH THE EVIDENCE

Help patients examine their thoughts and prove themselves wrong by using The DISPUTATION CHART. Following is an example of a DISPUTATION CHART that challenges assumptions influenced by dichotomous thinking:

The Disputation Chart

Situation: Argument with partner.

Belief: Partner won't love me.

Proof Supporting Belief	**Refuting Statement**
1. *We argued.*	1. *Conflict can help the relationship.*
2. *Partner disagrees with me.*	2. *Can disagree and still love the other.*
3. _____ .	3. _____ .
4. _____ .	4. _____ .

Worksheets 13 & 14: Behavioral Triggers & Suggested Interventions

WORKSHEET 13 (Patient Manual, p. 62) prompts patients to describe how they were reacting in a situation just prior to devaluing a previously idealized person. It also asks them to consider how they reacted after the devaluation. By monitoring early physiological, emotional, and cognitive warning signals, patients can begin to take control of their responses and behaviors. Identifying the behaviors they tend to exhibit when experiencing schemas related to idealization/devaluation is the first step in changing the entrenched course of behavioral expression (WORKSHEET 14; Patient Manual, pp. 63–64).

CONSIDER THE CONSEQUENCES

What behaviors are caused by the idealization/devaluation of the other, and what are the consequences of those behaviors? Utilize The NEGATIVE AND POSITIVE CONSEQUENCES CHART.

STOP

Ask patients to take a moment to stop. Remind them that often we tend to experience physiological sensations in reaction to something we are perceiving. If they are having thoughts like "Oh, no, my relationship is failing again," try to stop.

RELAXATION

Conflict in a relationship can lead to intense feelings. Patients may have experienced agitation or anxiousness, which involves physical reactions. These bodily reactions respond well to relaxation techniques.

RELAXING IMAGERY

In combination with relaxation techniques, ask patients to imagine their safe place. For their safe person, it is best if they imagine someone with whom they are not having a conflict.

Worksheets 16 & 17: Situational Triggers & Suggested Interventions

WORKSHEET 16 (Patient Manual, p. 65) prompts patients to specifically identify situations that tend to spark conflicts. For example, a patient may identify that when her significant other does not pay enough attention to her, she may try to remove herself from the situation, or she may try something different instead of her usual behavior, yelling. WORKSHEET 17 (Patient Manual, p. 66) suggests removing themselves, or trying something different.

REMOVE YOURSELF

If patients have determined that there are occasions when they have become so disappointed with others that any type of behavioral intervention would be futile, encourage patients to not allow themselves the opportunity to react in a way they may later regret. Suggest taking a walk, go into another room, or let their partner know that they are unable to discuss something at the current moment because they are too upset.

TRY SOMETHING DIFFERENT

Encourage patients to try different reactions to situations in which a shift from idealization to devaluation has occurred. This may give them the time necessary to reassess the situation. For example, if the patient tends to withdraw or ignore their partner when he or she begins to devalue them, ask him or her to try something different such as talking with a supportive friend, sharing an activity with their partner, or discussing something nonemotional or objective with the partner.

WORKSHEET EIGHTEEN: THE DPS

Complete WORKSHEET 18: THE DPS (Patient Manual, p. 67). Compare the results of the DPS after treatment goals were set. Is there a difference in the level of distress patients are experiencing in response to the criterion? If not, reexamine the interventions chosen to target the symptoms, and collaboratively determine whether changes or alterations should be made.

CASE EXAMPLE

In the first vignette, Sandi quickly devalued her boyfriend, Pete, when he forgot to mention his dinner plans with his parents. Sandi's therapist addressed this problem by helping Sandi elicit her beliefs and schema related to significant others. The DPS revealed that Sandi experienced great difficulty and distress in maintaining relationships as well as monitoring consistent, nonpolarized views of those for whom she cares. On her DTR, Sandi monitored her thoughts throughout the week and noticed a pattern: When Pete did not seem to comply with her needs, she approached the situation in a dichotomous manner, assuming he wanted to do nothing for her. She began tracing this belief to her interactions with her mother, who vacillated between being a giving caretaker and behaving as a cold, critical stranger. Sandi cared a great deal about her mother and expressed sadness about her view of her and the character of her relationship with her mother, and she made a commitment to challenge her dichotomous view of others. This required Sandi to be forgiving when her needs were not met and to explore why Pete was not always able to provide what she needed in the moment. Communication skills enhanced her ability to discuss the situation with Pete and helped her avoid the negative behaviors that ended up complicating the situation. Sandi utilized thought-stopping when she became angered or reactive to Pete, and she scaled back her emotions so that she could clearly express her needs before exploding.

| Identity Disturbance

This chapter addresses BPD Criterion 3: "identity disturbance: markedly and persistently unstable self-image or sense of self" (APA, 2000, p. 710). This criterion includes the tendency for patients to experience sudden, dramatic shifts in self-image. This shifting of self-identity can involve changes of goals, values, or even careers. Patients may take many types of roles during the course of their everyday life—at one moment acting as the nurturer or caretaker at home and then quickly shifting into the role of the dependent when with their friends or colleagues. Borderline patients often lack integrated characteristics; for instance, patients may identify with a social crowd completely foreign to their background or family values. Often this is an attempt to fill a vast internal void. Patients with BPD are most vulnerable to identity disturbance when they are experiencing a lack of something meaningful in their lives, for example, a relationship or a caretaker.

COMBINATION OF DEFINITIONS

To define this criterion, the Patient Manual uses the metaphor of a ship crossing an ocean in rough weather and limited visibility. Faced with those severe conditions, the ship docks at any port that will provide protection. In other words, those who lack a sense of identity may anchor at any harbor that provides safety in order to feel they belong or are a part of something bigger than themselves. Many of these identities, however, may not be a good fit, so the ship/person repeatedly sails forward (blindly) in the quest to find security. How can you determine if this is a problem for patients? They may try new clothing

Criterion 3

Identity disturbance: *markedly* and *persistently* unstable self-image or sense of self.

Identity
Definition: The set of behaviors or personal characteristics by which an individual is recognizable and that continue in spite of difficulty.
Synonym: Self.
BPD: Borderline patients are at times unable to recognize or distinguish the attributes or idiosyncratic traits particular to themselves. Their sense of self is not immediately or easily known; thus, those with BPD may sometimes assume the traits of those around them as a way to ground themselves.

Disturbance
Definition: A disruption of the establishment of a sense of self that will cause emotional or cognitive disturbance.
Synonym: Turmoil
Definition of *disturbing*: Troubling to the mind or emotions.
BPD: Those with BPD do not have a predictable sense of themselves or of the emotions they experience. They may be truly unable to gauge how they feel about a situation or experience or unable to predict their response in any given situation. This lack of knowledge or experience about the self often is troubling enough to cause distress. The disturbance usually occurs when patients experience a stressor or pressure (internal or external) and have difficulty coping due to their lack of access to a cohesive self.

Marked
Definition: Noticeable.
Synonym: Distinctive.
BPD: Those with BPD who experience an unstable identity will manifest their distress in a noticeable way. Friends and family are usually aware of the patient's difficulty in identifying what he or she wants or needs. It is often noticeable that patients consistently change their needs, wants, and even opinions to match the current environment. This is because they are unable to clearly identify or even recognize what their own needs are.

Persistent
Definition: Unremitting.
Synonym: Tenacious.
BPD: Those with BPD experience an unremitting difficulty with understanding themselves and recognizing their needs and wants. Their unstable sense of self and the related dysphoria rarely wavers. In this way, patients continually struggle with establishing direction and goals, as well as ensuring that their needs are met.

Self
Definition: An individual's awareness of what contributes to his or her essential nature and distinguishes him or her from all other persons.
Synonym: Identity.
BPD: Those with BPD experience a dramatic and sometimes painful sense of not knowing the basic aspects of their identity that differentiate them from others. The question of what makes one person similar or different from another often goes unanswered for those with BPD. This lack of knowing who or what they are relative to others is experienced as powerful psychological pain or distress.

styles, change social circles frequently, be willing to experiment with different things in order to remain part of a crowd, change hairstyles, or perhaps even move their home. They may have difficulty beginning or completing a course of study or sticking with a chosen career. They may change their overall direction in life very suddenly, only to adopt yet another set of life goals later. Patients may speak of an internal emptiness or vacancy. They may feel as if they live their life by looking through a glass window at everyone else who knows what he or she wants. This "identity hopping" may have caused difficulty with their family of origin.

What is the cause of such identity disturbance? The Object Relations school of thought proposes that a lack of integration of the main caregiver's self-object creates a polarized viewpoint on the part of the borderline individual (Freeman et al., 1990). Patients may not have felt safe enough to engage in the stage of rapprochement (Mahler, Pine, & Bergman, 1975) that allows the opportunity to test new ideas and environments with the safety and structure of the caregiver's encouraging separation. Thus the borderline individual retains a split sense of the other, polarized into all-good and all-bad. Cognitive-behavioral theory suggests that patients may have learned from an early age that they must adapt to and flow with the environment in order to avoid difficulty. They may have existing schemas which suggest that to be chameleonlike is to remain safe.

Both viewpoints suggest that a lack of integration of the internal environment causes a disruption in the integration of an identity manifested in the external environment. Not knowing in which niche, subculture, or group one belongs can create internal angst and propel those with BPD to desperately seek out something with which to identify. Their lives may be fraught with existential questions related to the purpose, meaning, and reason for who they are.

VIGNETTES

The first vignette introduces Marianne, a teenager whose plight is her unsuccessful attempts to find an identity that fits. Trying new hairstyles, clothing, and friends, she struggles to fit in with something and someone. Normal adolescent identity, according to Erik Erikson's fifth stage of psychosocial development, "identity vs. role confusion," states that adolescents question who they are and how they fit into the world. Throughout this stage, choosing the various roles that one will adopt can be difficult. It is also often difficult for all persons at this stage to differentiate that which with they want to identify with and that which with they do not want to identify (Erikson, 1963). However, those experiencing typical role confusion generally have a stable life value system, whereas those with identity disturbance display more radical changes.

In the second vignette, Terry drifts from one job to the next, never quite feeling as if something really matches him. He knows he wants to be something and somebody, but he continues to job hop, changes girlfriends and friends, and is unable to commit to a school or training program. He has few long-term goals that indicate a formed sense of self or identity.

Both vignettes describe individuals who lack of a strong sense of self. This lack of self-identity and accompanying determination causes the individuals to continually attempt to be a part of or follow different groups. The vignettes also portray not only the emotional and cognitive ramifications of the lack of a cohesive sense of self, but also the behaviors that indicate changes, shifts in relationships, and an altering of image.

Vignette 1: Marianne

There she goes again. A different hairstyle and color. The girls at the dorm wondered not only how Marianne could afford her frequent hair-dressing appointments, but also why she didn't get tired of changing so often.

Marianne looked at herself approvingly in the mirror. This bright pink color was just right for her; it fit in perfectly with the girls she had started hanging out with from a nearby college. They were really wild, and Marianne thought it was time to have more fun. Her friends here at school kept asking her to return all the things she borrowed from them. She had no idea where their stuff was. She didn't even wear that stupid style anymore; and it just didn't matter, she was sick of them anyhow.

Vignette 2: Terry

Terry was in his early forties. He kept pushing the thoughts that he would never amount to anything to the back of his mind. Sure, most other men at his age had homes, families, and careers. He just hadn't figured out what he wanted yet. He'd attended a community college for a year when he was 19, but he just didn't fit in with that crowd. The school . . . well he just couldn't get into that scene. He would try a job for a few weeks and then, bored with the work, quit. His friends seemed to change along with his jobs, not to mention his girlfriends— they changed all too often as well. How is a guy supposed to figure out what to do or what he wants? "Oh well," he thought, "by the time I figure it out, it'll be time to retire!"

Discussing the Vignettes & Prompting the Patient

In the first vignette, Marianne exhibits behavioral changes that indicate a lack of a cohesive sense of identity. This goes beyond the normal changes that everyone experiences or the new styles that many people try. Do your patients continually seek to belong to a group? Have they tried many different "selves" manifested through choices in clothing, values, or physical appearance?

In the second vignette, Terry experiences a lack of direction in his life. This is largely due to his not knowing what he really likes or dislikes. His own fragmented and incomplete sense of identity precludes him from identifying what he likes and needs. This lack of cohesion manifests in not knowing who could meet his needs, what job would satisfy him, and ultimately where his life may lead.

APPLYING TYPICAL BPD SCHEMAS & DISTORTIONS TO THE CRITERION

The identity disturbance criterion may be difficult for patients to identify. As your patients begin to describe their own experiences, be sure you have discussed the role schemas play in developing maladaptive behaviors and responses. These schemas may include themes that revolve around a lack of individuation, unlovability, and incompetence. Thought distortions may include all-or-nothing negative self-statements (such as believing they are incapable of forming an opinion) that lead to maladaptive behaviors. Schemas of incompetence combined with dichotomous thinking may lead patients to erroneous conclusions that they are unable to manage stressors or to feel competent in forming their own opinions. This may prompt them to adopt the stances or opinions of others, which may in turn challenge the values they currently do hold and further corrode their identity. Encourage patients to engage in self-reflection and self-evaluation on a day-to-day basis. Self-reflection is a necessary part of making a decision, forming an opinion, and identifying a general direction in which one wishes to proceed. Those with BPD tend to have a gnawing sense that they really don't know what they want or how to get it. Experiencing schemas related to a lack of individuation, they may look to others to help them make decisions or form opinions based on an external rather than internal source. The feeling of not knowing what they want and how to get it is felt frequently and causes great distress.

WORKSHEETS ONE & TWO: ASSESSMENT & ASSIGNMENT

As noted, states of intense anxiety can cause physical symptoms of panic, GI distress, and sweating. WORKSHEET 1: THE ASSESSMENT (p. 112; Patient Manual, p. 72) asks patients to consider times when they, too, have experienced a lack of a sense of identity. Not having a goal, sense of direction, or purpose can cause intense anxiety. Signs of intense anxiety can help the patient to recognize that they are experiencing turmoil related to their sense of a lack of an identity. If these symptoms are felt, patients can then take control, and not make decisions impulsively just to fit in or feel like they belong, but rather make choices out of self-knowledge and direction.

WORKSHEET 1
The Assessment for Criterion 3

Rate the severity of the following problems as you think they may relate to you.

0 = none   1= mild   2 = moderate   3 = severe   4 = extremely severe

1. You frequently change groups of friends. _____

2. You have tried many types of careers and still feel unsatisfied. _____

3. You are not sure what your self-image is. _____

4. You have questioned your sexual orientation on more than one occasion. _____

5. You have surprised family members or friends by changing long-held values. _____

6. You have found it difficult to maintain employment for any length of time. _____

7. You tend to forget about friends you've known for a long time to hang around new friends. _____

8. Your taste in clothes, style, and activities frequently changes. _____

9. In order to fit in, you're willing to "go with the crowd" even if it entails doing something you may be hesitant about. _____

10. You tend to get bored very easily. _____

If the patient answers five or more prompts at level 2 or above, consider focusing on this criterion.

After patients complete WORKSHEET 1: THE ASSESSMENT, complete WORKSHEET 2: THE ASSIGNMENT (Patient Manual, p. 73) which prompts patients to identify an incident in which they experienced distress related to questioning their identity.

SENSITIVITY & IDENTITY DISTURBANCE

With regard to identity, patients with BPD may be greatly distressed by any type of stressor that requires a decision, action, or deliberation. As patients search for what their emotions mean, they may experience a shifting sense of self. For example, a patient may experience a surge of anxiety, anger, or excitement, but have difficulty identifying what that particular emotion may mean. Early theories of emotion maintain that in order for an individual to experience an emotion, some sort of physiological arousal must occur, which then is interpreted and designated as a specific emotion in response to the cues in the environment (James 1890/1972). For example, a patient with BPD may experience symptoms similar to anxiety such as stomach distress, nervousness, or a racing heart. However, he or she may not look internally to identify the emotional state, but rather search the environment for cues. The BPD patient in this case may attribute the racing heart or nervousness to a positive emotion such as excitement, thrill, or even elation. The environment then serves as a means and method to categorize the felt physiological aspects of the emotion. In sum, in response to their not knowing how they experience emotional states, BPD patients may adopt a chameleonlike approach and closely monitor their external environments for direction or clues about how to define their emotions. They are, therefore, very sensitive to others' opinions, actions, and values, as well as to changes in their environment, including whether or not the opinion they express is "acceptable" to their audience.

WORKSHEETS THREE TO SIX, & EIGHTEEN: TREATMENT GOALS

A goal of treatment is to challenge the often abstract statements that question identity. For instance, the "Who am I?" statement obscures the fundamental definitions of identity by not recognizing the very basic parts and components of identity, such as one's sex, age, and even name. Your patients have identities—they are just not defined. Having patients self-monitor or concretely identify aspects of their identity will help them form a greater sense of self. Assist patients in identifying the already-existent aspects of themselves that indicate who they are. For example, each time a patient questions his or her basic sense of self, remind him or her of the parts of his or her life that are clearly defined, such as a role in a family (e.g., mother, sister), a profession, a home town, and prior decisions that were made about the direction of his or her life. This will allow patients to challenge amorphous statements such as "I don't know who I am" and help them ground themselves and improve their decision-making skills.

After patients complete WORKSHEETS 1 and 2, assist them in filling out WORKSHEET 3: THE INCIDENT CHART (Patient Manual, p. 74). Helping patients describe how they react to what they perceive as a lack of identity will aid them in constructively managing their fears rather than acting in ways that further complicate or deteriorate the situation. By clearly identifying these warning signals, patients can make informed choices and preemptively strike against acting on impulsive urges related to their fears.

Complete WORKSHEETS 4 and 5 (Patient Manual, pp. 75–76) to identify patients' automatic thoughts and schema. Then treatment goals can be identified. In order to help organize this process, complete WORKSHEET 6: TREATMENT GOALS (Patient Manual, p. 77). Once treatment goals are set, complete WORKSHEET 18: THE DPS (Patient Manual, p. 84) to determine a baseline level of distress or dysfunction for the particular criterion.

WORKSHEETS SEVEN TO SEVENTEEN: SUGGESTED INTERVENTIONS

Worksheets 7 & 8: Physical Triggers & Suggested Interventions

Once patients are able to identify and monitor particular physiological warnings (WORKSHEET 7; Patient Manual, p. 79), they can choose their reactions and next steps (WORKSHEET 8; Patient Manual, pp. 80–81). Because this criterion can be somewhat amorphous, physiological indicators may be difficult to define identify. The primary goal is to assist patients in determining what physical signals are present prior to the adoption of others' opinions or to the experience of sadness that may accompany a lack of a strong sense of self. Thought-stopping, relaxation techniques, and relaxing imagery can be used to combat patients' physiological reactions to situations in which they feel a lack of identity.

THOUGHT-STOPPING

Once patients notice their system turning itself up when they become convinced that they are alone and have no idea who they are, encourage them to take a moment to stop. Remind them that there are definite unique aspects about themselves that no other person shares. Reflect upon those unique differences.

RELAXATION

When patients relax, they are actually reinforcing their individuality. They are taking control, and accessing their body and its response system. The following questions can help patients identify how their unique system works:

When I am able to relax I notice my muscles _____.

When I am able to relax I notice my body _____.

When I am able to relax I notice my breathing _____.

When I am able to relax I notice my heart rate _____.

I have trouble relaxing when _____.

RELAXING IMAGERY

When patients are able to identify a safe place, they are identifying something uniquely their own. Their safe place is a place that for them feels comforting and good. Thoughts of their safe place can help with relaxation.

Worksheets 9 & 10: Emotional Triggers & Suggested Interventions

SCALE BACK

Scaling back (WORKSHEET 10; Patient Manual, p. 83) prior to making a decision or adopting an opinion can give patients the time needed to look inward rather than respond out of the feeling that they are unable to form their own opinions. Ask patients to rate the emotion they experienced when they felt as if they lacked a cohesive sense of self (WORKSHEET 9; Patient Manual, p. 82). Keep in mind that patients with BPD are extremely sensitive and may experience very powerful and intense emotions. Be sure patients consider their whole system, including their levels of physiological arousal. Ask: "Would your response to the situation be different now that you have *turned yourself down*?"

Worksheets 11 & 12: Cognitive/Automatic Thoughts & Suggested Interventions

Cognitive interventions in the context of this criterion are aimed at challenging patients' faulty beliefs about their lack of an identity (WORKSHEET 11; Patient Manual, p. 84). By challenging schemas related to an absence of individuation and to unlovability, these exercises help patients clearly identify the characteristics that make them uniquely different. As patients identify these characteristics, assist them in clarifying what each of their roles means and how they are competent in each of them. Doing this challenges the schema related to incompetence. The following interventions (WORKSHEET 12; Patient Manual, pp. 85–87) aid patients in clearly stating who they are.

IDENTITY INTERVENTION 1

The first intervention asks patients to describe themselves in narrative form. The patients' narrative description of themselves provides insight into how they view themselves, and the associated underlying schema related to self-image and self-concept. For those patients who find this exercise difficult, this very struggle can be utilized as a concrete example of the criterion. Providing a narrative about one's identity can also have drawbacks. These include patients becoming overwhelmed by negative statements, or becoming saddened by how they may define themselves in terms of relationships. (For instance: "I'm still single, I'll never find love.") The therapist needs to support patients during this process, reframing negative self-statements, and encouraging more positive responses.

IDENTITY INTERVENTION 2

Next, patients are asked to review the following list, marking an "x" next to the items that apply to them and filling in the blanks by providing a description for those items.

IDENTITY INTERVENTION 3

In this intervention, patients are asked to rank on a scale of 1 to 5 how much they identify with each prompt from the list (Intervention 2). For example, does the patient identify more with being a mother than a Philadelphian? Does he or she think of him- or herself more as a teacher than as a friend? Patients should not to get caught up in value judgments (e.g., "It's better to be a friend than a teacher").

The Identity Intervention Chart			
Category	**Yes/No**	**Description**	**Rank**
sex	_____	_____	_____
occupation	_____	_____	_____
race	_____	_____	_____
age	_____	_____	_____
ethnicity	_____	_____	_____
citizenship	_____	_____	_____
religion	_____	_____	_____
marital status	_____	_____	_____
sexual orientation	_____	_____	_____
political affiliation	_____	_____	_____
hair color	_____	_____	_____
clothing style	_____	_____	_____
height	_____	_____	_____
city of origin	_____	_____	_____
urban/suburban	_____	_____	_____
friend	_____	_____	_____
daughter/son	_____	_____	_____
neighbor	_____	_____	_____
student	_____	_____	_____
parent	_____	_____	_____
brother/sister	_____	_____	_____
other	_____	_____	_____

IDENTITY INTERVENTION 4

Once patients have ranked how much they identify with each item, they can start to mix and match them to clearly identify who they are. For example: "I am a 20-year-old male living in Trenton, N.J." As a 20-year-old male living in Trenton, this individual may have certain activities, interests, or music or food preferences that are unique to him. Ask patients to make these types of statements. These very basic signatures of identity can provide vast amounts of information regarding to what and to whom the patient is drawn. By defining the foundations of who they are, patients can begin to become aware of the many things they really are a part of, and pursuing their interests no longer seems such a difficult task. Use the following phrase to help patients create these combinations:

"I am a _____ who likes and identifies with _____ ."

WEIGH THE EVIDENCE

Use the DISPUTATION CHART to help patients prove to themselves the likelihood or unlikelihood that the worst is happening. Are patients assuming that they are unable to contribute to a conversation? Are they assuming that they are lost or directionless?

The Disputation Chart	
Situation: *Having difficulty contributing to conversation.*	
Belief: *I have nothing to contribute.*	
Proof Supporting Belief	**Refuting Statement**
1. *I have no idea who I am.*	1. *I know that I am _____* [use list].
2. *I don't ever know what to say.*	2. *I have a history and unique experiences that others might find interesting.*
3. _____ .	3. _____ .
4. _____ .	4. _____ .

Worksheets 13 & 14: Behavioral Triggers & Suggested Interventions

WORKSHEET 13: BEHAVIORAL TRIGGERS (Patient Manual, p. 88) prompts patients to describe how they were reacting both before they experienced a lack of a sense of self and after.

CONSIDER THE CONSEQUENCES

As patients struggle to identify how they may react in situations, encourage them to examine the potential consequences of their actions (WORKSHEET 14; Patient Manual, p. 89). Those who struggle with not knowing how to proceed afterward will often adopt the actions of others. It is similar to submitting to peer pressure. Ask patients: "What is the consequence of going along with others?" "Is this something that you would really want to do if you were alone?" Use The NEGATIVE AND POSITIVE CONSEQUENCE CHART to assist you.

Worksheets 16 & 17: Situational Triggers & Suggested Interventions

WORKSHEET 16 (Patient Manual, p. 90) prompts patients to specifically identify those situations that have led them to feel unsure about themselves or raised questions relating to their self-image. WORKSHEET 17 (Patient Manual, p. 91) suggests that they remove themselves from the situation or to try something different.

REMOVE YOURSELF

If patients find themselves in situations where they become overwhelmed with feelings of incompetence, they can choose to remove themselves from this type of situation. In this way, they can take charge of the situation, and feel more in control as they make their own decision to leave.

TRY SOMETHING DIFFERENT

In order to encourage patients to try something different from "following the leaders," ask them to do something novel or different from what they normally do. Remind them to tell themselves that their next move must be one that *they* not someone else have chosen. They should try to do something that comes directly from themselves and is not a result of influence or pressure from others or of their feeling as if they have no ideas about how to proceed.

WORKSHEET EIGHTEEN: THE DPS

Complete WORKSHEET 18: THE DPS (Patient Manual, p. 92). Compare the results of the DPS after treatment goals were set. Is there a difference in the level of distress the patient is experiencing in response to the criterion? If not, reexamine the interventions chosen to target the symptoms, and collaboratively determine whether changes or alterations should be made.

CASE EXAMPLE

In the second vignette, themes of unlovability and incompetence are present. Terry was so unsure about what he really felt that it took pressure from a friend to get him to enter treatment. Terry identified that he didn't know what he wanted because he never really gave himself the opportunity to look inward and listen to himself. After completing WORKSHEETS 1 and 2, Terry clearly identified several situations in his life in which he went along with what others thought he should do. After monitoring his automatic thoughts throughout the week, Terry realized that he particularly tended to focus on what others wanted when he was feeling down about himself. He noted that during those times his moods were low and he craved a "quick fix." This meant that he jumped at the next possible opportunity without taking the time to consider if it was something he truly wanted. For example, after he met a few art students at a local coffee shop, he immediately signed up and paid for an evening art course, convinced he had found a new career. This was despite never having any interest in art and doing little investigation about whether it was something he would succeed in. Within two weeks he tired of the course and was disappointed to discover that payment for it was unrefundable.

Upon completing WORKSHEETS 2 and 3, Terry recognized that although he at times appeared to be a drifter, he identified strongly with his role in his community as head of the "Neighborhood Watch" program and that he socialized quite easily with his neighbors. He especially enjoyed the weekend music festivals that occurred in the city and soon realized that by joining several clubs he could engage in activities that he enjoyed. Although his relationships with women tended to be short-lived, he did recognize a pattern. It came as a revelation that he did want to be in a relationship, but he mostly dated women that were married or otherwise unavailable, which directly contradicted his wanting to be in a relationship. Terry slowly ranked and categorized the things that meant the most to him, and soon he felt that he belonged to a few specific different groups of people. He was able to challenge ambiguous statements such as "I don't know who I am" and soon began enhancing the relationships with a circle of friends with whom he shared interests.

CHAPTER 4 | Impulsivity

This chapter addresses BPD Criterion 4: "impulsivity in at least two areas that are potentially self-damaging (e.g., spending, sex, substance abuse, reckless driving, binge eating). Note: do not include suicidal or self-mutilating behavior covered in criterion 5" (APA, 2000, p. 710). To be impulsive is respond to an urge to do something. Impulsivity is also acting on urges without careful consideration. Impulsive patients may jump into relationships very quickly, drive recklessly, experiment with drugs or alcohol, or show a pattern of not consistently considering the aftermath of their actions. An impulsive person may say, "I don't know why I did such a thing" or "It seemed great at the moment." Those patients may have been forced to suffer the consequences of acting impulsively by losing a significant relationship, endangering themselves or others, or damaging relations with employers.

Often those who are impulsive have learned that the only outlet for physiological excitement or overarousal is impulsiveness. Some may feel living life to the fullest entails being impulsive or "walking on the edge." However, most patients regret some of their impulsivity and, in particular, the consequences of their actions. How does impulsivity begin? We encourage you to help patients examine their whole system. Urges to do something can be emotional, physiological, cognitive, or behavioral. Most important for your patients is the understanding that to be impulsive is not just to do something illegal or dangerous. Rather, it extends into all the ways we interact with or conduct ourselves around others. If everyone acted on their urges, there would be no order. What patients may lack is the ability to modulate their urges or consider the consequences of acting on their urges. High-arousal seekers ultimately pay a huge price for their actions. An

Criterion 4

Impulsivity in at least two areas that are *potentially* self-damaging.

Impulsivity
Definition: Acting or happening without apparent forethought, prompting, or planning and characterized by unthinking boldness.
Synonym: Spontaneity, rashness, unpremeditatedness, reflexiveness.
BPD: Patients with BPD are prone to act without thinking ahead. Little planning is involved, which can lead to negative consequences. Impulsive behaviors are a key component to understanding the patient with BPD, and this impulsivity can be expressed in a myriad of ways. Impulsive behaviors include verbal statements as well as actually doing things that may be harmful.

Potentially
Definition: Possibily.
Synonym: Likely, probably.
BPD: Impulsivity can be unthinking, unemotional, or unplanned. But it is not simply acting or behaving without forethought; it involves a lack of comprehensive processing of stimulus from the internal and external environment. Patients who have a pattern of impulsivity lack the ability to mediate and modulate the messages they perceive from their arousal states to the actual action. Instead, they hastily respond from the gut without cognitively applying and associating prior experience, knowledge, and common sense to incoming, ongoing stimulus. The result is impulsive behaviors that can be (but aren't always) very self-damaging physically, emotionally, and interpersonally.

important part of treatment is recognizing that on some occasions patients' impulsivity has provided them with some pleasure. Not all spontaneous actions are deleterious; however, some potentially endanger both the patient and others.

VIGNETTES

The vignettes describe Karen and Jenny, both of whom experience impulses to do things with potentially hazardous outcomes. Karen, feeling annoyed about her job situation, happily accepts an offer from her girlfriends to go out but neglects to consider the ramifications of leaving for the day without her supervisor's permission. Jenny, excited by the prospect of a potential boyfriend, places herself in a very compromising situation with potentially disastrous results. Both characters act on urges that pervade every aspect of their system: emotional, cognitive, behavioral, and physiological.

The use of the systemic approach, is preferred, because it provides clues to managing impulsivity. This approach does so primarily by helping patients learn to identify which urges have led them into trouble. Encourage patients to examine all levels of their impulsivity, be they obvious acts of potential harm or derogatory remarks made inappropriately.

Vignette 1: Karen

Karen was frustrated with work. She felt tired, underappreciated, and she was annoyed with her supervisor. She really didn't feel like working the rest of the day; she had the urge to just walk out. So when her girlfriends called to ask her out, she readily accepted. Without much thought, she concluded that the company owed her some hours because she had been working so hard recently. She straightened her desk quickly, set her phone to voicemail, and left 2 hours early. She was shocked when she received her termination notice the following day.

Vignette 2: Jenny

Jenny had been waiting for this party all week. Her girlfriends told her there would be lots of great-looking guys. She had had such bad luck with men lately. She couldn't seem to find "the one." She took extra time getting ready and was sure to wear something sexy. When she arrived, she loosened up with a few drinks. She didn't want to appear stiff or stuffy. Then it happened. She met the man of her dreams. He was great-looking, talented, and with a great job; they talked together so easily. The night flew. He just seemed to know her. They told each other their innermost secrets; she never had felt this close to anyone before. Before long, she found herself at his apartment. She knew it was going too fast, but she was sure he was the one. His wife, however, tended to disagree.

Discussing the Vignettes & Prompting the Patient

Key to both of these vignettes is a lack of cognitive processing that could potentially divert distressing or negative consequences. In the first vignette, Karen made an impulsive decision largely due to feeling as if she "deserved" something in return for all her hard work. Reading that her body was fatigued, she sought some type of relief. Often justification becomes a modus for poor decision-making and impulsive actions. She decided to go with the physiological and emotional urge to leave rather than allow for a cognitive processing of potential consequences. Ask your patients: Do you use justification to satisfy your urges?

In the second vignette, Jenny fully responds to her emotional and cognitive need for intimacy. However, she does not consider the potential ramifications of having a casual encounter with someone she hardly knows. Those with BPD typically approach interpersonal situations in a dichotomous manner and view others in either an idealized or devalued way (see Chapter 3). Initially believing this was "the man of her dreams" (idealized), she acts on her impulses and places herself in a precarious position with someone not available emotionally for a future relationship.

APPLYING TYPICAL BPD SCHEMAS & DISTORTIONS TO THE CRITERION

If patients identify themselves as being impulsive, they have created a pattern or schema of reacting to stimulus without cognitive mediation. The stimulus, therefore, is interpreted according to a pattern or schema of not paying attention to clues that may indicate potential harm, danger, or negative consequences. Additionally, typical BPD schemas may include themes of emotional deprivation, dependence, and unlovability. Because patients may continually be searching to "feel" that they are alive and unique (see Chapter 3), often in order to counter feelings of deprivation, they seek stimulation. Compounded with dichotomous thinking—which may lead patients to believe that if they do not take the opportunity, one may never again present itself—this need for stimulation prompts patients to act on impulse. Additionally, patients may believe that if they are not spontaneous all the time, they will have no fun. As a means of maintaining connections and feeling a part of something, patients may allow others to encourage them to follow negative impulsive acts such trying a drug in order to "be in" or "be part of the crowd."

Those with substance-abuse problems often experience urges to use and are unable to stop. If patients identify themselves as having a substance-abuse problem, complete a thorough evaluation to determine if specialized substance-abuse treatment is warranted. Also support and discuss the healthy or positive responses patients may have had in reaction to an urge. Ask them: "What did you want to accomplish by doing that act?" This forces them to consider the whole situation—i.e, the aftermath and consequences of completing the act. It also reveals the motive behind the impulsive act. For example, was the patient impulsively driving fast in order to impress friends, "get a rush," or cause an accident? The motives behind actions often provide clues to schemas related to spontaneity, peer acceptance and rejection, and self-esteem. Does the motive derive from an internal or external locus of control? Is it a combination thereof? It is vital to understand the action in as much detail as possible, as it provides inroads to creating interventions.

WORKSHEETS ONE & TWO: ASSESSMENT & ASSIGNMENT

As noted, states of intense anxiety can cause physical symptoms of panic, GI distress, and sweating. WORKSHEET 1: THE ASSESSMENT (p. 126; Patient Manual, p. 96) asks patients to consider times when they, too, have been impulsive. Physical symptoms of anxiety can sometimes be a warning sign or trigger that impulsive behavior may follow.

WORKSHEET 1
The Assessment for Criterion 4

Rate the severity of the following problems as you think they may relate to you. If you aware of any other impulsive behaviors that you do that are not included on the list, please add them.

0 = none   1 = mild   2 = moderate   3 = severe   4 = extremely severe

1. I drink to excess or am unable to stop. ____

2. I use drugs to excess or am unable to stop. ____

3. I engage in sexual relations without adequately protecting myself or that place me in danger. ____

4. I place myself in unsafe situations, such as driving too fast or frequenting dangerous areas. ____

5. I run up bills that I know I am unable to pay for. ____

6. I eat excessively, knowing that it may make me feel bad. ____

7. I yell at others without first trying to resolve the situation quietly. ____

8. I miss school/work for reasons other than sickness. ____

9. I throw objects. ____

10. I physically fight with others. ____

If the patient answers five or more prompts at level 2 or above, consider focusing on this criterion.

After patients complete WORKSHEET 1: THE ASSESSMENT, complete WORKSHEET 2: THE ASSIGNMENT (Patient Manual, p. 97) which prompts patients to identify an incident in which they were impulsive.

SENSITIVITY & IMPULSIVITY

Patients with BPD have a highly charged physiological system and often gain relief or excitement from acting on an impulse. Not all impulsive actions have negative consequences. So, although patients may identify that they are impulsive, they may have learned to associate their highly charged physiological and emotional system and urges with positive consequences. Due to the phenomena of intermittent conditioning, the drive to seek the most positive consequence is very strong and difficult to break.

WORKSHEETS THREE TO SIX, & EIGHTEEN: TREATMENT GOALS

Treatment goals do not focus on eradicating all spontaneity from patients' lives. They do, however, revolve around encouraging patients to make informed choices and fully consider the potential consequences rather than hastily acting on their urges. This provides patients with the opportunity to drive their actions rather than passively receive and deal with the fallout of impulsive reactions. This requires intense self-monitoring and diligence in watching for the warning signs of impulsive decisions or acts. If patients look before they leap, many options will become available to them and they will begin to understand that they are able to make decisions about what they actually want. This will also help build confidence in self-identity and worth (see Chapter 3).

After patients complete WORKSHEETS 1 and 2, assist them in filling out WORKSHEET 3: THE INCIDENT CHART (Patient Manual, p. 98). Complete WORKSHEETS 4 and 5 (Patient Manual, pp. 99–100) to identify patients' automatic thoughts and schema. Then treatment goals can be identified. In order to help organize this process, complete WORKSHEET 6: TREATMENT GOALS (Patient Manual, p. 101). Once treatment goals are set, complete WORKSHEET 18: THE DPS (Patient Manual, p. 102) to determine a baseline level of distress or dysfunction for the particular criterion.

WORKSHEETS SEVEN TO SEVENTEEN:
SUGGESTED INTERVENTIONS

Worksheets 7 & 8: Physical Triggers & Suggested Interventions

THOUGHT-STOPPING

Thought-stopping is a particularly effective intervention for impulsivity. Because patients lack in-depth cognitive processing in response to stimuli, physiological sensations may be the only indicator of excitement, and stopping may actually thwart impulsive acts.

Ask patients to identify the physiological indicators of arousal (WORKSHEET 17; Patient Manual, p. 103). Often the same sensations are felt in response to both excitement and anxiety. Encourage patients to monitor not only the physiological sensations that indicate excitement, but also those that accompany their urges to do something. Once they have identified the physiological warning signs, they can try to stop it before they act (WORKSHEET 8; Patient Manual, pp. 104–105). This gives them time to consider the consequences and decide whether they truly wish to follow through on the act.

RELAXATION

After patients are able to utilize thought-stopping, relaxation techniques are particularly helpful with the physical sensation associated with excitement and anxiety. These bodily reactions respond well to relaxation techniques.

RELAXING IMAGERY

In combination with relaxation techniques, ask patients to imagine their safe place. Patients can also assure themselves that part of being in a safe place is not having placed themselves in harms way due to being impulsive.

Worksheets 9 & 10: Emotional Triggers & Suggested Interventions

WORKSHEET 9 (Patient Manual, p. 106) prompts patients to describe the specific feelings they experience when they perceive that they are about to act impulsively. In particular, sadness or anger may propel one to act impulsively almost as a means of "deserving" to feel better. For example, if your patient feels saddened by not finding a significant other, he or she may feel justified in acting on a sexual urge, even if it leads to a potentially dangerous situation. Another example is extreme rage: Patients may feel the only outlet is to act on an urge to hit or throw things.

SCALE BACK

Scaling back (WORKSHEET 10; Patient Manual, pp. 107–108) again provides an opportunity for further cognitive processing to take place, thereby allowing patients to examine the consequences (positive or negative) of acting impulsively. Ask patients to rate the emotion that prompted them to act impulsively. These emotions may include excitement, anxiousness, anger, or sadness. Once patients scale back, ask them to rate the emotion again. Encourage patients to note the differences and their ability to affect change.

ATTACH EMOTION TO IMPULSIVENESS

Help patients learn to attach their experienced emotion with pending impulsivity. In other words, if patients are able to identify from WORKSHEET 3: THE INCIDENT CHART that they tend to act on their urges when they are sad, they can begin to set up some safeguards to prevent acting irresponsibly. For example, patients may attach emotions to impulsiveness by stating: "When I am psyched and wound up, I tend to act impulsively, especially when I'm out with the guys." Help them understand their patterns. Additional questions include:

In the past, I have reacted strongly to _____ [*emotion*].

When I feel _____, I tend to act impulsively.

I have trouble controlling my impulses when _____.

LEARN TO IDENTIFY WHEN YOU'RE FEELING VULNERABLE

Can patients identify the times when they are feeling slightly more vulnerable? Are those times usually associated with some type of impulsive act? When do they feel vulnerable? When they are tired? When they feel ejected? When they are bored? After they drink alcohol? Ask patient to list the times when their vulnerability leads to impulsiveness.

I know I am vulnerable during _____.

I know I am vulnerable when _____.

I am especially vulnerable at _____ times in my life.

Worksheets 11 & 12: Cognitive/Automatic Thoughts & Suggested Interventions

Assist patients in understanding the role of cognition in mediating impulses or urges. It is imperative that patients are able to read the physiological and emotional cues (WORKSHEET 11; Patient Manual,

p. 109) that, if not mediated by cognitive processes, can lead to impulsive acts. The following interventions can be instrumental in derailing an impulse and providing a pathway to an appropriate action or behavior (WORKSHEET 12; Patient Manual, pp. 110–111).

CONSIDER THE CONSEQUENCES

Impulsive behaviors can be framed as specific acts for which patients are solely responsible. Those with BPD often engage in an other-blaming style when processing actions and behaviors. Due to the ego-syntonic nature of BPD, it becomes especially important for patients to become aware that *their* every action and behavior is a product of their own choice, and that, therefore, *they* are responsible for the consequences. This is powerful—both negatively and positively. On the one hand, taking responsibility for one's actions may cause feelings of guilt, regret, or remorse, potentially worsening a comorbid depression. On the other hand, it allows patients to recognize that they have the ability to take control not only of their impulses, but also of their future choices and their lives in general. Utilize The NEGATIVE AND POSITIVE CONSEQUENCES CHART.

The Negative and Positive Consequences Chart		
Behavior *Accepting ride from an attractive stranger.*	**Negative Consequences** *Potential danger.*	**Positive Consequences** *Excitement.*
_____ .	_____ .	_____ .
_____ .	_____ .	_____ .

After completing the chart, ask patients the following:

• Do the negative consequences outweigh the positive consequences?
• Is it worth it to decrease this behavior?
• Do you want to continue this behavior?

AVERT IMPULSIVITY

The following multistep model to averting impulsive behavior was first proposed by Pretzer (1990, p. 203). Be sure to elicit all contexts within each of the steps. This includes determining if certain situations are present when a tendency to act impulsive occurs. Within each

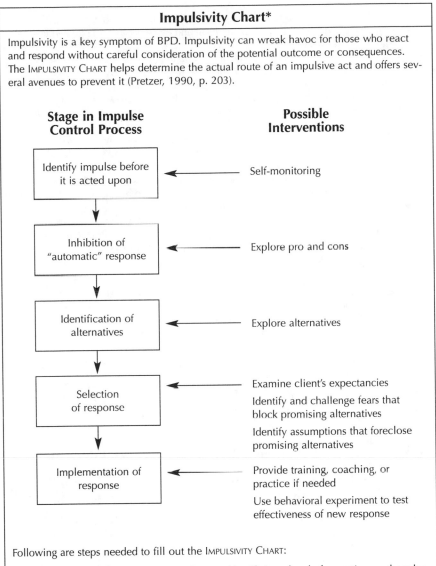

Impulsivity Chart*

Impulsivity is a key symptom of BPD. Impulsivity can wreak havoc for those who react and respond without careful consideration of the potential outcome or consequences. The IMPULSIVITY CHART helps determine the actual route of an impulsive act and offers several avenues to prevent it (Pretzer, 1990, p. 203).

Stage in Impulse Control Process	Possible Interventions
Identify impulse before it is acted upon	Self-monitoring
Inhibition of "automatic" response	Explore pro and cons
Identification of alternatives	Explore alternatives
Selection of response	Examine client's expectancies Identify and challenge fears that block promising alternatives Identify assumptions that foreclose promising alternatives
Implementation of response	Provide training, coaching, or practice if needed Use behavioral experiment to test effectiveness of new response

Following are steps needed to fill out the IMPULSIVITY CHART:

1. *Identify the impulse.* Encourage patients to identify impulses before acting on them by self-monitoring in all areas.
2. *Inhibit automatic responses.* What are the pros and cons of acting on a certain urge or impulse? How do they weigh out? Does a night of passion with a stranger outweigh the possibility of danger? When we enter situations, we usually have a preconception about how they will turn out. This is a result of our experiences growing up, living, and functioning in everyday society. For instance, we know that if we park in a no-parking zone, we may be able to get into the store more quickly (positive) but we

(continued)

*(From J. Pretzer [1990]. Borderline personality disorder. In A. Beck, A. Freeman, & Associates [eds.], *Cognitive therapy of personality disorders* [pp. 176–207]. New York: Guilford Press. Reprinted by permission of the Guilford Press.)

are also likely to get a ticket (negative). Often we can predict an outcome just by examining the situation at hand in more detail and by taking the time to read and monitor ourselves better.

3. *Identify alternatives*. Now that the patient is aware that he or she can make an informed choice about urges, does that mean no more spontaneity? Of course not. It's all a matter of degree, or finding the middle ground. For example, what could the individual considering sexual intimacy with a stranger have done to avoid placing him- or herself in a dangerous situation while continuing to attempt to make a connection with the new person?

4. *Select a response*. Identify and challenge fears related to alternatives. How does the patient make the choice to act or not to act? What are the patient's expectations regarding the act? What are the hopes related to carrying out the impulse? What, if any, are the disadvantages to not acting on an urge? Does actually looking before you leap make you boring or not alive? These responses need to be challenged, as acting on certain urges may actually threaten the patient's safety.

5. *Implement a response*. This fifth and final step entails actually choosing a response. If your patient is learning to take control of his or her impulses, it will take practice, training, and learning to identify vulnerable times when the likelihood of acting on an impulse that may be regretted later is high.

Encourage patients to ask themselves common-sense questions such as "Is this really a wise choice?" or " Could I get myself into trouble with this?" Also ask patients to consider the current situation: Are there prior situations that are similar?; What were the decisions that were made in this similar situation?; What was the outcome of the decisions that were made?; Are there similarities to the current situation and the potential decisions that are going to be made?

step lies a possible point for intervention in the impulse control process.

Worksheets 13 & 14: Behavioral Triggers & Suggested Interventions

When helping patients review their patterns of behavior, encourage them to identify how they felt or what they thought about the behaviors they exhibited. Once patients have identified the situations that usually lead to impulsive acts (Patient Manual, p. 112), utilize WORK-SHEET 3: THE INCIDENT CHART to outline potential interventions that will assist them in identifying and preventing the behaviors that they wish to change or alter (WORKSHEET 14; Patient Manual, p. 113).

AVOID THE SITUATION

Once patients have identified the specific situations in which they tend to act impulsively, ask them if they really need to allow themselves to be in those situations. For example, if patients know by their history that socializing with friends at the local pub has led to heavy drinking and impulsive acts like fighting, they might consider avoiding that situation.

IDENTIFY A FRIEND

Often impulsive decisions are made without "checking it out" with someone who is close or trusted. Ask patients to identify someone they can trust to help challenge or support a decision that may be made quickly or as a result of acting on an urge. This friend should not be someone who has engaged in risky behavior with the patient or who triggers further impulsivity.

CONSIDER TRIGGERS

Those who work in the substance-abuse field are well aware of the tenant "Avoid people, places, and things associated with your addiction." There are patterns pertaining to when and where patients tend to act on urges. Ask patients to identify and list these triggers clearly, so that when they appear, patients can recognize that they are heading into a situation that could result in impulsive behavior.

PLAY "WHAT IF" GAMES

Ask patients to play games that investigate the consequences of actions. For example, have them ask themselves questions such as "What if I did this? What if I didn't?" Or, if they are remembering something they did, ask: "What would have happened if I hadn't done that?"

REWARD YOURSELF

Ask patients to plan out ways of rewarding themselves for resisting an urge or saying no to something that may have had a negative consequence. This will help demarcate their successes. Obviously, the predetermined reward should not include triggers that may prompt impulsive actions. For instance, patients may reward themselves with a hot bath, saving personal time for themselves, or having lunch with friends.

Worksheets 16 & 17: Situational Triggers & Suggested Interventions

WORKSHEET 16 (Patient Manual, p. 114) prompts patients to specifically identify those situations that have led the patient to act impulsively. WORKSHEET 17 (Patient Manual, p. 115) suggests that patients remove themselves from the situation or try something different.

REMOVE YOURSELF

If patients find themselves in a situation where they have become impulsive, remind them that they can choose to remove themselves from the environment which may stimulate impulsive acts. By choosing to remove themselves from a situation known to result in impulsive acts, they can take charge of the situation.

TRY SOMETHING DIFFERENT

What actions can patients take instead of acting on an impulse? Patients may believe that if they do not act on an urge, they will be considered boring or dull. However, there are alternatives to acting impulsively; including planning an event that can provide as much enjoyment as acting on an urge does. A second component of this intervention is to identify and create other activities. Ask patients to list activities they can do instead of acting on an impulse, and create a plan for carrying out these behaviors. For example, patients who like to exercise could include daily runs on their list.

WORKSHEET EIGHTEEN: THE DPS

Complete WORKSHEET 18: THE DPS (Patient Manual, p. 116). Compare the results of the DPS after treatment goals were set. Is there a difference in the level of distress the patient is experiencing in response to the criterion? If not, reexamine the interventions chosen to target the symptoms, and collaboratively determine whether changes or alterations should be made.

CASE EXAMPLE

In the first vignette, Karen made impulsive choices without carefully considering the potential ramifications. Devastated at the loss of her job, Karen sought services through her Employee Assistance Program counselor, who helped her begin to dismantle her erroneous beliefs regarding acting on urges. Throughout her young years, Karen had always felt deprived. She viewed the other kids as getting so much more than she and felt that now, as an adult who could afford enjoyable things, she was entitled to take them. Karen also disliked being the only kid who couldn't join in the fun and feel part of a group. After completing WORKSHEET 1: THE ASSESSMENT, Karen began to recognize that impulsive behaviors had cost her a great deal over the years, including frequent job changes, losses of friendships and relationships, and frequent feelings of regret for what she called "my stupid events." Karen began to monitor her automatic thoughts—which included "I deserve that" and "Because I'm uncomfortable, I should make myself feel better"—throughout the week, as well as the triggers that tended to activate her urge to be impulsive. She noted that her triggers included stressful working situations, feeling overwhelmed and fatigued, or experiencing boredom. She soon recognized that not only did she do impulsive things such as shop excessively and at sometimes stay out too late, but she also tended to *say* things impulsively that alienated others. She learned to monitor for that excited feeling she got in her stomach when she thought about something new or thrilling and processed the urge through a decision chain. She also learned to seek guidance from other friends who were dependable and tended not to be impulsive. Karen soon learned that her early compelling schema that she was a "bore" if she didn't join in *all* the time was not really in her best interests. She also learned that by making decisions carefully, she did not have to wake up to the negative consequences of another day or night's "stupid events."

CHAPTER 5

Recurrent Suicidal Behavior,
Gestures, &
Self-Mutilating Behavior

This chapter addresses BPD Criterion 5: "recurrent suicidal behavior, gestures, or threats, or self-mutilating behavior" (APA, 2000, p. 710). Approximately 8 to 10% of individuals diagnosed with BPD eventually complete a suicide (APA, 1994). Self-mutilating behavior and self-destructive acts are also problematic with this population. When introducing this topic to patients, clearly differentiate suicide attempts and self-mutilative gestures. This helps patients understand the difference between actually trying to end one's life and attempting to alleviate internalized tension or pain. It is vital that clinicians conduct an ongoing evaluation throughout therapy, as patients with BPD are particularly sensitive to internal and external stressors that may overwhelm their coping system and potentially prompt a suicidal gesture or attempt. The goals of this step of the program are to clearly delineate alternatives to self-harm.

Suicide is defined as the act of taking one's life. Of individuals who complete suicides, approximately 60 to 70% have been previously diagnosed with major depression or bipolar disorder (Slaby, 1992). For clinicians, this aspect of treatment evokes much angst, as it demands complete and unrelenting consistency in evaluation, determination, and documentation. (For a complete review of evaluating a suicidal patient, see Reinecke [2000].) The key to the successful evaluation of a suicidal patient is the understanding that there are many different levels of suicidal thought. Patients may have fleeting ideation that indicates that their thoughts of suicide are more a passing fantasy than a comprehensive plan of action. Ideation is often connected to thoughts related to the punishment of others, such as "I bet he wouldn't be so hard on me if I weren't here." Your assessment should include how frequently patients experience ideation and if its occurrence is increasing. If patients have ideation, have they formulated a plan to carry it out? If patients have identified a plan, it is essential to assess its actual lethality (Roberts, 2000). Brent (1987) demonstrated a strong relationship between the medical lethality of the plan chosen and suicide intent. Roberts wrote that plans considered to be more lethal generally include concrete, specific, and dangerous methods. Additionally, the author stated: "Suicidal plans generally reveal the relative risk in that the degree of intent is typically related to the lethality of the potential method (e.g., using a gun or hanging infers higher intent whereas overdosing or cutting infers lower intent" (p. 140). However, it is not an exhaustive statement; all suicidal plans have the potential to be lethal and should be considered as such. Have patients identified that they actually intend to die? Do they have access to what they need to carry out the plan? Are they making arrangements in the event that they die—e.g., changing their will? These are key questions to be included in the evaluation of a suicidal patient. As individuals with BPD are particularly sensitive to separation and abandonment (see Chapter 1), the perceived loss of a partner or other important person can trigger an episode of suicidality. Additional consideration should be given to those who are particularly high-risk—i.e., those who have substance-abuse problems, have made prior attempts, are living alone, have medical problems, and/or who indicate that they are hopeless. Hopelessness is a key factor in predicting suicide (Beck, 1986). To assist you in your evaluation of patients, utilize the Beck Hopelessness Scale (Beck, Weissman, Kovacs, & Trexler, 1994).

As you continue to evaluate your patients, keep in mind one basic premise: Above all, ensure the safety of the patient. If you have any doubts or questions, or are unsure of the patient's ability to maintain his or her safety, do not take chances. This may seem very basic, but it becomes quite easy for a confusing situation to only become more unclear due to the heightened emotions, volatility, and unpredictability typical of those with BPD. It is imperative that you retain the following very fundamental treatment recommendations. Suicidal and self-injurious behavior, threats, or undiminished ideation require changing the treatment plan so that it includes the possibility of hospitalization, family sessions, psychiatric consultation, emergency services intervention, and involuntary commitment. As patients may tend to vacillate in their actual intent to die, clear and understandable limits such as patients agreeing to the treatment recommendations set by the therapist are intrinsic to retaining their patients' safety, to determining your own ethical decisions, and to knowing when you may require assistance and/or supervision.

Many patients with BPD have not learned to cope with ongoing stressors. Each and every crisis that occurs in their life presents the potential for choosing suicide as an option. Schematically, they may have learned that there are no alternatives to manage stress other than to die. Many patients engage in dichotomous thinking in their attempts to manage stress (e.g., "If I can't manage this as well as I should, then the only alternative is to die"). It is imperative that you elicit patients' automatic thoughts related to suicide and dying and their reasons for this behavior. This information can be utilized at a later time in challenging suicidal behaviors and thoughts, and in identification of adaptive alternative methods of managing stress.

You must be prepared to manage suicidal behavior, threats, or attempts when you first engage in treatment. This will ensure that the parameters of the treatment recommendations and interventions are not questioned when a crisis occurs. Very strict limits should be enforced when patients advise that they are suicidal. This includes a comprehensive evaluation of the current level of risk and a consideration of higher levels of care than outpatient treatment. Part of setting limits includes telling patients that ambiguous or vague responses to questions about their suicidal thoughts will not be tolerated and may require you to take steps to ensure their safety. At times there may be a manipulative quality to your patients' suicidality. Although you may sense this manipulation, a thorough and complete evaluation should occur irrespective of the patients' motive. It is important to remember that some completed suicides are the result of a patient's miscalculation of the projected rescue time or are a failed staged-attempt.

Self-mutilative behavior can be the actual harming of oneself with or without the intent to die. A common occurrence for those with BPD, it includes cutting, burning, acting recklessly, engaging in dangerous sexual situations, using drugs or alcohol, and knowingly placing oneself in a dangerous situation. Why does this occur? Often patients learn that mutilating themselves helps decrease internalized tension. Some theorists propose that self-mutilation allows the release of tension through the stimulation of endorphins, the body's natural pain reliever (for review, see Osuch, Noll, & Putnam, 1999). Through these self-destructive acts, patients in effect are self-medicating their anxiety, tension, or frustration. Schematically, they may have identified self-mutilation as a way of coping with stress, rallying support from others, or combating the overwhelming feelings of nonexistence by proving that if their physical self hurts or bleeds, they must be alive. Self-mutilating behaviors also require a comprehensive evaluation that includes determining the automatic thoughts associated with the acts, the intent of the acts, the purpose of the acts, and whether they are gestures indicative of a suicide attempt. Self-injurious behaviors must be taken as seriously as suicidal ideation, as studies have indicated of those who self-injure, 5%–10% eventually attempt suicide (Stone, Stone, & Hart, 1987).

Criterion 5

Recurrent suicidal behavior, *gestures*, or threats, or self-mutilating behaviors.

Recurrent
Definition: Happening or appearing at regular intervals; cyclical.
Synonym: Periodic.
BPD: The definition of recurrent—cyclical or at regular intervals—is misleading when applied to BPD. Recurrent episodes are not necessarily regular or cyclical. The unpredictability of the occurrence of episodes makes treatment very difficult. Although there are times when the likelihood of resorting to self-mutilating or suicidal behaviors may be high, this unpredictability often thwarts patients' implementation of interventions.

Suicidal
Definition of *suicide*: Efforts or attempts to be dead by acts of "self-damage inflicted with self-destructive intention" (Stengel, 1965, p. 74).
Synonym: In the depths of despair.
BPD: Patients with BPD can engage in two types of suicidal behaviors. The first is self-injurious behaviors (SIB), which can be defined as a "non-lethal self-inflicted, injurious suicide-like act" (Schneidman, 1985, p. 20). The act can be severe and sometimes life-threatening and can cause damage to the body, e.g., scratching, cutting, burning, or ingesting medications in larger quantities than prescribed. The intent may not be to actually kill oneself, but to receive some type of relief. The second type of suicidal behavior involves an actual gesture or attempt to end one's life. This type of behavior involves persistent and ruminative suicidal ideation and a plan to harm oneself that may escalate into an attempt. Impulsivity is characteristic of patients with BPD (see Chapter 4). If patients become overwhelmed or unable to regulate their emotional state, impulsive gestures or attempts may be made.

Gestures
Definition: Expressive, meaningful body movements.
Synonym: Indications, motions, signals, signs.
BPD: An SIB or suicidal gesture by a patient with BPD is usually an expression related to some type of extreme emotional state or dysregulation. The synonyms imply that some type of signal or sign underlies the actual action. The gesture potentially may indicate an eruption or disruption of mood, escalating into a need for some type of relief. Again, the gesture may be an attempt to decrease subjective distress or an actual attempt to end one's life.

The imperative for treatment is the elicitation of patients' motives. What were they attempting to accomplish by doing this act? What was the point of the act? Once the motive is disclosed, intervention then targets this harmful behavior by creating adaptive alternative methods to achieve the same goal. For example, if a patient was attempting to reduce an intolerable anxiety state by slashing at his or her arm, a less permanent action like drawing on his or her arm with a red marker can create a stopgap to this destructive behavior. Recreating the actual movement of the self-destructive act (drawing as if they were cutting) may stimulate the conditioned physiological response of endorphin release without leaving physical damage and permanent scars. Be creative in assisting patients in identifying adaptive coping methods to replace self-destructive behavior.

VIGNETTES

The first vignette introduces Sherri, who, overwhelmed with despair and hopelessness, chooses to overdose in an effort to escape her unbearable pain. The second vignette describes Kristy's attempt to manage her intolerable anxiety by cutting her arms. The vignettes are designed to clearly differentiate suicidal thinking and self-injurious behavior (SIB). In addition, warning signs and triggers are identified in an attempt to help patients learn their own warning signs of impending harm.

Vignette 1: Sherri

Sherri hated the mornings. While everyone else in the world was waking to the new day, showering, and preparing themselves for work, Sherri lay in bed, unsure, frightened, alone, and worst of all, convinced that things were never going to change. Losing her job 6 months ago was the last straw. Her husband Bob left her to live with his brother in a tiny one-bedroom apartment and said he would never come back. She must be really bad if he did that. Now she had no one. Sure, her friends said they cared, but they didn't really understand. She felt hopeless and was overwhelmed by her loneliness, her failures, her fears, and the horrible emptiness. She felt she no longer wanted to feel that pain anymore. She wanted to disappear. She went into the bathroom, poured a glass of water, and swallowed all of her medication.

Vignette 2: Kristy

Kristy was pacing in her apartment. She couldn't stand this feeling of panic and fear. Her therapist called it anxiety. Well, whatever it was, she wished it would just go away. She felt her hands shaking, her heart pounding, and her stomach twisted in knots. She picked up a steak knife sitting on the kitchen table. As she was fidgeting with it, she scratched her arm with it. She stared at the small trickles of blood oozing from her arm and fixated on the rate of the drops falling to the floor. She seemed to feel calmer. She was letting the pain go, drop by drop, to the floor. She decided to try cutting herself again, this time on the other arm in a place where no one could see the mark it left.

Discussing the Vignettes & Prompting the Patient

The key to both of these vignettes are the precursors or warning signs of self-destructive acts. Sherri experiences a series of external stressors, hopelessness, vegetative symptoms of depression, and the loss of normal functioning. Kristy's physiological indicators of pending self-destruction include feelings of panic and fear, a racing heart, shaking, and an upset stomach. These warning signs indicate that their systems have become overwhelmed, forcing them to make extreme choices. Unable to generate options between the polar extremes of adaptation and self-destruction, both characters choose the solution of self-harming.

APPLYING TYPICAL BPD SCHEMAS & DISTORTIONS TO THE CRITERION

Suicidal and self-destructive acts are unnecessary solutions to managing pain and stress. There are other solutions. The key to successful treatment begins with patients' recognizing that they are making a choice. They are choosing the permanent option of ending their life or being permanently scarred. Dichotomous thinking, ever-prevalent in self-destruction, becomes the overriding intervention target for the therapist. In order for patients to take control, they must first become aware that there are options other than suicide and self-destruction, and that they have the power to choose and enact them.

Patients who exhibit suicidal or self-injurious behaviors may have compelling schemas related to abandonment, unlovability, and incompetence. Often those who are suicidal approach their situations in a dichotomous way, believing that no matter what they do or how they approach things, nothing will change. Seligman (1975) suggested that many patients with depression have a learned helplessness, in that they are convinced that despite what they may do, their actions will have no impact or effect on their environment. This loss of a sense of control creates helplessness and hopelessness. For those with BPD, feelings of abandonment, unlovability, and an inability to manage the world are interpreted through a dichotomous filter that results in fatalistic thinking. No grays are seen, and self-harm becomes the only identifiable and viable solution.

If patients have become self-injurious or suicidal, it is also likely that their schemas related to coping and problem-solving are biased toward failing. This encourages the characteristic pattern of dichotomous thinking. If patients believe they are not able to cope, the only option is to end their life or harm themselves to ease their pain and distress.

WORKSHEETS ONE & TWO: THE ASSESSMENT & ASSIGNMENT

As noted, states of intense anxiety can cause physical symptoms of panic, GI distress, and sweating. WORKSHEET 1: THE ASSESSMENT (pp. 143–144; Patient Manual, pp. 121–122) asks patients to consider times when they, too, have been suicidal. Physical symptoms of anxiety can define early warning signs of pending self-harm, and provide a signal that the patient needs to seek help.

There are two versions of this worksheet in this chapter—one for suicidal thinking and one for self-mutilation. Often some overlap exists, but, generally, when patients knowingly self-mutilate to decrease anxiety or tension they are not attempting suicide. The obvious danger, however, is when these self-destructive acts lead to potential lethal harm, such as cutting an artery, causing an accident while driving, or overdosing on medication. Encourage patients to be as honest as possible throughout this survey, reminding them that taking control begins with clearly identifying what the problem is. If there are any positive indicators of suicide, a thorough and complete evaluation of suicide risk must be completed. For patients who have difficulty remembering or conceptualizing times such as this, frame the situation in language using dichotomous choices: "Do you remember a time when you felt so hopeless that you thought there was no choice but to end your life?" or "Do you remember a time when you felt you had no other options but to harm yourself in order to feel better?" If patients' have a history of suicidal behaviors or SIB, and are not suicidal currently, conduct an evaluation to ensure patients' current safety and to gain additional information regarding their prior high-risk behaviors.

WORKSHEET 1
The Assessment for Criterion 5 (Suicide)

Rate the severity of the following problems as you think they may relate to you.

0 = none   1 = mild   2 = moderate   3 = severe   4 = extremely severe

1. I have thoughts of dying.   ——

2. I have attempted to kill myself in the past.   ——

3. I have active thoughts of killing myself.   ——

4. I feel hopeless that life will never get better for me.   ——

5. Everything seems dark and cloudy for me.   ——

6. I think everyone would be better off without me.   ——

7. I have active plans to kill myself.   ——

8. No one understands how sad I really am.   ——

9. I wish I were never born.   ——

10. Death is a better option than the pain I feel.   ——

If the patient answers five or more prompts at level 2 or above on either of the assessments, consider focusing on this criterion. A full evaluation should also be completed if a patient rates a high-risk item such as "I have active thoughts of killing myself," as severe, even if no other items are rated as problematic.

WORKSHEET 1
The Assessment for Criterion 5 (Self-Harm)

Rate the severity of the following problems as you think they may relate to you.

0 = none   1 = mild   2 = moderate   3 = severe   4 = extremely severe

1. I have intense waves of emotion or anxiety. _____

2. I have cut or burned myself in the past. _____

3. I do things that may put me in harm's way. _____

4. I seem to get myself into trouble more than I should. _____

5. I pick at myself—sometimes I even cause bleeding. _____

6. I see no way to feel better other than to harm myself when I feel anxious. _____

7. I experience physical discomfort when I become upset, such as upset stomach, numbness, and difficulty breathing. _____

8. I think that the only way to relieve pain is to create it. _____

9. I feel I have little to no control over my actions. _____

10. If I start to harm myself I have difficulty stopping it. _____

If the patient answers five or more prompts at level 2 or above in either of the sections, consider focusing on this criterion. However, if a patient gives a high-risk item such as "I have active thoughts of killing myself," a full evaluation should still be completed even if no other items are rated as problematic.

After the patient completes WORKSHEET 1: THE ASSESSMENT, complete WORKSHEET 2: THE ASSIGNMENT (Patient Manual, p. 123) which prompts patients to identify an incident in which they harmed themselves.

SENSITIVITY & SUICIDAL OR SELF-HARMING BEHAVIOR

Due to their highly charged physiological system, patients with BPD may feel that the only way to gain relief from internal or external tension is through self-harm or death. Imperative to evaluating your patients' risk for harm is assisting them identifying when and if their system is becoming overwhelmed.

WORKSHEETS THREE TO SIX, & EIGHTEEN: TREATMENT GOALS

A goal of treatment is to eradicate SIB and suicidal thoughts and impulses. If patients have difficulty totally eradicating SIB, the goal is to decrease the SIB to a level at which more adaptive forms of managing their pain are enacted. For instance, patients may consider holding ice cubes in their hands instead of actually inflicting irreversible harm.

The Taking Control treatment program begins with patients' identifying the triggers to their self-destructive behaviors. This includes the physiological, cognitive, emotional, and behavioral cues that generally indicate that they are becoming overwhelmed and may consider self-harm.

After the patient completes WORKSHEETS 1 and 2, assist the patient in filling out WORKSHEET 3: THE INCIDENT CHART (Patient Manual, p. 124). The four areas of self-monitoring (physiological, emotional, cognitive, and behavioral) offer avenues to treatment interventions and provide concrete examples of specific areas of change the patient can address. Identifying the external or situational factors related to self-harm also is vital, as a combination of internal and external factors can lead to a lethal result. Through ongoing self-evaluation and monitoring, patients can learn to help themselves in healthy, adaptive ways before becoming overwhelmed with destructive impulses. In all circumstances, *patient safety is the top priority.*

Complete WORKSHEETS 4 and 5 (Patient Manual, pp. 125–126) to identify patients' automatic thoughts and schema. Then treatment goals can be defined. In order to help organize this process, complete WORKSHEET 6: TREATMENT GOALS (Patient Manual, p. 127). Once treatment goals are set, complete WORKSHEET 18: THE DPS (Patient Manual,

p. 128) to determine a baseline level of distress or dysfunction for the particular criterion.

WORKSHEETS SEVEN TO SEVENTEEN: SUGGESTED INTERVENTIONS

Worksheets 7 & 8: Physical Triggers & Suggested Interventions

Physiological sensations often play a major role in the body's reaction to or formation of anxiety. Patients often report physiological symptoms that closely parallel the fight, flight, or freeze responses. This includes heightened autonomic responses such as sweatiness, racing heart, gastrointestinal disturbances, or rapid breathing. Some patients may even report chest pain, dizziness, or numbness. Elicit the specific physiological manifestations that occur when patients become anxious or just prior to the urge to self-harm (WORKSHEET 7; Patient Manual, p. 129). Remind patients that anxiety and its physiological correlates are not permanent. In other words, the heightened anxiety state evident in a panic attack is relatively short-lived, generally lasting about 10 to 15 minutes (APA, 2000). The body will assume a homeostatic state in a short period of time.

THOUGHT-STOPPING

Thought-stopping is a key intervention when attempting to manage suicidal or self-injurious behaviors (WORKSHEET 8; Patient Manual, pp. 130–131). Often anxiety or pent-up frustration, pain, or discomfort is the instigator of the chain of thoughts leading to self-harm. As soon as patients have identified a sign or warning from their body, encourage them to *stop* and take a moment to organize how they want to react in the situation.

RELAXATION

When managing anxiety symptoms, relaxation techniques can be essential in disrupting the chain of thoughts leading to self-harm. Again, assisting patients in learning the alternative response of relaxation can help decrease their anxiety symptoms.

RELAXING IMAGERY

In combination with relaxation techniques, helping your patients identify safe, secure images can also help them return to a less aroused state. Be sure that the imagery is not in any way connected to something that adds to the patients' anxiety.

Worksheets 9 & 10: Emotional Triggers & Suggested Interventions

Those diagnosed with BPD often have overwhelming emotions that surge forth without the patients' understanding the nature of the feeling. Unsure of the emotions' source, patients may be driven to reduce their pent-up, volatile emotions. This welling up of emotion can create acts of impulsivity (see Chapter 4), which can lead to acts of self-harm. By asking patients to consider if they were fearful, angry, or sad, you can help them learn to prepare themselves for future situations, as they will know which feelings trigger self-harming behaviors (WORKSHEET 9; Patient Manual, p. 132). Additionally, the specific emotion state provides clues about the schema ignited by self-harm. For example, extreme sadness may be indicative of feelings of unlovability or abandonment.

SCALE BACK

This exercise is instrumental in helping patients identify the strength of the emotions that drive them to self-harm (WORKSHEET 10; Patient Manual, p9. 133–134). Keep in mind your patients' acute sensitivity and its relationship to intense emotional states. Once you have encouraged patients to scale back, have them "take their temperature" again to note the differences and their ability to affect some change. Be sure to ask patients to consider their whole system, including their levels of physiological arousal. Would their response to the situation be different now that they have "turned themselves down?"

ATTACH THE EMOTION TO SELF-HARM

Ask patients to try to identify and attach their experienced emotion to pending self-harm. In other words, if you know from their responses on WORKSHEET 3 that self-injurious urges occur when sadness is present, they can begin to set up safeguards to protect themselves from self-harm when they are sad. Patients should ask themselves the following types of questions:

When I feel _____, I want to harm myself.

In the past, I have reacted strongly to _____ [*emotion*].

I have trouble controlling my urge to harm myself when _____.

LEARN TO IDENTIFY WHEN YOU'RE FEELING VULNERABLE

Patients experiencing times of vulnerability may be at a higher risk to self-harm. Ask your patients to list those times.

I know I am vulnerable during _____.

I know I am vulnerable when _____ .

I am especially vulnerable at _____ during my life.

CHALLENGE FEELINGS OF HOPELESSNESS

Hopelessness is often associated with those who want to self-harm. It is a bleak emotion that makes people feel as if there is nothing for them, ever. However, this emotion tends to wax, wane, and change. To combat these feelings, ask patients to arm themselves with a list of times in their life when they were able to feel joy and happiness. This list provides reinforcement that they are able to experience emotions other than hopelessness. Encourage patients to carry around a picture of a loved one and look at the picture when they feel overwhelmed and want to hurt themselves.

Ask patients to complete this statement: When I feel hopeless I can _____ .

- Look at picture of someone I care about.
- Think of family/friends.
- Know I've felt better before and can again.
- Give myself a chance to feel good again.
- Remember that I may have felt helpless before and managed to feel better again.
- Know that the future has options that are good for me.
- Other: _____
  _____
  _____ .

Worksheets 11 & 12: Cognitive/Automatic Thoughts & Suggested Interventions

Assist patients in understanding the role of cognition in generating adaptive options to hopelessness or feeling overwhelmed. It is imperative that patients be able to monitor and therefore read their physiological and emotional cues, which often lead to dichotomous thinking.

What thoughts or cognitions were patients experiencing just prior to wanting to harm themselves (WORKSHEET 11; Patient Manual, p. 135)? Be particularly aware of themes of hopelessness—a clear indicator of potential suicidality. Are your patients catastrophizing events? Is dichotomous thinking present? Dichotomous thinking can be exhibited through beliefs or statements that indicate that self-harm is the only way to handle stress. Encourage patients to generate options other than self-harm (WORKSHEET 12; Patient Manual, pp. 136–132) . Brainstorm with patients about how they may have coped with or managed past situations in ways other than experiencing self-destructive impulses. They also may want to consider relaxation techniques or seeking support from an identified other whom they trust. Once patients begin to feel that they have other choices, create an anchor or a specific reminder (such as how they managed prior situations without self-harm) that can instigate the generation of alternative choices. Many patients state that if they are not stressed it is easy to formulate options and ideas, but if they are experiencing a runaway train of anxiety and impulses it can be nearly impossible to put the breaks on and actually think. By identifying an anchor, or something they can turn to when particularly stressed, they can remind themselves of another time when they were able to think of alternatives to self-harm.

CHALLENGE CATASTROPHIC THINKING

Assist patients in challenging catastrophic thoughts that may be spurring or exaggerating preexisting feelings of hopelessness and desperation. For example, patients may believe that if a person they care about does not share those caring feelings with them, *no one* ever will. Utilize The CATASTROPHIC THINKING CHART.

CHALLENGE DICHOTOMOUS THINKING

Dichotomous thinking often instigates a cascade of thoughts that leads to self-harm. Assist patients in identifying how they are approaching a situation and the extreme endpoints to which they are limiting themselves. For example, a patient may be thinking something like:

$$\textit{I have no control} \rightarrow \textit{means only that} \rightarrow \textit{Self-harm is the only option.}$$

The Dichotomous Thinking Chart		
Black	**Gray(s)**	**White**
I have no control.	I can practice relaxation, get support from a trusted other, or draw a line on my arm with a red marker.	Self-harm is the only option.
_____ .	_____ .	_____ .
_____ .	_____ .	_____ .

Have patients write down alternative options, or grays. This list can serve as an anchor that patients can carry with them in times of stress.

WEIGH THE EVIDENCE

Challenge patients to produce evidence supporting their negative assumptions and fears. For example, if they have decided to self-harm due to feeling unable to cope, ask patients to consider the following questions as counter-evidence.

How did you manage to . . .

- Arrive at your age?
- Parent children?
- Maintain employment?
- Maintain any relationship?
- Manage past stressors without hurting yourself?

Know what your patients' strengths are before entering into this exercise; otherwise you may get into a wrestling match about whether an aspect of their lives is positive or negative. Help patients recall times when they were able to manage intense feelings without self-harming. This provides encouragement that at times of undue stress they can cope without self-harm. Challenge feelings of hopelessness by drawing upon times that they have experienced joy, and remind them that it is possible to have emotions other than the deep depression they are currently enduring. Utilize The DISPUTATION CHART to assist you in this process.

The Disputation Chart

Situation: Too many bad things happened this week.

Belief: I have to harm myself to get relief.

Proof Supporting Belief	Refuting Statement
1. If I harm myself I won't have to deal with anything.	1. I can try talking to my therapist and learn new ways to cope.
2. If I harm myself my problems will go away.	2. I can try talking to my therapist and make a plan to tackle the problems.
3. _____ .	3. _____ .
4. _____ .	4. _____ .

Worksheets 13 & 14: Behavioral Triggers & Suggested Interventions

WORKSHEET 13 (Patient Manual, p. 138) prompts patients to identify their behaviors prior to, during, and after having thoughts of self-harm. It is imperative to fully understand those situations that trigger episodes of self-harm in order to undertake successful interventions (WORKSHEET 14; Patient Manual, p. 139).

Worksheet 15: The Expanded Incident Chart

Prompt patients to consider the full context of what they were actually experiencing and if any other individuals were present prior to the act of self-harm or suicidal thinking. The goal is to generate new, different behavioral options. This will be a process of combining the physiological, emotional, and cognitive exercises. Specifically utilize the "people" section of WORKSHEET 15: THE EXPANDED INCIDENT CHART (Patient Manual, pp. 140–142). This section helps patients identify if there are certain situations and events combined with particular individuals that tend to spark thoughts of self-harm. Once patients have identified the situations that usually prompt acts of self-harm, utilize the worksheets to outline potential interventions.

AVOID THE SITUATION

Help patients plan ways to avoid or differently approach situations that lead to self-harm. For example, if meeting with certain groups of people, or certain family members are usually associated with later acts of self-harm, encourage patients to avoid those situations that include these people as much as possible. If this is not possible, encourage patients to approach this type of situation differently, perhaps by bringing along a close and trusted friend for support or by limiting the amount of time spent in the situation.

IDENTIFY A FRIEND

Identifying friends is an important aspect of preventative planning for your patients. The friend that your patient identifies needs to be someone who is reliable and has not been associated with stressful states. Encourage patients to have a card that they carry in their wallet with phone numbers and means of contacting someone to whom they feel safe talking. A friend should not be a substitution for clinical intervention, but rather someone who can help prevent or thwart the escalation of negative feelings or thoughts. For example, if a patient knows that at the beginning of the weekend he or she typically feels very sad about not being in a relationship, have him or her call the friend to make arrangements to do something or to talk. This friend (with your patient's permission) also can be made aware of emergency numbers or of what to do if an emergency arises. In some situations, it may also be helpful to ask the friend to attend a therapeutic session with the patient in order to review a safety plan in the event that the patient experiences suicidal ideation.

IDENTIFY AN ANCHOR

An anchor is similar to a friend, but it doesn't necessarily have to be a person. An anchor can be any thought that helps patients feel grounded or safe. For instance, your patient may state that remembering a prior time when he or she was feeling better can be an anchor. Encourage the patient to write down the time, the context, and the feelings experienced during that time. He or she can then read what they have written when feeling compelled to self-harm.

CREATE A SAFETY PLAN

It is imperative that a comprehensive safety plan be made with your patients. Clearly list what to do, whom to call, and how to obtain immediate help in the case of an emergency.

CONSIDER TRIGGERS

Understanding the triggers and context of self-harm is an important part of preventing self-destructive behaviors. Be sure that patients have completed WORKSHEETS 3, 15, and 16 which specifically prompt them to identify those things that tend to be associated with intense negative feelings that have led to self-harm.

REWARD YOURSELF

Encourage patients to identify times when they were able to refrain from self-harm. What were they able to do? How did they manage the situation? This provides key information for future interventions. With your patients, identify a list of rewards. This will help clearly demarcate the times in which they engaged in adaptive behavior and were able to control or avoid their impulses to self-harm. Rewards could include a relaxing bath, a day trip they have been putting off, a movie with a friend, or something appropriate for your patient.

CONSIDER THE CONSEQUENCES

If patients have at times not been able to view self-harm as a negative behavior, review the following negative consequences of self-harm:

- Self-harm can be irreversible.
- Self-harm upsets and disturbs others close to patients.
- Self-harm causes scarring and permanent reminders.
- Self-harm may lead to an even worse situation (life support, brain damage, hurting someone else in the process).

- Self-harm is a short-term solution.
- Self-harm may lead to a family legacy of suicide.

IDENTIFY BEHAVIOR CHAIN

The following flowchart (Pretzer, 1990) can be used as a general guide in disrupting the cascade that may lead to suicidal or self-destructive behaviors:

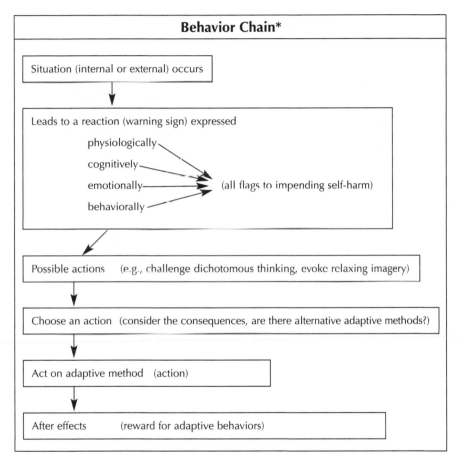

This flowchart also can be used in situations other than self-harm, as it promotes a more controlled method of reviewing available options. Life is full of challenges and we may be confronted with multiple difficult situations. Having a way to assist the decision-making process allows for a self-empowerment that patients may never have experienced before.

---

*(Adapted from J. Pretzer,. Borderline personality disorder. In A. Beck, A. Freeman, & Associates [eds.], *Cognitive therapy of personality disorders* [pp. 176–207]. Guilford Press, 1990©.)

Worksheets 16 & 17: Situational Triggers & Suggested Interventions

WORKSHEET 16 (Patient Manual, p. 143) prompts patients to specifically identify those situations that have led the patient to self-harm. WORK-SHEET 17 (Patient Manual, p. 144) suggests to remove themselves from the situation or try something different.

REMOVE YOURSELF

If patients find themselves in a situation where they have in the past self-harmed, they can choose to remove themselves from that specific environment. For example, if a patient knows that attending a memorial service or funeral causes intense pain and depression, he or she can choose whether attending the service is something that really needs to be done, or if he or she does attend, to do so with the support of a friend, or spend a limited time offering his or her respects.

TRY SOMETHING DIFFERENT

What can patients do other than self-harm? Can they try other means of creating a sense of relief? Can they generate alternatives to their negative thoughts? Layden, Newman, Freeman, and Morse (1993, p. 62) suggested the following alternative behaviors:

1. Telephone on-call therapist or professional.
2. Telephone a sympathetic friend or relative.
3. Go to the emergency room of the nearest hospital.
4. Hit oneself with pillows.
5. Use a water-soluble, red felt-tip pen to write on oneself as an alternative to cutting with a sharp object.
6. Immerse one's hand in cold water.
7. Crunch raw eggs on oneself.
8. Spend an hour reviewing an audiotape from a therapy session.
9. Spend an hour reviewing old homework assignments.
10. Spend an hour applying various self-help skills.

WORKSHEET EIGHTEEN: THE DPS

Complete WORKSHEET 18: THE DPS (Patient Manual, p. 145). Compare the results of the DPS after treatment goals were set. Is there a difference in the level of distress the patient is experiencing in response to the criterion? If not, reexamine the interventions chosen to target the symptoms, and collaboratively determine whether changes or alterations should be made.

CASE EXAMPLE

Sherri, in the first vignette, received medical attention and was evaluated by the emergency room crisis team. She was referred to an outpatient psychologist who immediately completed a thorough suicide assessment and risk history. Sherri agreed to stay with her mother for a few days until she felt stronger. In the course of therapy, Sherri began to describe the symptoms of a long-standing mood disorder that included prior episodes of major depression. She traced her feelings of hopelessness to her young adolescent years, when she had been hospitalized for a short period of time. Sherri was able to identify her signs of helplessness and hopelessness, which occurred as a result of her feeling that she was unable to manage her sadness and that she must be a "severely damaged person." Sherri felt powerless over her depression and recognized that the isolation she felt growing up and in her early adulthood only served to reinforce her belief that she was somehow different from others. When the recent stress of her husband's initiating the divorce occurred, the hopelessness schema became activated, and once again Sherri felt no control or competence in managing the growing pain inside. Obviously, she knew that when severe stressors occurred, her vulnerability to another depressive episode increased. Sherri soon identified the triggers that signaled a pending depressive episode: loss in sleep and lack of an appetite. With the help of her therapist, Sherri learned to monitor these warning signs and began disputing her dichotomous method of approaching stressful situations. Usually she saw no way out, and when she made the suicide attempt, she truly believed that there were no other options. But as her therapist challenged her to find evidence supporting her negative thoughts and encouraged her to see the grays, Sherri began devising alternatives. She was able to identify her mother and grandmother as key people in her life who meant a great deal to her. She gathered enough courage to ask her mother how she felt after the suicide attempt, and her mother very compassionately told Sherri that if she were to die, she would be devastated. Sherri could no longer believe that everyone would be better off if she died, and she began to carry her mother's picture with her to remind her to remain motivated in fighting the depression. Armed with new skills to combat her negative automatic thoughts, Sherri was able to consider alternatives to suicide.

CHAPTER 6 | Affective Instability

This chapter addresses BPD Criterion 6: "affective instability due to a marked reactivity of mood (e.g., intense episodic dysphoria, irritability, or anxiety usually lasting a few hours and only rarely more than a few days)" (APA, 2000, p. 710). Essential to understanding this criterion is an awareness of the subjective distress patients experience due to the lack of a consistent sense of well-being or satisfaction. Continually fraught with a basic dysphoric mood, patients with BPD must also contend with episodic panic, rage, and/or despair. Never quite finding a neutral ground, patients fluctuate between extremes, wearing down both their ability to cope as well as their internal and external resources.

As extremely sensitive individuals, your patients may have experienced rapid mood shifts that at times have no identifiable trigger. They may, however, be able describe how their entire mood can change when they hear an offhand comment or joke or perceive a "nasty" look from someone. Your patients probably have been told that they are moody and at times unpredictable. This in turn has caused interpersonal problems, as friends and family may decide that their mood changes have become somewhat troublesome. They may not know exactly who they are meeting or seeing; the happy, giddy person or the person sobbing uncontrollably over dinner. Patients may have described behaviors caused by these extreme moods that they later regret. They may have lashed out in anger at someone they care about or, if they were experiencing abandonment feelings, disclosed very personal details to a relative stranger. The goal, therefore, is to assist patients in establishing adaptive methods of managing mood shifts and in learning to prevent regrettable behaviors.

Throughout treatment, it is helpful to encourage patients to write down each time they experienced a mood shift through the week. By ask-

---

Criterion 6

Affective instability due to a marked *reactivity* of mood (e.g., intense episodic dysphoria, irritability, or anxiety usually lasting a few hours and only rarely more than a few days).

Affective
Definition: Emotional, to evoke a usually strong mental or emotional response from or impact.
Synonym: Stirring.
BPD: Patients with BPD have emotional and affective dysregulation. Emotions rapidly shift, are intense, and are not easily identified. Fully emotional, borderline patients are intrapersonally distressed, which inevitably leads to interpersonal distress. Intrapersonally, patients experience episodes of shifting moods consisting of anxiety, depression, and severe dysphoria. Riding a roller coaster of emotional states, patients become frustrated about the lack of their own self-determined emotional direction. They feel no sense of control over their own moods. This lack of direction can result in an ongoing state of apprehension about and anticipation of their next affective shift. The definition of *affect* captures others' very strong emotional and mental responses to patients' affective instability. Circular in nature, patients' moods are often erratic and unpredictable, which causes strong reactions from those around them. This in turn contributes to patients' frustration about their inability to regulate their emotional state.

Reactivity
Definition: Vehemently, often fanatically opposing progress or reform; behavioral responses.
Synonym: Responsivity.
BPD: The definition implies fanatical and, at times, opposing forces. This captures the very nature of the patient with BPD. Consistently vacillating between states of opposing forces, the reactivity of those with BPD causes additional vulnerability to both internal and external stressors. As patients struggle to manage stressors, their usual coping mechanisms are blocked by their own idiosyncratic tendency to oppose adaptive problem-solving.

---

ing patients in each session during the mood check how they are doing, you will help them learn to identify their moods and mood changes.

VIGNETTES

The vignettes demonstrate how an external misinterpreted cue leads to negative assumptions that change moods dramatically. Jackie, initially feeling good about her arrangements with her boyfriend, suddenly feels sad, angry, and unable to focus when she becomes convinced that her plans will fall through. Ellie experiences dramatic mood changes in response to various situations she encounters on her way to work. Her mood shifts cause her to feel tired and fatigued before the day even begins.

Vignette 1: Jackie

Jackie was in a great mood. She knew that Bob would be calling her around 10:00 A.M. to make final plans for the evening. Everything was set. It made doing her work so much easier. She was plowing through the stack of typing her supervisor left for her on her desk. She giggled at her officemate's colorful calendar and thought that she even looked good today. When Bob hadn't called by 10:15, Jackie's mood took a terrible nosedive. "Why hasn't he called?" she thought. "He's dumping me; I just know it." Jackie's tears streamed down her face as she considered another failed relationship. She snapped at her supervisor, lost the material she was typing, and flew into the bathroom sobbing— ultimately missing Bob's call.

Vignette 2: Ellie

Ellie was on her way to work. She drove the same route, at the same time, every day. It was a nice, clear, crisp autumn morning. When she left her apartment complex she saw that there was some ice on her windshield. She also saw that a man was scraping the ice from her neighbor, Susan's, windshield. Ellie immediately felt down. "I don't have anyone to do that for me," she thought.

As she pulled out onto the street, a big, black Mercedes cut in front of her. Ellie was furious. "Who the hell does that bastard think he is!?" she thought. She began cursing at the driver and tried to chase him and flip him the bird. Eventually, she lost him in the traffic.

The drive to work had less traffic than usual. Ellie enjoyed the sunshine, and the oldies station was playing some of her favorite songs. "Gosh, I miss those songs," she thought. She started to feel weepy as she pulled into the parking lot at work. "Here it is only 8:45 in the morning, and I feel exhausted," she thought.

Discussing the Vignettes & Prompting the Patient

As patients read the vignettes, ask if they, too, never quite experience feeling "in neutral" or in the "eye of the storm," where things just happen around them and they do not feel the need to process or emote. Do patients find it difficult to rest or relax? Is there always something, someone, or some situation to deal with or manage? As humans we are affected by our perceptions and interpretations of the environment. Constantly processing stimuli provided by our internal and external environments, we subject that data to our own filtering systems. Use the Whisper-Down-The-Lane metaphor (see pp. 29–30) to explain how we put our own spin on things.

APPLYING TYPICAL BPD SCHEMAS & DISTORTIONS TO THE CRITERION

Typical schemas related to affective instability include lack of individuation, emotional deprivation, and unlovability. A lack of individuation may be evident in patients' assuming or adopting the mood or feelings of others as a means of feeling connected. Often extremely sensitive patients are aware of other's emotional states and react strongly to others who are stressed or experiencing discomfort. Associated with BPD are poor or absent boundaries or differentiation from others, which exhibits as a melding of emotional states between the patient and the other person experiencing pain. For example, a patient may react very strongly to a movie character, to someone in the community who has experienced difficulty, or even to those that he or she has never met.

Individuals with BPD also experience emotional deprivation. This may seem at odds with hypersensitivity, but in this sense emotional deprivation refers to a lack of balance or of emotional states that constitute a restful, content mood. Frequent vacillation of emotions may create the appearance that patients are very emotional, whereas in fact they lack a consistent, stable emotional state and the ability to regulate and modulate their emotions. Also, as many with BPD hold beliefs about being unlovable, they be more attuned to triggers within the environment that confirm their belief. For example, if a patient believes he or she is unlovable, he or she may attend more to a frown from another person than a smile. This continual attention to stimuli that support negative beliefs may instigate a mood shift or change. Many of these negative beliefs are also exaggerated due to dichotomous thinking, which propels an already-fragile system into extreme stress.

WORKSHEETS ONE & TWO: ASSESSMENT & ASSIGNMENT

As noted, states of intense anxiety can cause physical symptoms of panic, GI, distress, and sweating. WORKSHEET 1: THE ASSESSMENT (p. 160; Patient Manual, p. 150) asks patients to consider times when they, too, have had affective instability. Often, symptoms of anxiety can be a clear indicator of a mood change.

WORKSHEET 1
The Assessment for Criterion 6

Rate the severity of the following problems as you think they may relate to you.

0 = none   1 = mild   2 = moderate   3 = severe   4 = extremely severe

1. Friends/colleagues have described you as being moody. ____

2. You experience many mood changes throughout the day. ____

3. Your friends would describe you as intense. ____

4. Your mood can fluctuate very rapidly and with little provocation. ____

5. You find it difficult to think of a time when you are in a neutral mood. ____

6. You have done impulsive things in response to your mood changes. ____

7. You become irritated, frustrated, and angry very easily. ____

8. You have disclosed private details about yourself to new acquaintances. ____

9. When you become emotionally overwhelmed you cry, yell, or snap at someone. ____

10. You wake up each day not knowing how you'll feel. ____

If the patient answers five or more prompts at level 2 or above, consider focusing on this criterion.

WORKSHEET 1 tests for mood changes that occur with little provocation and mood changes caused by internal shifts over which patients may feel a lack of control. The key to assisting patients with their moods is helping them identify the relationship between stressful internal or external events and the mood changes that accompany them. For instance, your patient may experience a mood shift due to being "cut-off" by someone on the road (external event) or to feeling bored (internal event). Keep in mind that patients whose moods meet the threshold of a mood disorder should be considered for a psychiatric consultation to determine if medication is warranted. After the patient completes WORKSHEET 1: THE ASSESSMENT, complete WORKSHEET 2: THE ASSIGNMENT (Patient Manual, p. 151) which prompts patients to identify an incident in which they experienced mood changes.

SENSITIVITY & AFFECTIVE INSTABILITY

Extreme sensitivity is a hallmark of affective instability. Patients' highly sensitive systems can cause almost instantaneous mood shifts as information is misinterpreted, distorted, or processed without a full gathering of data or evidence. As those with BPD tend to experience their worlds in extremes, mood changes can escalate quickly into hysteria, devastation, or utter despair.

WORKSHEETS THREE TO SIX, & EIGHTEEN: TREATMENT GOALS

Treatment goals focus on challenging the interpretations and perceptions that cause rapid mood changes and on helping patients learn to consider the consequences of acting upon the impulses that these emotional states can cause. WORKSHEET 1 prompts patients to establish whether they experience rapid mood shifts and if they have acted impulsively as a result of these mood changes. It is imperative for patients to begin to understand that they are not a product or victim of their emotions. They can have control. They can instigate a mood change as quickly as they feel they are subjected to one. Most patients initially do not believe in this basic principle. Usually those diagnosed with BPD assume they are not in control of outside forces and therefore are not in control of their reactions to them. This other-blaming style, consistent with disorders that are primarily ego-syntonic in nature, can become a treatment obstacle if not explicated in a supportive, directive way. The clinical challenge is to reinterpret patients' passivity to their internal events by nonpejoratively demonstrating their potential strength and resources in controlling their internal worlds.

The treatment program is predicated upon patients' learning to self-monitor their affective states-in other words, learning to identify what mood they are experiencing and therefore when a shift occurs. The basic mood states can be divided into times when the patient is happy or feeling good and times when the patient is angry or feeling sad. A large continuum of mood states exists. Patients with BPD have difficulty modulating these states and creating a midpoint that is neither joyful nor sad.

After the patient completes WORKSHEETS 1 and 2, assist the patient in filling out WORKSHEET 3: THE INCIDENT CHART (Patient Manual, p. 152). The four areas of self-monitoring (physiological, emotional, cognitive, and behavioral) offer avenues to treatment interventions and provide concrete examples of specific areas of change the patient can address. Assisting patients in clearly describing how their systems react prior to a mood change provides an inroad to constructively managing their moods. By clearly identifying warning signals, patients can make a preemptive strike against mood shifts by taking control of their actions and making decisions based not upon knee-jerk reactions but upon an informed choice. Complete WORKSHEETS 4 and 5 (Patient Manual, pp. 153–154) to identify patients' automatic thoughts and schema. Then treatment goals can be identified. In order to help organize this process, complete WORKSHEET 6: TREATMENT GOALS (Patient Manual, p. 155). Once treatment goals are set, complete WORKSHEET 18: THE DPS (Patient Manual, p. 156) to determine a baseline level of distress or dysfunction for the particular criterion.

WORKSHEETS SEVEN TO SEVENTEEN: SUGGESTED INTERVENTIONS

Worksheets 7 & 8: Physical Triggers & Suggested Interventions

Physiological indicators can often be helpful in identifying a mood change. Typical autonomic changes can indicate pending anxiety and feelings of doom and despair. A stomach churning at the notion of being rejected or abandoned can signify the activation of an anger response. Although autonomic responses can be interpreted in a myriad of ways (for example, a rapid heartrate could indicate anxiety or anger), by self-monitoring patients can learn to identify the mood changes their bodies signal (WORKSHEET 7; Patient Manual, p. 157).

Interventions are aimed not only at being aware of the physiological changes that accompany mood shifts, but also at how to use the physical changes as a means of scaling back the emotional shifts that follow them (WORKSHEET 8; Patient Manual, pp. 158–159).

THOUGHT-STOPPING

Intense emotions can be very difficult to contain. If patients experience an extreme mood shift, the first tactic is to take a moment to *stop*. As emotional lability is often seen in patients with BPD, it is important that patients recognize that they haven't lost control, they simply are experiencing mood changes that are a part of their patterned behavior and sensitive personality.

RELAXATION

Relaxation techniques can be helpful with many types of moods. For example, they can help create a sense of inner calm for those feeling angry. They can help return an anxious body to its resting state, and they can help disrupt spiraling negative thoughts that lead to increasing sadness and despair.

RELAXING IMAGERY

In combination with relaxation techniques, imagery that creates a sense of calm can help balance intense emotional states.

Worksheets 9 & 10: Emotional Triggers & Suggested Interventions

As noted earlier, patients with BPD experience a surge of emotions and a change of mood state and have difficulty identifying the source of the change or even what the change is. If they are responding to a negative stressor (WORKSHEET 9; Patient Manual, p. 160), they may cognitively attribute something negative to themselves or the environment. Most mood changes are negative, resulting from cognitive distortions and assumptions based on incomplete data.

IDENTIFY MOOD STATES

Many patients who have difficulty identifying the actual mood state they are experiencing will "assign" an emotion to the feeling caused by a negative interaction or thought. For instance, a physiological sensation such as a rapid heartrate may be interpreted as fear or anger prompted by another person's intentions or words, when in fact the increased heartrate was due to too much caffeine earlier in the day. Part of self-monitoring involves understanding and recognizing when or if a mood change has occurred. To help patients understand themselves better and take control of their mood states, you can help them learn exactly what those mood states feel like or are associated with.

The Patient Manual asks patients to begin by defining their moods by identifying which particular flags signal a certain mood (WORKSHEET 10; Patient Manual, pp. 161–162). Following are prompts with examples of how moods are identified.

My happy mood states are related to:

Thoughts including

He likes me, I'm okay.   .

Behaviors including

Giddiness, laughing, working hard.   .

Bodily sensations including

Butterflies in stomach.   .

Feelings including

Excitement, anticipation.   .

My bad mood states are related to:

Thoughts including

Being ignored/dumped.   .

Behaviors including

Losing concentration, snapping.   .

Bodily sensations including

Tightness in the chest.   .

Feelings including

Despair, hopelessness.   .

SCALE BACK

Ask patients to identify the intensity of the emotion they felt when they experienced a negative or distressing mood state.

Have them "take their temperature" again after they have scaled back. Be sure they note the differences between the ratings and their ability to affect some change in the modulation of their emotions.

Worksheets 11 & 12: Cognitive/Automatic Thoughts & Suggested Interventions

Mood changes are often related to dichotomous thinking or catastrophizing. Patients link something they are experiencing in the environment to a catastrophic conclusion and react as if that outcome has occurred or will occur (WORKSHEET 11 Patient Manual, p. 163). This type of thought leads to "tunnel vision," or a difficulty in seeing anything but the dreaded event. Techniques involve challenging the patient to consider the continuum of options that exist between the extremes, generating many explanations for the behaviors and actions of others (WORKSHEET 12; Patient Manual, pp. 164–165).

CHALLENGE CATASTROPHIC THINKING

As various stressors present themselves throughout the day, patients may be reacting to multiple situations. This reactiveness can lead to an emotional roller coaster. Part of the emotional reactiveness can be related to catastrophic thoughts and conclusions. Although negative events do occur in life, do they occur all the time? Challenge your patients' catastrophic thoughts by encouraging them to think of outcomes that are very different from the feared events. Utilize The CATASTROPHIC THINKING CHART.

CHALLENGE DICHOTOMOUS THINKING

Mood shifts can be readily traced to dichotomous thoughts and interpreting internal and external events in extremes. Once the pattern of thoughts that trigger mood shifts is identified, help patients identify the grays that exist.

The Dichotomous Thinking Chart		
Black	**Gray(s)**	**White**
He's leaving me.	He's late because he's stuck in traffic. I can relax and seek support.	He's perfect.

WEIGH THE EVIDENCE

Often the negative assumptions engendered by dichotomous thoughts can lead to erroneous conclusions. Utilize The DISPUTATION CHART to challenge these conclusions.

The Disputation Chart

Situation: *Friend forgot your birthday.*

Belief: *Friends let me down.*

Proof Supporting Belief
1. *Friend did not call or send card.*
2. *Friends can be disappointing.*

Refuting Statement
1. *Many people make honest mistakes.*
2. *Many friends have come through for me.*

3. _____ .

3. _____ .

4. _____ .

4. _____ .

HANDLING EMOTIONS

Encourage patients who experience a change in mood or are feeling out of control to take a moment to remind themselves that:

They can handle themselves in times of crisis.

They have handled _____ .

They are handling _____ .

They have many good qualities that will not go away just because they're moody.

They are an individual who has many options in life.

Worksheets 13 & 14: Behavioral Triggers & Suggested Interventions

CONSIDER TRIGGERS

Clearly identifying triggers that prompt mood changes will assist patients in knowing what situations cause those changes (WORKSHEET 13; Patient Manual, p. 166). Not all stressful events can be avoided, but patients' understanding that they are particularly sensitive to certain situations will allow them to intervene before a mood change causes a negative behavior and consequence (WORKSHEET 14; Patient Manual, pp. 167–168).

VALIDATE SELF AND EMOTIONS

Self-validation can be approached in two different ways. First, we all experience emotions. Some emotional changes throughout the day are expected and normal. Extreme fluctuations are not. Talking with patients about the varying levels of emotional change that accompany daily activities can help them self-validate their membership in the human race and not further aggravate their systems by believing that they are experiencing emotions that others do not. Second, self-validation can be utilized as a means of identifying their position in the world-that they have a right to have feelings and experience emotions in the same way that everyone does. Having emotions reaffirms their place in the human race and helps remind them that each person has a unique worldview and emotional expression.

STOP

Stopping in this context is similar to thought-stopping. Asking patients to *stop* before they act or behave in response to a mood shift can help prevent negative consequences.

BETTER USE OF EMOTIONAL ENERGY

Intense emotions require a great deal of energy. As patients identify situations in which they expend a great deal of emotion, ask them if they felt drained or tired afterward. Encourage patients to channel their emotional energy into something productive or positive. For example, a highly anxious individual might use extra energy to clean out a neglected area of the garage. This is helpful both in the short-term, as energy is directed toward something other than the patient's own body, and in the long-term, as a project he or she has been meaning to complete is finished.

A BACKUP PLAN

Creating a backup plan to help manage extreme emotional states can in itself be reassuring. If patients have already tried to use their energy in a different way, have validated their position, and continue to feel emotionally overwhelmed, have them activate a fail-safe plan that has been successful in the past. For example, if your patient knows that taking a walk helps promote a fresh perspective, or that thinking of a beloved aunt provides a sense of calm, encourage him or her to use this plan.

IDENTIFY A FRIEND

Do patients have a friend they know they can call on to act as a grounding force? Can they identify individuals in their lives that seems to provide consistent support without adding any additional stress? Be sure that patients have access to their friend and that the friend is aware that he or she may be part of helping the patient combat mood shifts.

CHANGE OF FOCUS

Although we are bombarded with external stimuli, our brains have a limited capacity to focus on multiple things at once. Encourage patients to redirect their focus toward something productive and nonemotional. Ask them to "turn up their thinking" and "turn down their emotions" as they attempt to change their focus. For example, if a patient has noted that he or she becomes enraged very easily by a coworker, encourage him or her to focus on the current task at work.

The goal is to encourage a balance. Moderating emotional states is not an easy process and requires much practice. Most importantly, it requires patients to recognize and appreciate that they can take control and learn to live with life's ongoing challenges and stressors.

Worksheets 16 & 17: Situational Triggers & Suggested Interventions

WORKSHEET 16 (Patient Manual, p. 169) prompts patients to specifically identify those situations that have led to intense mood changes. WORKSHEET 17 (Patient Manual, p. 170) suggests to remove themselves from the situation or to try something different.

REMOVE YOURSELF

For those situations that patients have identified as triggering intense mood changes, remind patients that they can always remove themselves from this type of situation. Once they have recognized their internal alarm indicating an unpleasant mood change, they can take control and attempt to alter the situation by not allowing themselves to be in it. For instance, if they are at a party and begin to recognize a mood change related to their belief that no one at the party will want to socially approach them, they can choose to leave and call a friend.

TRY SOMETHING DIFFERENT

If patients are in an identified situation in which they know they are likely to experience a mood change, ask patients to try something different from what they might normally do. For example, if a patient is in a social situation becoming upset due to negative thoughts about how attractive he or she is, challenge him or her to talk to at least two people concentrating only on the discussion, not physical appearance.

WORKSHEET EIGHTEEN: THE DPS

Complete WORKSHEET 18: THE DPS (Patient Manual, p. 171). Compare the results of the DPS after treatment goals were set. Is there a difference in the level of distress the patient is experiencing in response to the criterion? If not, reexamine the interventions chosen to target the symptoms, and collaboratively determine whether changes or alterations should be made.

CASE EXAMPLE

For Jackie, in the first vignette, treatment is focused on her frequent and intense mood changes. Ever-sensitive to her environment and the possibility of rejection, Jackie catastrophizes a situation, which results in an extreme mood shift. Throughout her life, Jackie felt as if her emotions ruled her. During her younger years, she received a great deal of attention when she was upset. She did not exactly want the attention; she simply felt she could not harness her emotions. She always seemed to be reacting. Jackie completed her assessment with her outpatient therapist, who helped her understand that external events often trigger emotional changes that at times become exaggerated. Jackie focused on the automatic thoughts that typically caused her mood changes and began to see that a theme of feeling abandoned or neglected instigated either great sadness or at times great fear. Jackie realized that she exerted a great deal of emotional energy in looking forward to certain events, only to be overwhelmingly devastated when the event did not occur. Her therapist helped her create her own "feeling thermometer," which assisted her in scaling back her emotions when she noted that her system was responding in an intense way-when she got butterflies in her stomach, had thoughts that raced through her mind, and couldn't concentrate. She was soon able to identify the mood states that occurred as a result of internal rather than external stimuli, and when external stimuli caused stress, she was able to scale back and look at the situation in a less catastrophic way. She also learned to challenge her dichotomous thinking and tendency to jump to conclusions. Jackie decided to write the word "stop" on an index card, which she looked at as soon as she felt a mood change. This helped her process the mood change, self-validate that some fluctuation is normal, and challenge the mood states that were extreme reactions to distorted thoughts.

| Chronic Feelings
of Emptiness

This chapter addresses BPD Criterion 7: "chronic feelings of empti-ness" (APA, 2000, p. 710). This criterion constitutes one of the more difficult constellations of symptoms to define and therefore treat. The *DSM-IV-TR* elaborates on the basic definition by stating: "Easily bored, [individuals with BPD] may constantly seek something to do" (APA, 1994, p. 651). This suggests that feeling empty can be likened to not having anything to occupy or fill one's internal experience, which is perceived by the individual as boredom. We agree with this formu-lation but would like to extend it to include a lack of a sense of mean-ing or life purpose. Patients diagnosed with BPD often indicate that they perceive their lives as being without meaning. Full of existential questions related to their own purpose, goals, and often future direc-tion, these individuals seek external stimulation to help define and create feelings and meaning. They tend to monitor their environment closely searching for clues to the direction in which to proceed. The direction and subsequent feelings they derive from external sources, therefore, are closely related to their future purpose and direction. Without these external clues, those with BPD may experience a gnaw-ing sense of a lack of purpose and meaning. This relates to how they define their identity, both interpersonally, and intrapersonally with regard to their role as a member of society. You may have heard patients describe symptoms of extreme isolation including feeling as if they are totally alone even when they are in a crowded room or in the company of family and friends. They may have said that they watch the world go by with their noses pressed against the window, wishing they could experience all that others do. They may have described never feeling content, or feeling as if they never have achieved a significant milestone in their lives. Nothing quite fills their

---

Criterion 7

Chronic feelings of *emptiness*.

Chronic
Definition: Of long duration.
Synonym: Consistent, lingering, persistent.
BPD: For patients with BPD, chronic feelings of emptiness do not abate or resolve themselves. They are ongoing and persistent with limited relief.

Emptiness
Definition of *Empty*: Total absence of matter; total lack of ideas, meaning, or substance; desperate sense of loss; lacking a desirable element.
Synonym: Barrenness, hollowness, destitution, blankness.
BPD: This definition offers insight to the chronic and persistent feeling of emptiness that is experienced by those with BPD. Patients experience an overall absence of direction or meaning. They may describe a "throbbing numbness" or an excruciating ache throughout their whole being. Typically they have difficulty describing this sensation. This is experienced in both intrapersonal and extrapersonal realms, as one's direction and meaning in life is both internally and externally driven. Internally, goals are defined according to one's internal reference points of cognition and emotion. Experiencing extreme vacillation and reactivity, the patient often has the sensation of drifting without a solid, cohesive sense of self-identity (see Chapter 3). This lack of internal reference points encompasses a sense of emptiness that becomes a painful reminder of their vacant or hollow existence. Externally, the drifting identity of borderline patients causes dysfunction and distress in interpersonal relations, as no sense of internal cohesion exists. This creates an unpredictability within relationships and a potential source of conflict.

---

void. Never experiencing contentment, they are forever seeking to experience, feel, and create inner meaning.

VIGNETTES

The vignettes demonstrate the overwhelming feelings of emptiness that those with BPD can sometimes experience. In the first vignette, Pam's social role shifts from colleague to socialite, but with no internal guidance. She lacks direction and seeks it from outside sources, including the attention from a man she meets at a bar. Tom feels isolated and alone even among a group of people. Having what he determines as nothing to contribute or say, he isolates himself and withdraws from the group, feeling desperately alone. Both vignettes demonstrate how loneliness, emptiness, and despair affect intrapersonal and interpersonal functioning. The emptiness can also create a context in which patients attempt to establish feelings by engaging in inappropriate behaviors. In this way they at least are able to feel some-thing defineable, such as excitement or interest.

Vignette 1: Pam

It seemed like it would never end. The tight sensation in her chest proved that she was different. Being different seemed as much a part of her as did her arms and legs. There was nothing to look forward to or be excited about, no one to help fill the void inside her. The bore-dom she felt was turning into despair. She thought of her colleagues at work, always smiling, humming, looking forward to the long week-end ahead. "Why are they able to feel and I can't?" thought Pam. She then decided to respond to the flirtations of the man sitting across the bar. "If I don't have feelings," thought Pam, "I'll just make them." She strained to see the tattoos covering his muscular arms and decided to ignore his wedding ring. She had to—she was finally experiencing a spark of excitement inside, a feeling.

Vignette 2: Tom

"Here we go again," Tom thought. "I'm being excluded." When the topic of conversation shifted to something about which he had little interest, Tom felt an even greater separation from the group. His stom-ach knotted and he felt like he would never be able to eat in the cafe-teria again. As he thought some more, he began to feel more like an outcast—not just excluded, but rejected. "I knew this would happen. Once people get to know me, they find out how boring and stupid I am," Tom thought. "I'm almost 26 years old and I feel like I have no personality at all." Tom began to focus on how much the other people in the group had going for them. Compared to them, he felt like an empty shell. Where did they get all of their ideas or their thoughts on all of these topics? As the hollow feeling in his chest grew, Tom sneaked away from the group too embarrassed to say good-bye.

Discussing the Vignettes & Prompting the Patient

As patients review the vignettes, ask if they, too, experience a gnaw-ing sense of emptiness. This emptiness may manifest as a sense of numbness or feeling totally without direction. Everyone questions his or her purpose in life. However, patients with BPD not only question the larger, more abstract issues, but also their daily existence. They are constantly challenged by an internal uninhabited space or a life without meaning. Do they attempt to fill this void with excitement or act impulsively? A key part of tackling this symptom is assisting patients in understanding that they do experience feelings. This is achieved by patients becoming aware and perceptive of the feelings that they experience, and learning to "turn them up." When patients are able to experience and identify their own emotional states, they can soon learn what these emotions may mean and how they relate to the situations they are currently experiencing. This can help provide a sense of cohesion and a greater self-understanding.

APPLYING TYPICAL BPD SCHEMAS & DISTORTIONS TO THE CRITERION

Schematic themes related to a lack of individuation, emotional deprivation, and incompetence often are present with this criterion. Feeling empty inside, patients with BPD often monitor others to determine the appropriate response. In this way, they remain out of contact with their own internal systems and continue to be drawn to others. The belief that one cannot experience emotions often creates a long-standing, intense, and compelling assumption that one is emotionally deprived. Patients may actually make statements such as "Well, there's nothing inside me anyway." Feeling without any direction and at times without purpose can exaggerate beliefs that they are incompetent and unable to contribute to their direction or goals. As dichotomous thinking can sway these beliefs to polarities, patients may question their own existence and continue to look to others for direction.

WORKSHEETS ONE & TWO: ASSESSMENT & ASSIGNMENT

As noted, states of intense anxiety can cause physical symptoms of panic, GI distress, and sweating. WORKSHEET 1: THE ASSESSMENT (p. 174; Patient Manual, p. 176) asks patients to consider times when they, too, have experienced emptiness. Identifying symptoms of anxiety can help patients confirm that they have feelings, and are not empty.

WORKSHEET 1
The Assessment for Criterion 7

Rate the severity of the following problems as you think they may relate to you.

0 = none   1= mild   2 = moderate   3 = severe   4 = extremely severe

1. I feel lonely even in a group of people I know. ____

2. I often have the sensation of feeling emotionally hollow or empty inside. ____

3. People close to me often don't seem to satisfy my needs. ____

4. I often experience intolerable boredom. ____

5. I have been told by significant others that I am too needy or demanding. ____

6. My life seems to lack a sense of meaning or purpose. ____

7. I seek relief from boredom in potentially dangerous or self-destructive activities or outlets. ____

8. I often feel disconnected from the group I'm in-not really a part of things. ____

9. I struggle to feel connected or a part of anything. ____

10. I often feel as if I have no direction in life. ____

If the patient answers five or more prompts at level 2 or above, consider focusing on this criterion.

After the patient completes WORKSHEET 1: THE ASSESSMENT, complete WORKSHEET 2: THE ASSIGNMENT (Patient Manual, p. 177) which prompts patients to identify an incident in which they experienced feeling empty.

SENSITIVITY & CHRONIC FEELINGS OF EMPTINESS

Incredibly sensitive to their internal experiences, individuals with BPD have chronic feelings of emptiness that become overwhelmingly evident and pervasive throughout everyday existence. This lack of feeling and subsequently of meaning can lead patients to seek out experiences that will create more feelings. They tend to perpetually scan their environment for clues, and how they perceive their environment dictates their feeling or mood state. As feelings of emptiness work as a painful reminder of their lack of direction or purpose, a heightened sensitivity to the environment can quickly be utilized to incorporate a new or exciting feeling state. Impulsive patients may make uninformed choices in an attempt to replace the feelings of emptiness with excitement, joy, or purpose. This can lead to poor choices.

There is also an apparent vacillation between hypersensitivity and chronic feelings of emptiness. This criterion often coexists with affective instability. This is due to patients' exquisite sensitivity to internal changes and perceptions, which results in an overall mood shift. As patients become overwhelmed by feelings of emptiness and boredom, stimulations become exaggerated or magnified. Life then can become erratic, as patients oscillate between sheer boredom and ebullience.

WORKSHEETS THREE TO SIX, & EIGHTEEN: TREATMENT GOALS

The Taking Control treatment program is predicated upon patients' learning that they actually do experience feelings but have learned to shut them off or are unable to perceive them. In order to articulate this, we use *The Wizard of Oz* and the quest of the Tin Man, Straw Man, the Lion and Dorothy to find a heart, a brain, courage, and, ultimately, home. Home can be likened to the self in that patients are experiencing difficulty in identifying and filling in their own space with feelings, thoughts, and direction (i.e., heart, brain, and courage). This analogy helps organize the identification of the self and its components.

You can assist patients in understanding how they may have learned to shut off their feelings. They may have learned to do this due to the very nature of the feelings they have experienced (pain and loss) or to protect themselves from danger (physical or emotional). Schematically, patients may have learned as children that feelings are dangerous or can cause undue pain. They may have been taught to "stuff" their feelings, "pull themselves up by their bootstraps," or ignore their existence. Perhaps, when they did manage to express themselves, they were punished or, in worse case scenarios, abused. Challenging these schemas is difficult because they tend to be an entrenched aspect of the personality. However, with practice at identify feelings and subsequent meanings, patients can learn to recognize that they do feel and are indeed very human with human-like feelings.

Remind patients that although this method of coping and managing external pain and stress may have been adaptive when they were children, it is no longer a helpful or useful tool in managing feelings as an adult. The protective belief that "life has no meaning and therefore I can't be hurt any longer" is relevant to daily survival and existence. Feelings, as discussed earlier, help give meaning to our lives. It therefore stands to reason that if we allow ourselves to feel, we may then experience purpose, and ultimately experience meaning.

How do we create this internal experience? We must build upon what is either not perceived or not utilized by patients. In other words, within patients lie experiences, emotions, and perceptions that have not been clearly identified as such. If you help patients to recognize the experiences they have as part of their meaning, they can begin building upon the structure. It is important to relay to patients that they are certainly not alone in their quest to define their meaning or the meaning of life. It is a question that has engaged both philosophers and scientists since the beginning of time. The treatment program attempts not only to help patients understand and recognize when they may be more prone experiencing emptiness, but also to learn how to label or identify the feeling states they do experience. Overall, the goal is to combat the notion that they are an empty shell void of feeling.

After the patient completes WORKSHEETS 1 and 2, assist the patient in filling out WORKSHEET 3: THE INCIDENT CHART (Patient Manual, p. 178). The four areas of self-monitoring (physiological, emotional, cognitive, and behavioral) offer avenues to treatment interventions and provide concrete examples of specific areas of change the patient can address. By clearly identifying these warning signals, patients can make a preemptive strike against feeling empty by taking control of their actions and making decisions based not upon knee jerk reactions but rather upon an informed choice.

Complete WORKSHEETS 4 and 5 (Patient Manual, pp. 179–180), to identify patients' automatic thoughts and schema. Then treatment goals can be identified. In order to help organize this process, complete WORKSHEET 6: TREATMENT GOALS (Patient Manual, p. 181). Once treatment goals are set, complete WORKSHEET 18: THE DPS (Patient Manual, p. 182) to determine a baseline level of distress or dysfunction for the particular criterion.

WORKSHEETS SEVEN TO SEVENTEEN: SUGGESTED INTERVENTIONS

Worksheets 7 & 8: Physical Triggers & Suggested Interventions

As feelings of emptiness can be very difficult to describe, they also may be difficult to identify. Encourage patients to monitor for physical signals that indicate feelings of emptiness, such as a sinking feeling in the stomach or symptoms of anxiety (WORKSHEET 7; Patient Manual, p. 183). These symptoms can serve as clues or identifiers of these feelings. Once patients have identified such symptoms, they can begin to provide themselves with the opportunity to react in a thoughtful and purposeful way rather than out of impulse (WORKSHEET 8; Patient Manual, pp. 184–185).

THOUGHT-STOPPING

What physiological sensations are attached to patients' identified symptoms or feelings of emptiness? Are the sensations similar to those of fear? If they are experiencing these symptoms, encourage them to *stop*. In addition to being beneficial in and of itself, stopping allows for further interventions to take place.

RELAXATION

Relaxation techniques can be helpful if symptoms of anxiety are present. For example, a patient may say that when he or she is among a group of friends and feels disconnected with nothing to say, anxiety rears its ugly head. Deep breathing and focusing on the present can help this situation and refocus thoughts away from feeling alone and toward considering how to reconnect with the group.

RELAXING IMAGERY

Encourage patients to utilize their safe place. Their special place provides reinforcement that they are an individual with unique likes, dislikes, and emotions.

Worksheets 9 & 10: Emotional Triggers & Suggested Interventions

Chronic feelings of emptiness can be unbearable. Although it may seem counterintuitive, the experience of emptiness can become both intense and exaggerated. The accompanying mood changes and fluctuations render patients victims of their own painful emotional states (WORKSHEET 9; Patient Manual, p. 186). They may then seek to define their feelings from external stimulus or cues.

INTERVENTION 1

To help patients begin to experience meaning (WORKSHEET 10; Patient Manual, pp. 187–188), first have them complete the EXPERIENCES AND EMOTIONS CHART. This chart is designed to elicit the emotions patients experience throughout the day and the specific experiences which triggers those emotions.

Encourage patients to go through a full day's worth of significant experiences (those that they can easily recall) and enter them into the EXPERIENCES AND EMOTIONS CHART. You are attempting to define for patients that they do, indeed, have experiences throughout the day that have subsequent reactions, feelings, and sensations. They are not void of meaning or purpose. The chart can be filled out bidirectionally. They may experience the physical sensation first and then attach emotions, or vice versa. Encourage patients to examine like a detective their experiences in detail by completing what physical sensations, thoughts, behaviors, and time of day that the experience occurred. Assisting patients in understanding the varying emotional states they experience throughout the day directly contradicts the belief that they are empty. By internally magnifying of their experience, they probably will be relieved that they, too, will begin to recall that they experienced feelings and emotions and do exist not as an empty shell, but as a fully functioning human.

Once they have gone through an entire day's worth of experiences and situations, have them list the attached emotions that occurred. Therefore, if a similar experience occurs in the future, they will understand what the emotional state probably will be. Ask patients to pick a particular experience in the day and rank (from 1 to 5) their emotional states. This ranking can help to predict what emotion will occur in similar experiences. Specifically, say to patients, "Let's look at your chart again, this time with prompts for you to rank what feelings you may have if this experience occurs again."

The Experiences and Emotions Chart

Rank the probability of the felt emotion (e.g., anger, sadness, frustration) on a scale of 1 to 5, with 1 being the lowest intensity and 5 being the highest intensity. Because emotions are highly subjective, work with your client to establish the precise meaning of the ratings on this 5-point scale.

Experience 1 _____

Physical sensation	Thoughts	Behavior	Time of day	Emotion	Intensity
_____	_____	_____	_____	_anger_	__
_____	_____	_____	_____	___	__
_____	_____	_____	_____	___	__
_____	_____	_____	_____	___	__
_____	_____	_____	_____	___	__
_____	_____	_____	_____	___	__

Experience 2 _____

Physical sensation	Thoughts	Behavior	Time of day	Emotion	Intensity
_____	_____	_____	_____	_anger_	__
_____	_____	_____	_____	___	__
_____	_____	_____	_____	___	__
_____	_____	_____	_____	___	__
_____	_____	_____	_____	___	__

INTERVENTION 2

Next, prompt patients to identify the meaning that is attached to or associated with specific experiences and the emotional responses. As patients' begin to define the experiences and the related emotions, the meanings of specific situations can now be defined. We use the term *meaning* to convey an experience with associated feelings. To help describe this to patients, connect feelings and meaning: feelings = meaning, and meaning = feelings. By specifically looking at their experiences and emotions, patients can begin to figure out what carries deep meaning in their life. Identifying meanings directly contradicts any schema related to being empty or without feeling.

The MEANINGS CHART prompts patients to specifically connect their experiences with their emotions and the meanings created. For example, if a patient experiences a derogatory remark from a fellow staff member, the meaning assigned to that situation often becomes the emotion that accompanies the situation. Attached to the experience is the thought "I'm no good at this job" or "I've failed again." Thus, the derogatory remark leads to: I'm no good (meaning) = sadness (feeling).

The chart prompts the patient to provide a summary of their experiences or situations that have specific emotional reactions. Patients are then asked identify the attached meaning with the specific experience and emotional state.

The following brief list of words may help patients describe and define the meanings derived from their emotions:

• loss	• understanding	• sense of belonging
• acceptance	• conscientiousness	• empowerment
• fear	• sensitivity	• specialness
• being overwhelmed	• happiness	• tough-mindedness
• anger	• aggressiveness	• indifference

The Meanings Chart		
Experience	**Emotion**	**= Meaning**
demand from boss	*frustration*	*want to work independently*
cut off in traffic	*anger*	*don't like to be disregarded*
_____ .	_____ .	_____ .
_____ .	_____ .	_____ .

Now have patients list other ways to describe the meanings of their experiences.

Worksheets 11 & 12: Cognitive/Automatic Thoughts & Suggested Interventions

Chronic feelings of emptiness are often due to patients' assigning a particular feeling state to a meaning of emptiness (WORKSHEET 11; Patient Manual, p. 189). Patients may experience some type of physiological arousal that they interpret as an empty feeling. Once the feeling state has been designated as emptiness, patients may subsequently experience despair and loneliness.

CHALLENGE CATASTROPHIC THINKING

Catastrophic thinking related to loneliness may occur. Utilize the CATASTROPHIC THINKING CHART to challenge these beliefs (WORKSHEET 12; Patient Manual, p. 190). For example, if the patient is in a group of strangers with whom they have little in common, does the patient think, "I am nothing and alone?" Challenge patients to identify the noncatastrophic thought-for instance, "I may not know these people, but I have a chance to meet new people and learn new things."

WEIGH THE EVIDENCE

Assumptions about being alone in the world, being entirely misunderstood, or having little value can be disputed with the DISPUTATION CHART. Assumptions may also be made about how others perceive patients in social situations. For example, a patient may be convinced he or she "sticks out" in social situations because he or she does not have anything to offer during conversations or relationships.

The Disputation Chart

Situation: *You are alone at a party.*

Belief: *Because I am alone, I have no one.*

Proof Supporting Belief	**Refuting Statement**
1. *I have no one with me.*	1. *I have friends and family.*
2. *I don't know anyone.*	2. *I have met strangers who became friends.*
3. _____ .	3. _____ .
4. _____ .	4. _____ .

Worksheets 13 & 14: Behavioral Triggers & Suggested Interventions

When you examine behaviors that occur as a result of feelings of emptiness, themes of adopting others' beliefs or opinions may arise (WORKSHEET 13; Patient Manual, p. 191). Patients may truly believe that they do not have opinions, or they may be concerned that they will have to stand alone with their differences. Additionally, impulsive behaviors may occur as patients desperately try to *feel* something, whether it be excitement, danger, or even intoxication.

CONSIDER THE CONSEQUENCES

When experiencing feelings of emptiness, patients often will not stop to consider the consequences. For example, in the second vignette, Tom choose to leave the group because he felt he had nothing to contribute. The positive consequence was that he no longer had to feel embarrassed or "put on the spot." However, he forfeited his chance to get to know other people or even practice being in a conversation and letting people get to know him.

Encourage patients to examine their behaviors and the related consequences: Utilize the NEGATIVE AND POSITIVE CONSEQUENCES CHART (WORKSHEET 14; Patient Manual, p. 192).

STOP

Stopping is completed in conjunction with examining the consequences of behaviors. It can be used to thwart both immediate and long-term behaviors. For example, a patient who is experiencing feelings of intense emptiness and impulsively joins a group of people engaging in potentially harmful acts (e.g., speeding down a highway) can take a moment to *stop* and consider the consequences of wanting to feel that something can occur. In the long-term, patients who must make a decision about something can take some time to derive their own answer-this can help reinforce the belief that they are not empty inside but rather need to "turn up" their internal sensors.

Worksheets 16 & 17: Situational Triggers & Suggested Interventions

WORKSHEET 16 (Patient Manual, p. 193) prompts patients to specifically identify those situations that have led to feeling empty. WORKSHEET 17 (Patient Manual, p. 194) suggests to remove themselves from the situation or to try something different.

REMOVE YOURSELF

For those situations that patients have identified as triggering feelings of emptiness, remind patients that they can always remove themselves from this type of situation. For example, if a patient is in a situation in which he or she feels unsure, confused, overwhelmed with a sense of not fitting in, feeling empty, or not knowing how to react, leaving the specific situation can reinforce the belief that he or she has specific needs and emotional states.

TRY SOMETHING DIFFERENT

For those situations that patients have identified as triggering feelings of emptiness, encourage patients to try something different in the situation. For example, instead of scanning the room looking for topics of discussion from other party-goers, ask the patient to make a statement related to an area of their own interests, such as a recent book they have read or a movie they have seen.

WORKSHEET EIGHTEEN: THE DPS

Complete WORKSHEET 18: THE DPS (Patient Manual, p. 195). Compare the results of the DPS after treatment goals were set. Is there a difference in the level of distress patients are experiencing in response to the criterion? If not, reexamine the interventions chosen to target the symptoms, and collaboratively determine whether changes or alterations should be made.

CASE EXAMPLE

With Pam, in the first vignette, treatment issues revolved around choices that she made when feeling numb or empty inside. The morning after she had engaged in the risky situation with the man at the bar, Pam was actually frightened enough to realize that she needed to seek help. With the help of WORKSHEET 1, her therapist helped her learn to identify and describe the intense feelings of emptiness. Pam remembered always "shutting down" her emotions. She described a childhood full of discipline and strict rules-an environment in which emotions meant weakness. When she did express feelings, she received physical and emotional abuse from her father, who wanted to "teach" her to be strong. Now she just felt like a robot. After monitoring her behaviors and automatic thoughts, she began to realize that she sought outside stimulation to define how she was feeling inside. She at times heard her own small voice trying to speak, trying to say what it wanted, but she recognized that she soon squashed it. Pam's belief system consisted of schemas related to believing that she no longer had any emotional capacity-that she had shut down forever. With the help of her therapist, Pam began to monitor the tiniest of changes within her body, within her emotions, and within her mind. She then turned them up and tried to exaggerate the feeling that was occurring. She jotted them down and began to make associations with certain events, times, places, and other sensations. Soon she was able to rank those emotions, which helped her realize that she, too, was an emotional being, she just needed to turn up the volume and challenge the old, compelling schemas consisting of beliefs that she was nonemotional.

| Inappropriate &
Intense Anger

This chapter addresses BPD Criterion 8: "inappropriate, intense anger or difficulty controlling anger (e.g., frequent displays of temper, constant anger, recurrent physical fights)" (APA, 2000, p. 710). This criterion is particularly relevant for patients who have shown poor impulse control and who are not adept at self-monitoring. Anger and angry outbursts are expressed in many ways. Patients may not be overtly hostile but in times of stress make sarcastic, debasing, or even degrading remarks. They may seem extremely bitter or negative. Alternatively, some patients demonstrate an inability to control or modulate their expression of anger, which if further aggravated, may result in physical aggression or fights. These behaviors have caused difficulties in interpersonal relationships, employment problems, and perhaps legal charges.

How does this anger become activated? Patients may be able to identify that their anger is often instigated by the perception or threat of the loss of a significant other or by feelings of abandonment. Sensing that their needs may not be met by their significant other, they may become extremely angry about what they perceive as a rejection. Schematically, patients may have learned that when significant others are unable to respond to their needs, the only way to take control of the situation is to become angry. Perhaps they have learned that anger creates intimidation and fear and ultimately may cause the other person to become closer or more intimate with them. Again, reiterate to patients that as humans we are a system of sensors and alarms. Alarms warn us of pending danger. However, our system of interpreting events may be sounding the alarm when there is no need to do so. In effect, patients may be reacting to an incredible loss or rejection that may not have occurred. This results in extreme anger, hurt, and despair.

Criterion 8
Inappropriate, intense anger or difficulty controlling anger (e.g., frequent displays of temper, constant anger, recurrent physical fights).

Inappropriate
Definition: Improper or unfit.
Synonym: Unsuitable.
BPD: Those with BPD may express anger at times when the situation does not necessarily warrant it. It may also be an extreme reaction of anger. If anger *is* appropriate in a given situation, patients tend to experience it in intense waves and are typically unable to modulate the intensity.

Intense
Definition: Extreme in degree, strength, or effect.
Synonym: Pronounced.
BPD: Those with BPD often experience unwarranted displays of anger that are not only inappropriate, but also tend to be extreme or disproportionate to the situation. The degree of expressed anger is great and, combined with impulsivity (see Chapter 4), may lead to an outburst or expression of feelings that results in self-damage or damage to others. Patients may experience great difficulty in controlling the anger and subsequently regret their actions.

VIGNETTES

The vignettes describe two individuals who experience anger but have difficulty attaching the emotion to its true source. Kenny, frustrated at his inability to complete a contracted job, becomes furious with his wife for her nagging. After making a derogatory remark to her, he storms out and becomes enraged while driving. Unable to contain his rage, he engages in reckless driving, which results in an accident with another driver. He now has to contend not only with the original problem of not having a job, but also with large bills to fix both cars. In the second scenario, Carrie, consumed with self-doubt and thoughts related to her feelings of worthlessness, assumes her friend Jean is insulting her. Failing to consider the true source of her anger (low self-esteem), Carrie is unable to control her rage, tosses wine in her friend's face, and makes a derogatory remark. In both scenarios the characters personalize an external situation: Kenny, by thinking he was being personally attacked by another driver, and Carrie, by assuming her talkative friend was making negative references to her specifically. It is important for patients to understand that although anger is not necessarily negative or bad, it sometimes can be irrational, as it is created from our unique perception of situations. Additionally, the tendency to catastrophize exacerbates the already-distorted interpretation of the event or meaning.

Vignette 1: Kenny

Kenny was getting really annoyed with his wife. She seemed to nag him constantly about his not working. This time he had admitted that he hadn't completed a job he was hired to do and had lost a valuable contract. Yeah, he knew he had screwed up, but her nagging wasn't helping. "How are we supposed to pay the bills?" she asked him. "Who's going to pay the rent?" She just wouldn't let up. "I wish I never married a bitch like you!" Kenny yelled as he stormed out. As he drove around town, her irritating voice played over and over in his head. The last straw came when some idiot in a station wagon cut him off when switching lanes. Kenny saw red. He was unable to feel anything but rage. He tapped the other driver's rear bumper just to let him know how angry he was. What he didn't anticipate was the other drivers' slamming on his breaks.

Vignette 2: Carrie

Carrie was getting annoyed. Sipping her third glass of red wine over dinner, she was becoming infuriated with her friend, Jean's, constant chattering. Jean was laughing and talking about other people, but Carrie thought it seemed to pertain directly to her. Jean talked about her other friend's jobs, clothes, and backgrounds. Carrie's mind raced back to this morning, when she had stood in front of the mirror for at least an hour trying to fit into some of her good clothes. Didn't Jean know that she was feeling incredibly bad about herself right now? "If she cuts up other people that way, what does she think of me?" Carrie thought. She couldn't stand it any longer. She was furious. Tightness welled up in her throat and she felt like she couldn't breathe. She didn't think she could contain herself any longer. Jean was amazed when Carrie tossed what was left of her wine in her face and stormed out of the restaurant.

Discussing Vignettes & Prompting the Patient

As patients read the vignettes, ask if they, too, experience losing their cool or episodes of inappropriate anger. In both vignettes, anger is discharged in an extreme, intense, and misdirected manner. It is natural for people to get angry. However, for those with BPD, anger becomes a patterned mode of responding and usually is carried to an extreme. Ask patients if they, too, often and easily "see red." They may also act impulsively on the basis of this anger and later regret these actions.

Assist patients in concretizing their experience so that they can begin to recognize and understand the specific way they interpret events that may have led to extreme outbursts of anger and ultimately negative consequences.

APPLYING TYPICAL BPD SCHEMAS & DISTORTIONS TO THE CRITERION

Typical schemas for patients with intense anger often include themes of abandonment, mistrust, and incompetence. As emotional lability complicates how external stimuli are interpreted, jumping to conclusions can lead to intense anger. Sensitive to their environment, patients may experience intense anger as a result of mistrust and believing they are being abandoned or left. Dichotomous thinking also engenders extreme emotional responses like anger. Finally, beliefs related to unlovability and incompetence can overwhelm patients with intense anger and rage.

WORKSHEETS ONE & TWO: ASSESSMENT & ASSIGNMENT

As noted, states of intense anxiety can cause physical symptoms of panic, GI distress, and sweating. WORKSHEET 1: THE ASSESSMENT (p. 189; Patient Manual, p. 199) asks patients to consider times when they, too, have had intense anger. Identifying symptoms of anxiety prior to being explosive can act as a helpful warning sign. These warning signs offer opportunities for patients to take control and not act upon their anger in a way they may later regret.

WORKSHEET 1
The Assessment for Criterion 8

Rate the severity of the following problems as you think they may relate to you.

0 = none   1 = mild   2 = moderate   3 = severe   4 = extremely severe

1. You lose your temper easily. ____

2. People have described you as an "angry person." ____

3. You have regretted things you've said in arguments. ____

4. You have used physical force when you argue. ____

5. During arguments your voice gets loud. ____

6. You feel completely out of control when you are angry. ____

7. When you're annoyed, you feel tightness in your chest and your muscles seem tense. ____

8. You find it difficult to think of anything else when you are angry. ____

9. Your anger has gotten you in trouble. ____

10. Others are frightened of your anger. ____

If the patient answers five or more prompts at level 2 or above, consider focusing on this criterion.

After the patient completes WORKSHEET 1: THE ASSESSMENT, complete WORKSHEET 2: THE ASSIGNMENT (Patient Manual, p. 200) which prompts patients to identify an incident in which they experienced intense anger or rage.

SENSITIVITY & ANGER

Due to the intensity of their emotional reactions, those with BPD who become angered easily usually compound their situation by magnifying this anger. This can lead to verbal or physical rage reactions. Eversensitive to clues in their environment that indicate threatening events, patients can become enraged easily or retaliate in an effort to protect themselves or their relationship. This can lead to poor choices, or choices made out of rage rather than out of a rational decision-making process.

WORKSHEETS THREE TO SIX, & EIGHTEEN: TREATMENT GOALS

The treatment program is predicated upon patients' learning to identify when they may lose their cool, the events or situations that trigger this anger, the physiological warning signs of anger, and, finally, how to generate informed choices rather than act on their rage. Self-monitoring is a vital part of managing anger and rage reactions, as patients who are of unsure of why or how they become enraged do not have the opportunity to gauge whether or not their responses are appropriate in the given situation.

It is important for your patient to understand that everyone gets angry. Anger helps us survive, and all humans have the capability and capacity for anger and aggression. However, patients with BPD tend to misinterpret or misread cues, interpreting innocuous data as a threat. This leads to an emotional overreaction and an intense, exaggerated response. The treatment program addresses this problem and attempts to help patients understand that certain times are appropriate for anger but not inappropriate levels of anger.

Prompt patients to identify the various components involved in processing incoming information (this may include distortions related to rage). In order to "see red" or become enraged, patients have sensed, perceived, and interpreted an external or internal clue as threatening. This threat causes an intense reaction of rage. Patients may have learned as children to respond ragefully in order to survive, or that outbursts of rage were an acceptable form of communicating. If this is the only way they know how to discharge emotions, they may actually feel entitled to be angry or to use anger as an emotional outlet.

Common causes of rage are threats to self-esteem, threats of abandonment, and misreadings of interpersonal cues. The goal, therefore, is to assist patients in learning to describe and identify the process by which they become angry, including the perceptions and situations that lead them to anger. You then can help patients create alternative methods of handling this anger. In short, if patients can clarify how they first see red, they won't have such difficulty keeping their cool.

After the patient completes WORKSHEETS 1 and 2, assist the patient in filling out WORKSHEET 3: THE INCIDENT CHART (Patient Manual p. 201). The four areas of self-monitoring (physiological, emotional, cognitive, and behavioral) offer avenues to treatment interventions and provide concrete examples of specific areas of change the patient can address. Assisting patients in clearly describing how their systems react prior to experiencing anger or rage provides the inroad to constructively managing this feeling state rather than acting in ways that further complicate or deteriorate the situation. After completing WORKSHEETS 4 and 5 (Patient Manual, pp. 202–203) to identify the patient's automatic thoughts and schema, treatment goals can be identified. In order to help organize this process, complete WORKSHEET 6: TREATMENT GOALS (Patient Manual, p. 204). Once treatment goals are set, complete WORKSHEET 18: THE DPS (Patient Manual, p. 205) to determine a baseline level of distress or dysfunction for the particular criterion.

WORKSHEETS SEVEN TO SEVENTEEN: SUGGESTED INTERVENTIONS

Worksheets 7 & 8: Physical Triggers & Suggested Interventions

As outbursts of anger can be potentially dangerous for both patients and those around them, it is particularly important that patients not only learn to monitor when their rage is occurring (WORKSHEET 7; Patient Manual, p. 206), but also make attempts to "cool down" before responding (WORKSHEET 8; Patient Manual, pp. 207–208). How are their bodies indicating that they are angry? Cooling down can help circumvent the severe consequences resulting from physical violence, negative statements, or even self-harm.

THOUGHT-STOPPING

Thought-stopping is imperative when attempting to manage anger. Physical clues may be more powerful and easier to identify. For example, a patient may notice a clenching of his or her jaw or fist or a tightness in the chest. These physical warning signs can be a direct line to pending anger and potential negative consequences. Patients who feel these physical cues are encouraged to *stop* and consider the situation and all options.

RELAXATION

Relaxation techniques can be particularly helpful for those with anger problems. As many physical symptoms are felt as muscle tension, relaxation techniques can assist in relaxing the muscles, which helps relax the mind.

RELAXING IMAGERY

Encourage patients to combine relaxation techniques with soothing images. For example, patients might imagine themselves floating in a calm, warm pool, or soothing tub.

Worksheets 9 & 10: Emotional Triggers & Suggested Interventions

For those with BPD who are both physiologically and psychologically sensitive, feelings of anger can be unbearable. At times, this rage may render patients victims of their own painful emotional states (WORKSHEET 9; Patient Manual, p. 209). They may then regret actions or words that come out of a rageful feeling state.

SCALE BACK

Using WORKSHEET 10 (Patient Manual, p. 210) ask patients to rate on a scale of 1 to 10 the severity of the emotion they felt before, during, and after they experienced anger. Once patients have scaled back, have them "take their temperature" again, noting the difference in the ratings and their ability to affect some change in their modulation.

Worksheets 11 & 12: Cognitive/Automatic Thoughts & Suggested Interventions

Rage emotions and reactions are often prompted by misinterpreted cues (WORKSHEET 11; Patient Manual, p. 211). Although there are times when it is appropriate to be angry, patients who have a tendency to act out of rage probably are allowing cognitive distortions to play a role in their interpretation of events. WORKSHEET 12 (Patient Manual, p. 212) proposes some interventions.

Worksheet 15: The Expanded Incident Chart

What thoughts were patients having as they became increasingly angry? Were their thoughts related to anger toward the other person or to something negative about themselves? Were they assuming they were being left or abandoned? Was their rage directed at others or themselves? Were they catstrophizing or using dichotomous thinking? Utilize the "people" column in WORKSHEET 15: THE EXPANDED INCIDENT CHART (Patient Manual, pp. 213–216) to determine what thoughts patients experience when they become enraged, and if there are particular individuals associated with that rage.

THE ANGER CHAIN

Certain people may instigate a chain of events that leads to anger. This chain of events usually begins with a distorted or negative perception of a situation. Vital to treatment is your patients making a very important decision: Do they wish to change how they react? Do they choose to alter this chain of events that has led to behaviors they are uncomfortable with? The decision to take control and alter their pre-set reactive patterns is a conscious choice.

The following flowchart traces the chain of events that leads to angry reactions. It defines how patients see red and ultimately how they react in response to that perception. An in-depth breakdown of the individual phases follows the flowchart. Assist the patient in filling out how their specific reactions relate to each of the steps in The ANGER CHAIN.

The Anger Chain

1. Perception of event (physiologically through senses).
2. Schematic interpretation.
3. Application to self.
4. Chain of events triggered.
5. Physiological responses.
6. Increased internal pressure.
7. Anger response to relieve pressure (short-term solution!).

---

1. PERCEPTION OF EVENT (PHYSIOLOGICALLY THROUGH SENSES).

Our bodies are equipped with a very advanced system of sensors. Our five senses constantly perceive incoming information and send neuronal signals to the brain for interpretation. Our alertness and consciousness allows this perpetual process. These sensors provide the data necessary for our survival. Perception of our environment activates the very primitive mechanisms by which we respond, react, and interpret our surroundings. However, our perceptions are also learned. Through experience and time, the way we perceive our surroundings becomes patterned. We may selectively perceive events in a way that is favorable to us or, in the case of a negative distortion, that perpetuate the cycle of skewing incoming information.

Challenge Perceptions Encourage patients to challenge their perceptions. They can ask themselves questions such as "Is this really happening?" or "Is it likely that I'm really seeing what I think I'm seeing?"

Weigh the evidence What is the actual likelihood that what they are perceiving is true?

The Disputation Chart

Situation: *Friend yawns when I'm talking to her.*

Belief: *My friend thinks I'm not important.*

Proof Supporting Belief	**Refuting Statement**
1. *Friend's yawn means I bore her.*	1. *Friend could be tired.*
2. *Friend is disrespectful to me.*	2. *Friend is usually interested in what I say.*
3. _____ .	3. _____ .
4. _____ .	4. _____ .

2. SCHEMATIC INTERPRETATION.

This stage involves the very mechanisms that define our beliefs and belief systems.

Challenge Dichotomous Thinking Challenge the patient to draw a straight line with black and white endpoints, with black being destructive rage and white being blissful happiness. Assist patients in examining what lies between two endpoints.

The Dichotomous Thinking Chart

Black	**Gray(s)**	**White**
Rage.	I can be annoyed and still care for someone.	Happy.
Relationship is over.	Conflict is normal in relationships.	Relationship is safe.
_____ .	_____ .	_____ .
_____ .	_____ .	_____ .

Common-Sense Questions Help patients begin to ask themselves, "Does this really make sense?" or "Is this really likely to happen?"

Reflect on Previous Experiences Have there been times when patients have made similar assumptions, only to discover later they were very wrong? Is this situation similar?

3. APPLICATION TO SELF.

Once information is interpreted through our schematic structures, an application is made to the self. This is imperative in the survival of the self and the social system. How one interprets information and applies it to the self occurs as a patterned response. This patterned response has associated behavioral reactions. Awareness of patterns allows a decision to be made regarding whether the patterned behavioral reactions should occur. These applications can be very primitive and instinctual or conscious and thought out. For example, a woman may perceive through her senses of sight and hearing that someone is approaching her. Her schema interprets the information as a stranger walking toward her. Because she has been attacked previously by a stranger, she interprets this information as danger and reacts accordingly. Once patients have interpreted the data, help them look outside of their own experience to make a realistic assumption. Remind them that the interpretations we make may actually have nothing to do with us, but rather be products of someone else's experience.

4. CHAIN OF EVENTS TRIGGERED.

This stage involves the linking of incoming information with the many associations that this data may be related or connected to. For example, the woman who sees the stranger walking toward her may link the previous situation of a stranger approaching with her information that strangers are dangerous. Associations are contextual in nature: The woman might perceive the stranger as dangerous if she is in a dark alley but not make the same associations if a stranger approached her carrying a briefcase and talking with a colleague in a well-lit office.

Break the Chain of Events Once the chain of events is triggered, thoughts and emotions are generated. These thoughts and emotions lead to subsequent physiological responses and ultimately behaviors. How can patients learn to put a cog in the wheel?

5. PHYSIOLOGICAL RESPONSES.

As part of our system of warnings and signals, our body reacts to the information perceived and interpreted. It then reacts to the suspected outcome of the interpreted information. The woman frightened by a stranger in an alley might experience a tightening of muscles, an upset stomach, sweating, or a racing heart. Although she may be fearful of meeting new people, she probably would not have the same physiological response to the stranger approaching her in the well-lit office.

Relaxation Relaxing can particularly be helpful in reducing physiological arousal.

6. INCREASED INTERNAL PRESSURE.

As we become increasingly aware of our physiological reactions and our interpretations of those reactions, a negative loop perpetuates the response. Pressure increases. The woman's pounding heart may add fuel to the flames of her fear. This in turn makes her heart race even faster.

Decrease the Pressure Once patients have identified that pressure is building, they can choose to break the chain and to decrease the pressure. They need to identify ways in which to cool off, like lifting the lid off a pressure-cooker on a stove. Scaling back can help with this.

Avoid the Situation Have patients list the places or people that encourage anger-related behaviors. Create an "escape hatch" or "safe place" that patients can go to when overwhelmed or angered. When examining the behaviors that occur prior to the patient's wanting to explode with rage, be sure to elicit the context of the situation and the behavioral responses correlated with it.

7. ANGER RESPONSES TO RELIEVE PRESSURE.

In an effort to relieve the internalized tension, pressure, or fatigue, the body reacts. It naturally seeks an outlet to provide rest and relief. The woman in the alley might choose to run, shout, or even attack in preparation for what she feels is incumbent harm. Reacting to this cycle without questioning and challenging our perceptions, interpretations, and triggered events can create situations that may ultimately worsen the circumstance. It does not have to happen this way. Within the cycle of distorted thoughts that lead to angry outbursts are many opportunities for derailment and intervention. Again, patients must make the conscious choice that they want to take control of their reactions and to commit to learning the processes that create them.

Consider the Consequences Utilize the NEGATIVE AND POSITIVE CONSEQUENCES CHART to outline the negatives of relieving pressure through angry reactions, and the positives of using responses other than anger to relieve pressure. For example, rather than discharging built up pressure by hitting someone, hit a pillow instead.

The Negative and Positive Consequences Chart

Behavior	Negative Consequences	Positive Consequences
Yelling.	Frightening the person.	Release of tension.
Throwing items.	Harming someone or something.	Getting my point across.
Hitting pillow.	No negative consequences.	No one gets hurt.
_____	_____	_____
_____	_____	_____

After completing the chart, ask patients the following:

- Do the negative consequences outweigh the positive consequences?
- Is it worth it to decrease this behavior?
- Do you want to continue this behavior?

Worksheets 13 & 14: Behavioral Triggers & Suggested Interventions

Review WORKSHEET 15: THE EXPANDED INCIDENT CHART and the ANGER CHAIN to determine what behaviors occurred as a result of rage (WORKSHEET 13; Patient Manual, p. 217). Ask patients if they wish to address or change these behaviors. Prompt patients to specifically identify which behaviors they wish to take control of, change, or eradicate.

Once patients have identified the situations that usually incur rage reactions and can identify the chain of events that lead to maladaptive behavioral responses, they are in the position to take control and make choices about how they wish to respond (WORKSHEET 14; Patient Manual, p. 218).

BETTER USE OF EMOTIONAL ENERGY

Like mood changes, anger uses a great deal of energy. Ask patients if they can direct their energy into something positive or toward a project they have been wanting to complete. Physical exercise can help reduce pent-up anger. (Be sure the patient has been examined by a physician to ensure that no risks are taken.)

Worksheets 16 & 17: Situational Triggers & Suggested Interventions

WORKSHEET 16 (Patient Manual, p. 219) prompts patients to specifically identify those situations that have led to feeling intense anger or rage. WORKSHEET 17 (Patient Manual, p. 220) suggests to remove themselves from the situation and to try something different.

REMOVE YOURSELF

For those situations that patients have identified as triggering intense anger or rage, remind patients that they can always remove themselves from this type of situation. For example, if a patient is in a situation in which he or she is feeling angered, instead of losing control, removing him- or herself can prevent doing something regrettable.

TRY SOMETHING DIFFERENT

Is there something else patients can try in a situation? For example, instead throwing something out of anger, could they go for a walk? Call a friend?

WORKSHEET EIGHTEEN: THE DPS

Complete WORKSHEET 18: THE DPS (Patient Manual, p. 221). Compare the results of the DPS after treatment goals were set. Is there a difference in the level of distress the patient is experiencing in response to the criterion? If not, reexamine the interventions chosen to target the symptoms, and collaboratively determine whether changes or alterations should be made.

CASE EXAMPLE

In the second vignette, Carrie experienced intense emotional reactions and rage, which disrupted and potentially damaged her long-term friendship with Jean. Carrie quickly cooled down as she was driving home and began to feel very embarrassed. Why had she gotten so angry? She began to notice a long history of failed relationships due to her tendency to become easily enraged. With the help of a therapist, Carrie sought to understand why she reacted so intensely to others and to situations that, upon reflection, really didn't warrant such anger. Carrie completed the assessment and noted many themes-one of which was that when she felt bad about herself, she tended to have limited patience for others around her. She began to feel as if they were purposefully trying to make her feel worse. Carrie monitored her automatic thoughts through the weeks and determined that she often made rash conclusions based on feelings of low self-esteem or disappointment in herself. She often was truly angry with herself as she was forced to deal with the embarrassment caused by her overreactions and with the loss of friends throughout the years. By looking at the schema related to her internal anger, she also identified themes of unlovability. She described these beliefs as very strong. However, on some level she knew that she deserved to be loved. She just had no means of making it happen. Carrie began to monitor for the churning feeling in her stomach that often signaled impending anger. She learned to stop and take stock of the situation when she experienced those feelings. Utilizing the ANGER CHAIN, Carrie soon realized that she was jumping to conclusions about the motives of others and that her actions were largely based out of a distortion of incoming information. She scaled back her anger, learned relaxation techniques and deep breathing, and imagined herself on that beautiful Caribbean island she wanted to go to. Carrie soon began to feel more competent in her interactions and, with some encouragement, even was able to apologize to Jean.

CHAPTER 9

Transient,
Stress-Related
Paranoid Ideation

This chapter addresses BPD Criterion 9: "transient, stress-related paranoid ideation" (APA, 2000, p. 710). Criterion 9 also includes dissociative symptoms, which are covered in Chapter 10. The *DSM-IV-TR*
further states that paranoid ideation is usually in response to a perceived loss or potential abandonment. If the caregiver's nurturance
returns, these symptoms usually remit. It is important to differentiate
those who have delusional systems impenetrable by reality testing
from those with BPD who experience transient, brief episodes of paranoia. If your patients exhibit paranoia that is more entrenched and not
transient, additional Axis I diagnoses should be considered. In addition, a consultation with a psychiatrist should occur to determine if
medication is warranted. If, however, patients experience transient
paranoid symptoms, they usually are reacting in the context of interpersonal conflict and to externalized events. Vital to understanding
BPD is the identification of the distorted thought processes that occur
in response to external stressors that activate intrapersonal crises.
These intrapersonal events lead patients to react, defend, or protect
themselves from the loss or harm they perceive is occurring.

VIGNETTES

The vignettes describe two characters that exhibit paranoid thoughts
related to a perceived rejection or abandonment. In the first scenario,
Kim returns home from a long night's work and sees her boyfriend
packing boxes into a car. Already tired, she is unable to pose reasonable questions about what he is doing. She immediately jumps to the
conclusion that he is leaving her, although there had been no indica-

Criterion 9
Transient, stress-related *paranoid* ideation or severe dissociative symptoms.

Transient
Definition of *Transitory*: Lasting or existing only for a short time.
Synonym: Fleeting, temporary.
BPD: *Transient* refers to symptoms that are short-lasting-from a few minutes to a few hours. If these states last longer, additional Axis I diagnoses should be considered.

Stress
Definition: Pressure; the act or effect of exerting force on someone or something.
Synonym: Strain.
BPD: Stress can be identified as any force creating tension or pressure. Tension or pressure includes both internal and external forces. Often stress-related states are the result of perceived abandonment (see Chapter 1). If external stressors (such as an argument or shift in a relationship) occur, enough tension may be triggered to result in a brief and transitory change in mental status.

Paranoid
Definition of *paranoia*: Psychosis marked by delusions and irrational suspicions.
Synonym: Doubtfulness, dubiousness, leeriness.
BPD: Stressful situations, particularly those involving themes of potential abandonment, can instigate a transient or short-lasting episode of paranoia. In times of extreme stress (usually of an interpersonal nature), the patient may distort the intentions of others. The synonyms also indicate that patients experience leeriness or doubt, particularly when internal or external stressors are apparent.

tion of conflict or dissatisfaction in the relationship. For Clare, decisions based on distorted thinking led her to act impulsively and violently. In both scenarios, the characters jump to conclusions based on distorted thinking and engage in behaviors they later regret. It is important to keep in mind that transient paranoid states can not only be caused by perceived abandonment, but also can occur as a result of intense rage or an extremely stressful event.

Vignette 1: Kim

Kim was tired. She had been working double shifts at the diner just to make the bills this month. When would it all end? When she returned to her apartment after a long night of serving greasy burgers, she noticed her boyfriend, Bill, packing items into the back of his truck. Just what did he think he was doing? Her mind raced as she got out of her car. Her heartbeat pounded in her temples. "He's moving out," she thought. "He's leaving me. He's met someone else. Probably some twit he works with at the hospital." Furious and terrified, she ran from her car and yelled, "You bastard, how could you do this to me?" Puzzled by this display of anger, Bill tried to calm her down. She starting yelling at him and kicking his tires. While she was taking a breath she noticed that the boxes in his truck were items marked to be distributed to charities.

Vignette 2: Clare

Clare sat at her desk overwhelmed by what seemed to be hundreds of feelings. There was a collection for a baby shower gift for one of the women in the public relations department. Nobody came to collect anything from her. What did that mean? Were they not going to invite her? Did they not even want her name on the card? She felt alternately angry, sad, annoyed, hurt, and vindictive.

"I would really like to get even with them," she thought. She spent the next hour reviewing everything that had transpired between her and the other women in the office. She started to see a pattern emerge. Little slights, minor rebuffs, tiny experiences of being avoided. As she thought about these things it seemed more and more obvious. Clare's heart pounded, her stomach was upset, and she was feeling very jittery. She left her office to get a drink of water.

When Sue came into Clare's office for the third time to collect money for the gift and to have Clare sign the card, she found Clare away from her desk again. As she was leaving she ran into Clare, who blurted out that she would be unable to come to the party and therefore did not think that she would contribute to the gift.

Discussing the Vignettes & Prompting the Patient

As patients read the vignettes, ask if they, too, experience times when they have become overly suspicious of someone they care about or are involved with. Again, it is natural for us to make assumptions about our environment. However, suspicions about a pending loss may lead patients with BPD to respond as if the dreaded event actually is occurring or will occur. This often worsens an already-difficult situation for both patients and those they are relating to. Do patients tend to leap to erroneous conclusions due to being suspicious? They may argue and yell at their significant others and demand a minute-by-minute itinerary of their moves throughout the day. It may take additional reassurance for the patient to feel safe again.

WORKSHEET 1 prompts patients to consider how they process external events in relation to themselves. Often, BPD patients personalize external events that occur with significant others. In reality these events usually are unrelated to them. After reacting to the perceived threat, loss, or rejection, patients respond in ways they later regret. Once a safety zone is reestablished, the paranoia goes into remission and patients recognize that they were overreacting or being inappropriate.

APPLYING TYPICAL BPD SCHEMAS & DISTORTIONS TO THE CRITERION

Typical schemas for patients who experience transient paranoia are related to themes of abandonment and mistrust. Ever-aware of potential losses, patients may scan for signs of betrayal. Fearing abandonment, patients may demonstrate suspicion when stressed, jealous, or disappointed. They may demonstrate an intense need to remain connected at all times. Usually extreme stress needs to be present for a transient episode to occur, but it invariably results from a fear of abandonment. Once the fear has been removed (e.g., the significant other returns or reassures the patient), the paranoia is no longer a compelling force. Catastrophic thinking propels fears and creates additional suspicion. Dichotomous thinking allows competing evidence to be dispelled quickly, with patients interpreting vague information in a suspicious manner.

We live and survive by minute-by-minute assumptions. Those who experience paranoia misread or misinterpret incoming information. Over time, if we have learned through either unsafe environments or misinterpreting stimuli that it is not safe to trust or that others may harm us, a chronic pattern forms. Schemas therefore may relate to being abandoned or abused, and paranoia may be the most natural mode of responding to a perceived potential loss or danger. Because of consistent and perpetual loss, some patients have a very entrenched mode of viewing the world. They may have real difficulty establishing trust in others, and when they are stressed, they easily exhibit these symptoms. No matter how entrenched the schema is, however, patients can learn ways to manage these symptoms so as to not further alienate others and so that they can obtain some degree of relief from these very uncomfortable sensations.

WORKSHEETS ONE & TWO: ASSESSMENT & ASSIGNMENT

As noted, states of intense anxiety can cause physical symptoms of panic, GI distress, and sweating. WORKSHEET 1: THE ASSESSMENT (p. 204; Patient Manual, p. 225) asks patients to consider times when they, too, have been suspicious. Symptoms of anxiety are useful triggers to alert for impending danger. Therefore, the identification of anxiety symptoms can prompt patients to examine what they are perceiving as a threat, and if their reactions to the threat are appropriate.

WORKSHEET 1

The Assessment for Criterion 9 (Paranoid Ideation)

Rate the severity of the following problems as you think they may relate to you.

0 = none   1 = mild   2 = moderate   3 = severe   4 = extremely severe

1. If someone close to you doesn't stick to scheduled plans, you assume that it is directly related to how he or she feels about you.   ____

2. If someone close to you is late, you assume the worst possible scenario.   ____

3. You tend to regret your actions after an argument.   ____

4. You tend to jump to conclusions very quickly.   ____

5. You tend to be on guard for disloyalty on the part of others.   ____

6. You've discovered that you tend to switch emotions very quickly.   ____

7. When you disagree with someone, you feel as if he or she not only doesn't agree with you, but also wants to harm you.   ____

8. You tend to feel singled out when bad things happen.   ____

9. You think that bad things happen to you more often than they happen to others.   ____

10. You tend to distrust others when you are stressed.   ____

If the patient answers five or more prompts at level 2 or above, consider focusing on this criterion.

After the patient completes WORKSHEET 1: THE ASSESSMENT, complete WORKSHEET 2: THE ASSIGNMENT (Patient Manual, p. 206) which prompts patients to identify an incident in which they experienced suspiciousness or paranoia.

SENSITIVITY & PARANOIA

As extremely sensitive individuals, patients may be particularly aware of changes in others' moods, tone of voice, or body language. As they subject cues from others to their own interpretive systems, they may tend to distort those cues.

As the body naturally has created a system of warning devices, *do not* encourage patients to disregard or challenge all of their suspicions. In certain situations paranoia is entirely appropriate and provides vital information to ensure our survival. The paranoid symptoms patients *should* examine are those that come from distorted thinking and have resulted in behaviors that have later proved embarrassing or inappropriate.

WORKSHEETS THREE TO SIX, & EIGHTEEN: TREATMENT GOALS

The treatment program is predicated upon patients' learning to identify when they may become suspicious or paranoid. Transient episodes often occur when patients experience a stressor, particularly within interpersonal relationships. It is vital that patients be able to identify when they are becoming stressed or overwhelmed by sensations that indicate a threat to themselves.

It is important that patients understand that there are appropriate times to be suspicious. However, the tendency to exaggerate or intensify emotions is a common trait of those with BPD. Patients who sense a threatening event may distort it by catastrophizing or exaggerating a suspected outcome. Their actions, therefore, are directly made out of a survival mode.

After the patient completes WORKSHEETS 1 and 2, assist the patient in filling out WORKSHEET 3: THE INCIDENT CHART (Patient Manual, p. 227). The four areas of self-monitoring (physiological, emotional, cognitive, and behavioral) offer avenues to treatment interventions and provide concrete examples of specific areas of change the patient can address.

Complete WORKSHEETS 4 and 5 (Patient Manual, pp. 228–229) to identify patients' automatic thoughts and schemas. Then treatment goals can be identified. In order to help organize this process, complete WORKSHEET 6: TREATMENT GOALS (Patient Manual, p. 230). Once treatment goals are set, complete WORKSHEET 18: THE DPS (Patient Manual, p. 231) to determine a baseline level of distress or dysfunction for the particular criterion.

WORKSHEETS SEVEN TO SEVENTEEN: SUGGESTED INTERVENTIONS

Worksheets 7 & 8: Physical Triggers & Suggested Interventions

Paranoia leads to fearing others, and the resulting physiological symptoms can look like those of fear or anxiety (WORKSHEET 7; Patient Manual, p. 232). As you describe bodily reactions to paranoia, compare them to the feelings your patients had during times when they were extremely frightened (e.g., narrowly missing an automobile accident). As these symptoms can be very transient, it may be difficult to actually demarcate when suspicion becomes paranoia. However, behaviors prompted by paranoia can be long-lasting and damaging. WORKSHEET 8 (Patient Manual, pp. 233–234) details pertinent interventions.

THOUGHT-STOPPING

Thought-stopping may be difficult for patients experiencing symptoms of paranoia. This is largely because the episodes are generally transient and short-lived. However, if patients can recognize when they are experiencing a flow of thoughts about others harming or abandoning them, they can utilize thought-stopping to provide the necessary time to rationally process the information. The key, therefore, is to monitor bodily reactions to feelings of fear and when they become present, stop.

RELAXATION

As the bodily reactions to paranoia or suspiciousness are similar if not identical to those of a fear response (autonomic responses activated by the sympathetic nervous system cause tension, rapid heartrate, and general overall arousal), relaxation techniques can help the body return to a relaxed resting state.

RELAXING IMAGERY

Encourage patients to utilize imagery that allows for a safe feeling, where there is no potential harm or loss. Imagery should not include people or situations that incur suspicion, such as the image of a partner providing a hug.

Worksheets 9 & 10: Emotional Triggers & Suggested Interventions

For those with BPD who are both physiologically and psychologically sensitive, paranoia and suspicion can lead to feelings of intense fear or terror (WORKSHEET 9; Patient Manual, p. 235). These feelings may render patients victims of their own painful emotional states. They may regret actions or words stated out of their paranoia and fear. Once the triggers are recognized, interventions can be proposed (WORKSHEET 10; Patient Manual, p. 236).

SCALE BACK

Have patients rate the severity of the emotion they felt when they experienced paranoia. Once they have scaled back, have them rate the emotion again, noting the difference between the ratings and their ability to affect some change in their modulation.

Worksheets 11 & 12: Cognitive/Automatic Thoughts & Suggested Interventions

Paranoia and fear often arise from automatic thoughts that are linked to experiential cues (WORKSHEET 11; Patient Manual, p. 237).

CHALLENGE CATASTROPHIC THINKING

Use the CATASTROPHIC THINKING CHART (WORKSHEET 12; Patient Manual, pp. 238–239) to help patients challenge their catastrophic conclusions. Again, these conclusions may be particularly prevalent during times of extreme stress. Some additional interventions are:

- "What if?" questions. Ask patients, "So what if this is true?" or "What would happen if your fears were true?" Make sure patients are in a stable state before performing this intervention so as not to worsen the situation and exacerbate fears.
- "Common sense" questions. Help patients ask themselves common-sense questions such as "Is there really a chance that this could be happening?" or " What is the likelihood that what I'm fearing will really occur?"
- Reflect on previous experiences. Ask patients whether their conclusions were correct during past experiences of paranoia. Were they able to manage the stress? How did they do it?

CHALLENGE DICHOTOMOUS THINKING

Help patients challenge extremes in their beliefs by having them draw a straight line with black and white endpoints, black being the dreaded outcome and white being a completely safe situation. This helps patients examine what lies between these two endpoints.

The Dichotomous Thinking Chart

Black	Gray(s)	White
	--	--	
She didn't say hello to me in the café, so she must be avoiding me.	She'll chat with me later. She's preoccupied.	She isn't avoiding me.
_____ .	_____ .	_____ .
_____ .	_____ .	_____ .

Weigh the Evidence

Suspicion is often the result of making assumptions without carefully looking at the evidence. For example, when a significant other states that he or she needs some space, a patient may conclude that the partner is leaving permanently, when in reality the "space" may just be a few hours. Utilize the DISPUTATION CHART to challenge these assumptions.

The Disputation Chart

Situation: *Friend didn't call as planned.*

Belief: *Friend likes others more than me.*

Proof Supporting Belief	**Refuting Statement**
1. *Friend didn't contact me.*	1. *Friend usually contacts me unless she's busy.*
2. *Friend may be with other friends.*	2. *Friend can go out with others and still like me.*
3. _____ .	3. _____ .
4. _____ .	4. _____ .

The Expanded Incident Chart

Use WORKSHEET 15: THE EXPANDED INCIDENT CHART (Patient Manual, p. 240) to detail your patient's chain of thoughts. In addition to asking what their cognitions, emotions, physiological symptoms, and behaviors are, ask patients to identify the people and situations that seem to trigger paranoid thinking. Challenge patients to view these events in a two-step process. First, the initial interpretation of events leads to an activation of their internal sensory system. Schematically, associations are made with the information filtered through their sensory system. If a negative association is made with the external events, physiological responses, negative thoughts, reactive behaviors, and emotional upset occur. Second, patients perceive that they are no longer in control and that their worst fears are being realized. Loss of control is related to feelings of paranoia. When one feels out of control, one loses the ability to assert oneself. Patients may feel so overwhelmed with emotion that they are unable to clearly express their fears and feelings. In sum, they are not able to verify if what they are perceiving is real information or the product of a schematic association that has led to a patterned response to perceived rejection, abandonment, and despair.

Worksheets 13 & 14: Behavioral Triggers & Suggested Interventions

Acting out of fear can lead to negative consequences and may further stress an already-fragile system. The behaviors that often follow paranoid ideation are meant to protect the patient or thwart the dreaded event (WORKSHEET 13; Patient Manual, p. 241). Sometimes these behaviors come in response to no apparent provocation. Examine exactly *what* thought the patient is responding to (WORKSHEET 14; Patient Manual, pp. 242–243).

STOP

Stopping is similar to thought-stopping. Stopping before acting allows for additional time to fully examine the situation and not respond out of an impulse or fear.

MONITOR YOURSELF & OTHERS

This exercise is important for patients who experience paranoia and suspicion. Encourage patients to examine their environment to determine if what they are perceiving is true or likely. This is almost an evidence-gathering exercise in that patients can seek the opinion of a neutral party to help contradict paranoid beliefs. Patients may want to identify a specific person that they trust to guide them and to objectively challenge their beliefs.

IMPROVING COMMUNICATION OF FEELINGS

Encourage patients to examine the messages they are receiving from others. Is there is misinterpretation of a message being sent from the sender? Are there specific senders that are associated with danger? What are the messages that are particularly frightening?

ASSERT YOURSELF

Often assumptions are made from communication of messages without checking things out. Encourage your patients to assert themselves and ask basic questions that support or refute their beliefs. For example, a patient might say, "I feel anxious right now, can we take a moment and talk about this?" When patients are able to identify what they are experiencing rather than blame the other person, miscommunications can be prevented.

Worksheets 16 & 17: Situational Triggers & Suggested Interventions

WORKSHEET 16 (Patient Manual, p. 244) prompts patients to specifically identify those situations that have led to feeling suspicious or paranoid. WORKSHEET 17 (Patient Manual, p. 245) suggests to remove themselves and to try something different.

REMOVE YOURSELF

Once patients identify potentially stressful situations, they can choose to remove themselves from similar situations. For example, if patients identify that during arguments they tend to become overwhelmed and jump to conclusions about the motives of the other person, encourage them to make a plan to discontinue the interaction or exit the situation.

TRY SOMETHING DIFFERENT

If patients can identify those situations that cause suspicion, encourage patients to try a different behavior in similar situations. For example, if patients find they are becoming suspicious with a particular individual, instead of becoming quiet or withdrawn, ask patients to begin a conversation with a different individual.

WORKSHEET EIGHTEEN: THE DPS

Complete WORKSHEET 18: THE DPS (Patient Manual, p. 246). Compare the results of the DPS after treatment goals were set. Is there a difference in the level of distress the patient is experiencing in response to the criterion? If not, reexamine the interventions chosen to target the symptoms, and collaboratively determine whether changes or alterations should be made.

CASE EXAMPLE

Kim, in the first vignette, managed to calm down, regroup, and apologize to Bill. But she certainly felt stupid. She called her therapist, who encouraged her to examine how stressed and fatigued she had been that evening. Her therapist mentioned that in times of great fatigue or stress, Kim seemed to have great difficulty trusting others. Kim soon was able to identify that she actually became suspicious of others and tended to jump to conclusions that the worst was happening. Kim's assessment revealed a pattern that consisted of reacting to stressful situations in the same way, and that she usually regretted her actions afterward. Throughout the following weeks, Kim monitored her stress and fatigue level and the automatic thoughts she had during times of greater stress. She was able to see the pattern clearly, and could even identify the physical states that usually accompanied those feelings. It felt just like a panic attack. Kim tried to understand how her belief that others didn't have her best interests in mind became activated, particularly when she felt she was being abandoned or left. She soon recognized that her internal alarm system was turned up so high to "catch" any signs that something bad would happen that she was picking up *everything* bad that might happen. She viewed vague situations in a negativistic and catastrophic way, and always assumed the worst without checking things out. With the help of the therapist, Kim learned to monitor for high levels of stress and fatigue, and for the bodily signs that felt like anxiety. She learned to check out her perceptions by asserting herself and asking questions when she was unsure of the situation. She also learned to challenge her catastrophic thoughts by asking herself common-sense questions such as "My boyfriend and I have been fine for weeks; is it really possible that he would just leave?"

CHAPTER 10 | Severe Dissociative Symptoms

This chapter addresses the second part of Criterion 9: "severe dissociative symptoms" (APA, 2000, p. 710). Individuals diagnosed with BPD may experience dissociative states that are generally transient and stress-related. These episodes usually last minutes or, at most, hours, and are not prevalent enough to warrant an additional diagnosis. For patients who demonstrate more prevalent dissociative symptoms, additional Axis I diagnoses and a medical evaluation should be considered. As extremely sensitive individuals, your patients may report dissociative-type symptoms at times of real or imagined abandonment and extreme stress. Patients may feel as if they are automatons or not in complete control of their actions or speech. During these dissociative episodes, patients' sense of reality typically remains intact—i.e., they are aware that they are not really robots. Patients often report an increase in these symptoms when they are physically tired and experiencing stress.

Dissociative symptoms are generally a difficult condition to define and describe. You may hear patients make statements such as: "I felt as if I was watching myself"; "I just didn't feel like I was there"; or "I felt like I was in a fog." They may be unable to account for time completely or remember certain aspects of an event or conversation. Depersonalization is defined as "an alteration in the perception or experience of the self so that one feels detached from, and as if one is an outside observer of, one's mental processes or body (e.g., feeling like one is in a dream)" (APA, 1994, p. 766). Again, these are transient experiences, but they can be quite frightening to patients. Patients may be unconvinced that these experiences will remit in the future, and they may fear that the episodes will increase in severity and dura-

---

Criterion 9

Transient stress-related paranoid ideation or severe *dissociative* symptoms.

Transient
Definition of *Transitory*: Lasting or existing only for a short time.
Synonym: Fleeting, temporary.
BPD: *Transient* refers to those symptoms that are short-lasting-from a few minutes to a few hours. If these states last longer, additional Axis I diagnoses should be considered.

Stress
Definition: Pressure; the act or effect of exerting force on someone or something.
Synomym: Strain.
BPD: Stress can be identified as any force creating tension or pressure. Tension or pressure includes both internal and external forces. Often stress-related states are the result of perceived abandonment (see Chapter 1). If external stressors (such as an argument or shift in a relationship) occur, enough tension may be triggered to result in a brief and transitory change in mental status.

Dissociative
Definition of *Dissociate*: Break.
Synonym: Detached, separate, disengaged.
BPD: For those with BPD, dissociative states are short-lasting and involve feelings of depersonalization or feeling outside or not part of oneself. The patient may describe themselves as numb or floating. These symptoms are usually the result of a perceived loss or abandonment and ordinarily remit upon the real or perceived return of the caregiver. If dissociative states become more than transient episodes, additional Axis I diagnoses should be considered.

---

tion. They may even believe that one day they will be living their whole life as if they are in a dream.

It is imperative for you to be aware that certain cultural traditions embrace dissociative states as an accepted expression of religious experiences or activities. Only when dissociative states cause distress or disrupt functioning are they deemed a pathological symptom. Patients may have learned that the only safe way to manage abandonment and rejection is to enter into a state where they may not be as sensitive or feel as much. As a method of protection, patients may be dissociating in order to avoid the incredible hurt, shame, and fear that is produced when they perceive they are being rejected.

VIGNETTES

The vignettes describe Mary and John, two individuals under extreme stress who fear that their loved ones are leaving them and consequently experience dissociative phenomena. Mary, exhausted and overwhelmed by stress at work, reacts to her mother's threat to kick her out by slipping out of the conversation and floating to a safe vantage point. John hopelessly stands by as his wife packs her belongings in preparation for leaving him. Frozen by fear and angst, he is unable to move, speak, or react. Both vignettes contain themes of real abandonment. Dissociative states can, however, be instigated by imagined abandonment.

Vignette 1: Mary

Mary had gotten little sleep in the past two nights. Her constant arguments with her mother were exhausting, and now her mother was threatening to kick her out. She was so tired that she was dozing off at her desk. She meant to finish the director's report, but the computer screen in front of her seemed to be blending the letters together. Her supervisor, noticing that Mary had stopped typing for at least 30 minutes, stormed into her cubicle and began firing a series of questions at her: "Why aren't you finished yet? What's taking so long? What are you doing?" Her supervisor concluded, "This is a final warning!" Mary's heart was pounding faster and faster, and she felt sick. Then suddenly, it didn't matter. She felt herself slipping out of the conversation, out of the chair, and nearly out of the room. She saw her supervisor's finger wagging at her and saw her mouth moving, but she just couldn't for the life of her answer in any kind of organized way. Finally her supervisor pounded her desk. This jerked her back to her senses which only make her feel lousy again.

Vignette 2: John

"I'm leaving John!" Suzie shouted. She was picking out items of clothing; her favorite ones at that; and throwing them into a large duffel bag. "I just can't take your drinking anymore or your incredible bad moods. I'm staying with Mom for a few days until this is sorted out." John watched, bewildered, as his wife continued to collect things to leave. He saw her moving, he saw her talking to him, he saw her hair flouncing about as she moved throughout their bedroom. He suddenly felt as if this whole scene wasn't real. It just didn't feel like it was happening. It seemed as if he was watching one of those Woody Allen movies where a couple is supposed to have some kind of sophisticated conversation or something. He couldn't speak; he couldn't move. He hopelessly and helplessly stood by, not really there, watching his wife leave him.

Discussing the Vignettes & Prompting the Patient

As patients read the vignettes, ask if they, too, experience dissociative states. They may especially feel these states when they are stressed, overwhelmed, or tired. They may be experiencing chronic forms of stress and, with any additional pressure, experience dissociation. Patients may have difficulty describing these states, but they can clearly demarcate these experiences from other experiences.

WORKSHEET 1 asks patients to recall times when they experienced dissociative symptoms. These responses are generally patterned and, as noted earlier, in response to extreme states of stress. If many symptoms are evident, you may consider administering the Dissociative Experiences Scale (DES; see Bernstein, 1986) to determine if your patients are exhibiting enough symptomology to warrant an additional diagnosis.

APPLYING TYPICAL BPD SCHEMAS & DISTORTIONS TO THE CRITERION

Typical schemas related to this criterion include themes of abandonment, unlovability, and incompetence. Themes of unlovability can cause great internal tension and a sense of helplessness. Helplessness in this sense is related to feeling as if one has no control over events in life and that because one is an unlovable person, being content is not possible. As individuals struggle to manage these intense feelings, an overwhelming sense of incompetence can cause a "shutting down" of the system.

When does this occur? If information is perceived as threatening and unbearable, patients may dissociate as a means to manage the situation. As information can be misread or misinterpreted, subsequent reactions are based on distortion. Growing up, patients may have learned to manage high-stress situations by detaching from themselves. However, in adulthood this coping mechanism is no longer adaptive and may have severely disrupted functioning.

WORKSHEETS ONE & TWO: ASSESSMENT & ASSIGNMENT

As noted, states of intense anxiety can cause physical symptoms of panic, GI distress, and sweating. WORKSHEET 1: THE ASSESSMENT (217; Patient Manual, p. 250) asks patients to consider times when they, too, have felt as if they were in a trance-like state, or dissociating. When highly stressed, symptoms of anxiety are sometimes present prior to a dissociative state. Therefore, the identification of symptoms of anxiety can help the patient know if a dissociative state is likely to occur, and gives patients the opportunity to take control and use coping strategies.

WORKSHEET 1
The Assessment for Criterion 9
(Dissociative Symptoms)

Rate the severity of the following problems as you think they may relate to you.

0 = none   1= mild   2 = moderate   3 = severe   4 = extremely severe

1. You feel as if you have watched yourself from outside your body. ___

2. You can easily tune others out when you are talking with them. ___

3. When stressed, you sometimes feel as if you are in a dream. ___

4. You have felt a lack of control of your body when stressed. ___

5. You have experienced feeling like a robot or automaton. ___

6. When arguing with a loved one, it almost seems as if you are existing in a movie. ___

7. Stressful situations or events seem unreal to you. ___

8. If you are overtired, you sometimes don't feel attached or grounded to anything. ___

9. Your friends and family describe you as "spacey." ___

10. There are brief periods of time you can't account for or have an unclear memory of. ___

If the patient answers five or more prompts at level 2 or above, consider focusing on this criterion.

After the patient completes WORKSHEET 1: THE ASSESSMENT, complete WORKSHEET 2: THE ASSIGNMENT (Patient Manual, p. 251) which prompts patients to identify an incident in which they experienced dissociative states.

SENSITIVITY & DISSOCIATION

The hypersensitivity typical of individuals with BPD can wear down or fatigue the system. In times of heightened stress those predisposed to dissociative states may experience a trancelike state as a means of coping with an unbearable stressor. Everyone experiences "not feeling like themselves today," but those who have dissociative states feel detached from the self and out of control. They fear the return of these episodes, as they can be disorienting and frightening.

WORKSHEETS THREE TO SIX, & EIGHTEEN: TREATMENT GOALS

The Taking Control treatment program is predicated upon patients learning to identify when they are more vulnerable to experiencing a dissociative state. WORKSHEET 2 asks your patients to recall a time when they have felt detached from themselves or as if they were watching themselves from a distance.

After the patient completes WORKSHEETS 1 and 2, assist the patient in filling out WORKSHEET 3: THE INCIDENT CHART (Patient Manual, p. 252). The four areas of self-monitoring (physiological, emotional, cognitive, and behavioral) offer avenues to treatment interventions and provide concrete examples of specific areas of change the patient can address. Patients can then take steps to protect themselves during such episodes. It is vital that your patient be able monitor for a pending dissociative state so that they can take preventative precautions to ensure their safety. Complete WORKSHEETS 4 and 5 (Patient Manual, pp. 253–254) to identify the patient's automatic thoughts and schema. Then treatment goals can be defined. In order to help organize this process, complete WORKSHEET 6: TREATMENT GOALS (Patient Manual, p. 255). Once treatment goals are set, complete WORKSHEET 18: THE DPS (Patient Manual, p. 256) to determine a baseline level of distress or dysfunction for the particular criterion.

WORKSHEETS SEVEN TO SEVENTEEN:
SUGGESTED INTERVENTIONS

Worksheets 7 & 8: Physical Triggers & Suggested Interventions

Physiological symptoms are usually the first symptoms of a dissociative state (WORKSHEET 7; Patient Manual, p. 257). Often a sense of lightness, numbness, or general disconnectedness can occur. Patients who experienced these symptoms can take steps to prevent or lessen the severity of the dissociation (WORKSHEET 8; Patient Manual, pp. 258–259). Their physiological triggers may be similar to those related to fear or anxiety.

THOUGHT-STOPPING

Thought-stopping can be extremely helpful with dissociation. Stopping should occur when patients first begin to feel overwhelmed with stress. Monitoring for physiological symptoms associated with intense stress and perceived abandonment will provide an opportunity for regrouping, eliciting support, and relaxing.

RELAXATION

Relaxation techniques can be helpful when patients respond to stress with physiological indicators of fear. For example, if they are experiencing muscle tension, rapid breathing, or a rapid heartrate, relaxation can help return the body to resting, relaxed state. This can then allow for additional support.

RELAXING IMAGERY

In combination with relaxation exercises, imagery that involves a sense of grounding can be helpful. As noted earlier, dissociative states are often the result of intense feelings of disconnectedness, abandonment, and loss. Patients may almost feel as if they will float away. Encourage use of images such as being wrapped in a warm blanket in a safe place.

Worksheets 9 & 10: Emotional Triggers & Suggested Interventions

For those with BPD who are both physiologically and psychologically sensitive, dissociative feelings can be frightening and inappropriate (WORKSHEET 9; Patient Manual, p. 260). At times, dissociation may render patients victims of their own painful emotional states. They may then regret actions or words that occurred during the dissociative state. They may learn to fear these random trancelike states and their loss of control.

Scale Back

Worksheet 10 asks patients to rate, on a scale of 1 to 10, the severity of the emotion they felt prior to an experienced dissociative or trancelike state (Patient Manual, p. 261). Once patients have scaled back, have them rate the emotion again, noting the difference between the ratings and their ability to affect some change in their modulation.

Worksheets 11 & 12: Cognitive/Automatic Thoughts & Suggested Interventions

Dissociative symptoms for the BPD patient can often be related to automatic thoughts of abandonment or intense anger (Worksheet 11; Patient Manual, p. 262). It is therefore important to identify those specific situations which may trigger dissociative episodes in order to propose interventions (Worksheet 12; Patient Manual, p. 263).

The Expanded Incident Chart

Use Worksheet 15: The Expanded Incident Chart (Patient Manual, pp. 264–265) to detail your patient's scenario. In addition to asking what their cognitions, emotions, physiological symptoms, and behaviors are, ask patients to identify the people and situations that seem to trigger dissociative episodes. Challenge patients to view these events in a two-step process. First, the initial interpretation of events leads to an activation of their internal sensory system. Schematically, associations are made with the information filtered through their sensory system. If a negative association is made with the external events, physiological responses, negative thoughts, reactive behaviors, and emotional upset occur. What were your patient's thoughts prior to detaching themselves? Were there themes of abandonment, hopelessness, or self-depreciation?

Second, patients perceive that they are no longer in control and that their worst fears are being realized. Loss of control is experienced during a trancelike state. When one feels out of control, one loses the ability to assert oneself. Patients may feel so overwhelmed with emotion that they are unable to clearly express their fears, feelings, and assumptions. In sum, they are not able to verify if what they are perceiving is real information or a product of a schematic association that has led to a patterned response to perceived rejection, abandonment, and despair. A method of intervening in this process is to challenge catastrophic thinking and to use grounding techniques.

CHALLENGE CATASTROPHIC THINKING

Catastrophic thoughts can often lead to feelings of being overwhelmed. If patients have the potential to dissociate, being able to challenge the very catastrophic thought that is propelling their fear state can help prevent further distress; the goal being to prevent a dissociative state from occurring. Utilize the CATASTROPHIC THINKING CHART. For example, if patients become overwhelmed with distress and multiple stressors, do they have thoughts such as "I can't handle this" or "I want to feel numb"? Challenge these thoughts with "I can handle this" or "Not being numb will help me handle the situation."

Some additional interventions are:

- "What if?" questions. Encourage patients to ask themselves "What if this did happen?" This directly challenges patients to examine the feared outcome and to sensitize themselves to the experience. The goal is to reduce the fear response to the feared outcome.
- "Common-sense" questions. Help patients ask common-sense questions such as "Is this really happening?"
- Reflect on previous experiences. How have patients managed prior experiences of extreme stress? In prior experiences of dissociation, what was the outcome? Did any harm come to the patient? How were they able to manage their states?

GROUND YOURSELF

After patients have identified what triggers usually instigate dissociative states, have them focus on something that grounds them or helps them feel in control. They may decide to imagine someone or something in their life that is stable-for example, imagine being wrapped in a large warm blanket or having a family member holding onto them. Use a picture to reinforce this.

Some other grounding techniques:

- Imagine wearing a heavy pair of boots that won't let you float away.
- Imagine a trusted family member holding onto you. (Use a picture to reinforce this.)
- Sit in a chair and allow all of your weight to sink into the chair.
- Imagine wrapping yourself in a warm blanket.

Worksheets 13 & 14: Behavioral Triggers & Suggested Interventions

WORKSHEET 13 (Patient Manual, p. 266) prompts patients to identify their reactions prior to, during, and after a dissociative episode. What is their typical response to feeling overwhelmed and stressed? How do they cope? How do they manage an episode if the are beginning to experience dissociation? Based on these responses, interventions can be undertaken (WORKSHEET 14; Patient Manual, p. 267).

MONITOR YOURSELF & OTHERS

Monitoring helps patients "check out" their reactions to situations. Extremely stressful situations can often precipitate a dissociative state- therefore it is imperative that patients make realistic and nondistorted interpretations of the environment. Encourage patients to scan their environment or to elicit feedback from others to determine if their response is proportional to the situation. If patients can identify some- one whom they trust to run situations by, encourage them to contact this person. Some additional questions to have patients ask themselves are:

When I have detached in the past I noticed that I _____.

When I detach I notice that others _____.

When I detached but was later reassured that nothing bad was happening, around me others were behaving _____.

IDENTIFY A FRIEND

A supportive friend also can distract patients and even help with grounding. A familiar voice or a hug can help patients interrupt their reactions to a stressful situation. A friend can help remind patients of prior times when they were able to cope successfully and can encour- age use of coping techniques such as relaxation or challenging assumptions.

IDENTIFY AN ANCHOR

In combination with grounding techniques, it is important for patients to identify an anchor, or something that helps them feel safe, supported, and grounded. As feelings of detachment, floating, and drifting are associated with dissociative states, images of being grounded or "landed" within themselves can help thwart these states. For example, these anchors could include:

• Imagine holding a heavy object.
• Imagine feeling solid ground beneath their feet.
• Imagine laying on warm sand on a beachtowel.

Worksheets 16 & 17: Situational Triggers & Suggested Interventions

WORKSHEET 16 (Patient Manual, p. 268) prompts patients to specifically identify those situations that have led to feeling detached or experiencing a dissociative state. WORKSHEET 17 (Patient Manual, p. 269) suggests to remove themselves or try something different.

REMOVE YOURSELF

Not all stressful situations can be avoided, however if patients are able to identify themes of situations that trigger dissociative states they can choose to remove themselves, or structure the situation in such a way it is less distressful. For example, patients may note that conflict-laden family gatherings usually produce extreme levels of stress. If the situation is unavoidable, there may be ways to manage it, such as limiting the duration of the visit.

TRY SOMETHING DIFFERENT

Help patients identify a list of alternative responses to enact when experiencing extreme stress. As with any behavior, there is typically a patterned chain of events and reactions that may lead to a dissociative state. Encourage patients to disrupt this chain by generating alternatives. For example, patients who experience severe anxiety symptoms prior to detaching could attempt to use that energy in a positive direction, such as going for a walk.

WORKSHEET EIGHTEEN: THE DPS

Complete WORKSHEET 18: THE DPS (Patient Manual, p. 270). Compare the results of the DPS after treatment goals were set. Is there a difference in the level of distress the patient is experiencing in response to the criterion? If not, reexamine the interventions chosen to target the symptoms, and collaboratively determine whether changes or alterations should be made.

CASE EXAMPLE

For Mary, in the first vignette, treatment issues revolved around her growing inability to manage extreme stress, combined with threats of being kicked out of her mother's home. On some level Mary was aware that her mother wouldn't really throw her out. But she continued to think: "Where would I live? Who would help me?" Mary was able to regroup and sought the help of an Employee Assistance Program counselor at her office. With the assistance of her counselor, Mary was able to identify that she had a long history of "floating away" and even remembered being yelled at as sixth-grader for "day-dreaming too much." These episodes felt very different from her normal feeling state, and she didn't feel she could control them. She felt her emotional reactions were too intense for her and considered herself unable to manage any emotional pain. As she became increasingly tired and stressed, she became more fearful that she would experience a dissociative episode and had, in fact, been fearing one for some time. Mary learned to monitor some of the triggers that usually precipitated pending trancelike states. She recognized that her heart pounded quickly and that she experienced some stomach distress. She also noted some dizziness. She had already been seen by her family physician, who assured her she was medically fine, but these symptoms frightened her. When she became frightened, the symptoms appeared to worsen. With the help of her therapist, Mary learned to identify those warning signs and to take a moment to stop when they occurred. She identified her college roommate as someone she could call when she began to feel these symptoms-someone who would quickly remind her that she was really there, grounded, and not about to float away. Mary also learned to visualize herself in heavy combat boots that wouldn't allow her to float away as she battled with herself not to dissociate. After learning some coping skills to manage her current stressors (which included bringing her mother into the therapy office to assure Mary that she wasn't evicting her), Mary soon began to feel more competent in handling her emotions and was able to challenge her compelling schema that she was incapable of managing stress.

Wrapping Up

The therapy of patients with BPD has been discussed in clinical literature since the beginning of the recorded history of psychotherapy. It was not however, until the publication of *DSM-III* in 1980 that the syndrome had not only a name but also defining characteristics. Since then the general literature on the psychotherapeutic treatment of BPD has emerged, and it is growing quickly.

Our goal in developing this program was manifold. First we wanted to provide patients with a name and understanding of their disorder. We wanted to demystify the disorder and its characteristics. We also wanted to offer patients a structure and means of focusing that would allow them to develop coping mechanisms for dealing with the symptoms of BPD.

Second, we wanted to offer therapists a parallel focus that would allow them to guide and support patients. These two companion volumes serve those purposes. Therapists are given specific definitions of the somewhat vague *DSM-IV-TR* (APA, 2000) BPD criteria to assist in understanding the specific presentation of BPD. It is hoped that these definitions will promote a more unified understanding of the disorder and subsequently, less misdiagnoses.

From a cognitive-behavioral perspective, therapists can help patients to learn about themselves, their thought and behavioral patterns, and to anticipate difficult situations. Self-monitoring helps patients thwart behaviors that have negative consequences. As the patients learns about their patterns, the patient gains access to their deepest held schemas. Therapists can then assist patients to challenge these schemas, and to make changes.

Therapists can add the interventions outlined in these volumes to their present armamentariums. We need at this point to offer a caveat.

No one technique, no single intervention or homework, will completely eradicate a pattern of perceiving, feeling, and acting that has been in place for years, if not decades. Patients must first be helped to decriminalize their disorder, which has often been made worse by a fear simply of the diagnosis.

Once patients can view their behavior as part of the normal spectrum (albeit sometimes at the extremes), they can proceed, as does any patient in therapy. The more therapists can integrate this program with their existing model of treatment, the better. Trying to use the program "straight from the box" will probably be unsuccessful.

Given the long-term nature of the patients' characterological problems, their general avoidance of psychotherapy, their frequent referral through family pressure or legal remand, and their seeming reluctance or inability to change, they are often the most difficult patients in a clinician's caseload. Therapy burnout can easily occur with the BPD patient. BPD patients generally require more work within the session, a longer time for therapy, and more therapist energy than do other patients. The therapist needs to ensure they maintain appropriate boundaries and structure, and if necessary seek peer supervision for guidance and support.

However, all of these difficulties can, with focus, structure, and collaboration be overcome. Patients can learn to understand themselves better and learn to predict how they may react to particular situations. Self-knowledge provides valuable information to use in those situations that have in the past caused difficulty. Once patients understand themselves, they can in effect, empower themselves and how they react to particular situations by making a basic choice. This choice is to utilize what they have learned. By taking control, they have chosen to make informed, adaptive, and healthy choices.

References

American Psychiatric Association (1980). *Diagnostic and statistical manual of mental disorders (3rd ed.)*. Washington, DC: Author.

American Psychiatric Association (1994). *Diagnostic and statistical manual of mental disorders (4th ed.)*. Washington, DC: Author.

American Psychiatric Association (2000). *Diagnostic and statistical manual of mental disorders (4th ed. text revision)*. Washington, DC: Author.

American Psychiatric Association. (2001). Practice guidelines for the treatment of patients with borderline personality disorder. *The American Journal of Psychiatry, 158*(10), 2 52.

Beck, A. (1976). *Cognitive therapy and the emotional disorders*. New York: International Universities Press.

Beck, A. (1986). Hopelessness as a predictor of eventual suicide. *Annals of the New York Academy of Science, 487*, 90–96.

Beck, A., & Emery, G. (1979). *Cognitive therapy of anxiety and phobic disorders*. Philadelphia: Center for Cognitive Therapy.

Beck, A., & Freeman, A., & Associates (1990). *Cognitive therapy of personality disorders*. New York: Guilford Press.

Beck, A., & Steer, R. (1987). *Manual for the revised Beck Depression Inventory*. San Antonio, TX: The Psychological Corporation.

Beck, A., & Weishaar, M. (1986). *Cognitive therapy*. Philadelphia: Center for Cognitive Therapy.

Beck, A., Weissman, A., Lester, D., & Trexler, L. (1974). The measurement of pessimism: The Hopelessness Scale. *Journal of Consulting and Clinical Psychology, 42*, 861–865.

Beck, J. (1995). *Cognitive therapy basics and beyond*. New York: The Guilford Press.

Bernstein, E. (1986). Development, reliability and validity of a dissociation scale. *Journal of Nervous and Mental Disorders, 174*, 727–735.

Bernstein, D., & Borkovec, T. (1976). *Progressive relaxation training: A manual for the helping professionals*. Champaign, Il.: Research Press.

Brent, D. (1987). Correlates of the medical lethality of suicide attempts in children and adolescents. *Journal of the American Academy of Child and Adolescent Psychiatry, 26*, 87–91.

Erikson, E. (1963). *Childhood and society*. New York: Norton.

Freeman, A. (1992). The development of treatment conceptualizations in cognitive therapy. In A. Freeman and F. Dattilio (Eds.), *Comprehensive casebook of cognitive therapy* (pp. 13–26). New York: Plenum Press.

Freeman, A. (1998). *The Diagnostic Profiling System*. Unpublished manuscript

Freeman, A., & Dattilio, F. (2000). Introduction. In F. Dattilio and A. Freeman (Eds.), *Cognitive-behavioral strategies in crisis intervention (2nd ed.)* (pp. 1–26). New York: Guilford Press.

Freeman, A., & Fusco, G. (2000). Treating high-arousal patients: Differentiating between patients in crisis and crisis-prone patients. In F. Dattilio & A. Freeman (Eds.), *Cognitive-behavioral strategies in crisis intervention (2nd ed.)* (pp. 27–58). New York: Guilford Press.

Freeman, A., Pretzer, J., Fleming, B., & Simon, K. (1990). *Clinical applications of cognitive therapy*. New York: Plenum Press.

Jacobson, E. (1962). *You must relax*. New York: McGraw-Hill.

James, W. (1972). *The principles of psychology (vol. 2)*. New York: Dover. (Original work published 1890)

Layden, M., Newman, C., Freeman, A., & Morse, S. (1993). *Cognitive therapy of borderline personality disorder*. Boston: Allyn & Bacon.

Linehan, M. (1987). Dialectical behavior therapy: A cognitive behavioral approach to parasuicide. *Journal of Personality Disorders, 1*, 328–333.

Linehan, M., Armstrong, H., Allmon, D., Suarez, A., Miller, M. (1988). *Comprehensive behavioral treatment for suicidal behaviors and borderline personality disorder: II. Treatment retention and one year follow-up of patient use of medical and psychological resources*. Unpublished manuscript, University of Washington, Department of Psychology, Seattle, WA.

Mahler, M., Pine, F., & Bergman, A. (1975). *The psychological birth of the human infant: Symbiosis and individuation*. New York: Basic Books.

Mayne, T., Norcross, J., & Sayette, M. (1994). Admission requirements, acceptance rates, and financial assistance in clinical psychology programs. *American Psychologist, 49*, 806–811.

Mays, D. (1985). Behavior therapy with borderline personality disorder: One clinician's perspective. In D. Mays & C. Franks (Eds.), *Neg-*

ative outcome in psychopathology and what to do about it. New York: Springer.

McGinn, L., & Sanderson, W. (2001). What allows cognitive behavioral therapy to be brief: Overview, efficacy, and crucial factors facilitating brief treatment. *Clinical Psychology: Science & Practice, 8*(1), 23–37.

Meichenbaum, D. (1977). *Cognitive-behavior modification: An integrative approach.* New York: Plenum Press.

Merriam-Webster (1993). *Webster's third new international dictionary of the English language unabridged.* Springfield, MA: Author.

Millon, T. (1987). On the genesis and prevalence of the borderline personality disorder: A social learning thesis. *Journal of Personality Disorders, 1,* 354–372.

Osuch, E., Noll, J., & Putnam, F. (1999). The motivations for self-injury in psychiatric inpatients. *Psychiatry, 62*(4), 334–346.

Pretzer, J. (1990). Borderline personality disorder. In A. Beck, A. Freeman, & Associates (Eds.), *Cognitive therapy of personality disorders* (pp. 176–207). New York: Guilford Press.

Raj, A., Kumaraiah, V., & Bhide, A. (2001). Cognitive-behavioural intervention in deliberate self-harm. *Acta Psychiatrica Scandinavica, 104*(5), 340–345.

Reinecke, M. (2000). Suicide and depression. In F. Dattilio & A. Freeman (Eds.), *Cognitive-behavioral strategies in crisis intervention (2nd ed.)* (pp. 84–125). New York: Guilford Press.

Ritter, K. (1985). The cognitive therapies: An overview for counselors. *Journal of Counseling and Development, 64,* 42–46.

Roberts, A. (2000). *Crisis intervention handbook (2nd ed.).* New York: Oxford.

Rosen, H. (1989). Piagetian theory and cognitive therapy. In A. Freeman, K. Simon, L. Beutler, & H. Arkowitz (Eds.), *Comprehensive handbook of cognitive therapy* (pp. 189–212). New York: Plenum Press.

Rush, A., & Shaw, B. (1983). Failure in treating depression by cognitive therapy. In E. Foa & P. Emmelkamp (Eds.), *Failures in behavior therapy.* New York: Wiley.

Satir, V. (1967). A family of angels. In J. Haley & L. Hoffman (Eds.), *Techniques of family therapy* (pp. 97–173). New York: Basic Books.

Schneidman, E. (1985) *Definition of suicide.* New York: John Wiley & Sons.

Seligman, M. (1975). *Helplessness: On depression, development, and death.* New York: Freeman.

Slaby, A. (1992). Creativity, depression and suicide. *Suicide and Life-Threatening Behavior, 22*(2), 157–166.

Stengel, E. (1965). *Suicide and attempted suicide*. Bristol, U.K.: MacGibbon & Kee Limited.

Stone, M. (1993). *Abnormalities of personality*. New York: Norton.

Stone, M., Stone, D. K., & Hurt, S. W. (1987). Natural history of borderline patients treated by intensive hospitalization. *Psychiatric Clinics of North America, 10*, 185–206.

Trull, T., Stepp, S., & Durrett, C. (2003). Research on borderline personality disorder: An update. *Current Opinion in Psychiatry, 16*(1), 77–82.

Turner, R. (1989). Case study evaluation of a bio-cognitive-behavioral approach for the treatment of borderline personality disorder. *Behavior Therapy, 20*, 477–489.

Young, J. E. (1990). *Schema-focused cognitive therapy for personality disorders: A schema-focused approach*. Sarasota, FL: Professional Resource Exchange.

Index

231